SILENT COURAGE

George P. Lee, age twelve, during his first
year on the Indian Student Placement
program

SILENT COURAGE

AN INDIAN STORY

The Autobiography of
GEORGE P. LEE
a Navajo

Deseret Book Company
Salt Lake City, Utah

This book is not an official publication of The Church of Jesus Christ of Latter-day Saints, and the views expressed in it do not necessarily represent the official position of the Church. The author alone is responsible for its contents.

Photo of George P. Lee on page 347
© copyright The Church of Jesus Christ of Latter-day Saints. Used by permission.

No part of this book may be reproduced in any form or by any means without permission in writing from the publisher, Deseret Book Company, P.O. Box 30178, Salt Lake City, Utah 84130. Deseret Book is a registered trademark of Deseret Book Company, Inc..

First printing March 1987
Second printing April 1987
Third printing November 1987
Fourth printing February 1988
Fifth printing November 1988

Library of Congress Cataloging-in-Publication Data

Lee, George P., 1943–
    Silent courage.

    Includes index.
    1. Lee, George P., 1943–   . 2. Navajo Indians—Biography.   3. Converts, Mormon—Biography.   4. Navajo Indians—Social life and customs.   5. Indians of North America—Southwest, New—Social life and customs.
I. Title.
E99.N3L535   1987   978'.00497 [B]   86-29324
ISBN 0-87579-056-9

CONTENTS

FOREWORD

We have looked forward to the day when this book would be published. It brings honor not only to our family, but to our clan and tribe as well. Our understanding is that George intended for this book to be more a story about what Indian people have had to face rather than exclusively about his own life.

In writing about his childhood and family, George has expressed the struggles and trials that every Native American family has undergone. By and large, it is the story of what the literal seed of Israel has had to face in mortality.

The Indians have been strangers in their own land. It should be understood that the prologue, "The Trail of Tears," is not over for any tribe; we still struggle for our rights and lands in America. Native Americans, whether Latter-day Saints or not, pray for the fulfillment of the Book of Mormon prophecies concerning the day when our Creator will see that our native rights are protected forever. For this we pray.

We hope that this book will bring hope and inspiration to many people, both Indian and non-Indian. The spiritual world of the Indian becomes confusing when the material aspects of the dominant society are infused with it. Our brother's life is an example of how both may successfully be combined. He has told us, and he tells us in this book, how the gospel as contained in the Book of Mormon brings him understanding so he is able to function well in both worlds. Enduring without understanding is difficult; but with understanding, one endures through hope.

Our brother is not only a great Native American, but he is also a great American. His success is America's success. Our brother's accomplishments, we feel, can be classified as a miracle. In spite of the disadvantages he had to overcome, not only was he a leader throughout his school years, but he was also a great leader as he served a mission among his own people, the Navajos. Later he became president of the Arizona-Holbrook Mission, he served as president of a community college, and he served as a United States Office of Education Fellow. He was voted an outstanding young man of America by the National JayCees, was selected to Phi Delta Kappa National Honor Society, received a Ford Foundation fellowship, and received his bachelor's, master's, and doctorate degrees. He has been a teacher, a coach, a guidance counselor, and a consultant for the U.S. Department of Health, Education, and Welfare on national educational matters. Most important, he was called as a General Authority, to serve as one of the top officials of The Church of Jesus Christ of Latter-day Saints for the rest of his life. All of these achievements were fulfilled by the time he was thirty-two years old.

One of George's childhood dreams was to be able to help his people, the Navajos, in a big way. That chance came when he was asked to run for tribal chairman by the then-incumbent chairman, Peter McDonald. He received his call as a General Authority for the Church almost simultaneously. He chose the latter. Now we hope that his story will bring strength and courage, not only to Navajos, but to all who read it.

Like his people, our brother has faced many trials and struggles. The world, at times, has not been too kind to him. But he has risen above them all and continues. He has learned to accept adversity as his companion and has functioned well in the two worlds.

Because of our brother's belief in himself, in his country, and in God, he has come from rock-bottom poverty to the highest pinnacle of success. This is the success story of one of America's native sons.

We have seen and heard our brother in prayer many times in behalf of all of God's children. We love him dearly, and we are very proud of him.

JOEY, PATRICK, BOB, AND LUCY LEE

ACKNOWLEDGMENTS

I express sincere and deep gratitude and appreciation to the people who have helped make this book possible:

First, to my sweet wife, Kitty, and our children, Duane and Chad, Tricia and Robyn, Todd, Scott, and Jacob, who have been my source of inspiration and in whom I have great pride, joy, and love.

To my wife's great parents and family for their faith and encouragement.

To my foster parents, Glen and Joan Harker, and their family, Michael, Steven, Kerry, Bret, and Jana, for their helpful suggestions and encouragement.

To my father, mother, brothers, and sisters for their superb, helpful suggestions about the manuscript.

To Fay Howell, my secretary, for her patience, understanding, and superb typing of the manuscript, and to all who gave help and support in its preparation.

To David Flake and Jack Lyon for their editorial assistance.

And, finally, I express special thanks for the blessings of my Maker.

GEORGE P. LEE

THE TRAIL
OF TEARS

The story of the Navajos' long walk is told to me through a tradition that has been passed down from father to son for as long as can be remembered.

I am one of the *Dineh,* or the People, as the Navajos called themselves. Our ancient name, *Dineh,* survives through our children, descendants, many relatives, and friends. I am a full-blooded Navajo Indian. My father, Jaaneez Yee Biye (Son of Donkey Man), a medicine man, poetically and beautifully expresses his native feelings about his beloved Navajoland, heritage, and Mother Earth. His thoughts represent well the feelings of traditional Navajos: "The Navajos are one with Mother Earth and nature. The unseen wind speaks my name, and I have uttered kind words in its passing. When the high treetop sways, it is I who sighs the melodious movement, for wisdom has come my way as I have bent to the breath of the Great Spirit.

"Above, spreading around, the blue sky is my name. Tearful clouds have gentled my eyes, have filled my soul with clean gratitude and growing reverence. The red of Mother Earth is my heart bringing forth green blades, emerald forests, yellow-brightened flowers, white snows, and the heaven-tipped mountains.

"In all these things I know and am known. In harmony I have lived as a man should. Mother Earth and Father Sun have seen my manly walk in nature. Though my voice yet whispers from the dust, you may hear, my beloved ones, and shall come to know, and then understand.

"The land of my fathers, the Navajos, as far back as I can remember, has been filled with movement and life. Upon the monumental red rock, I have sat in silence as the golden eagle soared overhead. From this wingmaster of the sky, I have learned to elevate my thoughts to the heavens above. I have seen the mesas, their dark cliff pockets among the varying colors that gather to dance upon the steep sides. These things I have pondered. The dark, green forest that crawls agelessly up the slant of mountains, ancient in wisdom—I am one with this splendor and beauty.

"My spiritual eyes are taught while gazing upon the vastness of the endless desert vision. So unending is the vista that the supple curve of Mother Earth's horizon heals the hungering heart. Always, as far as memory goes, this land has been one of the everlasting enchantment.

"This is our home, the land of the Navajos. My own heart can be found enwrapped with the same beauty. And my people, the same goes for them. This land is our destiny and our being; it is our soul, for we are known as *Dineh,* the People."

There came a time when our beautiful land was invaded by people from the south, then the east. They asked no permission to use our land. So there were many times we justly confiscated their cattle as payment for rent due. They did not like to pay, but considered our land their own. In retaliation for the rent we demanded, our women and children were abusively taken from our arms, then sold as slaves.

History records that the Spanish explorers, and later Anglo settlers, were the ones who invaded our beloved Navajoland. We treated them kindly until they began taking liberties with our needed game and our young women, even with young widows. Then we grew angry.

We rode long and hard to retrieve our stolen families who had been sold as slaves by our enemies. When we could not find them, we began taking sheep, goats, and horses. Still, to us, the trade was not fair. We took thousands of sheep from these enemies, yet our hearts mourned for the unfound slave child, and the suckling child still cried for the missing mother. Only once in a great while were we successful in locating missing members of our tribe.

The ranchers soon tired of seeing their flocks disappear. They appealed to the United States government for protection. A man named Kit Carson was sent to teach us a lesson. Nothing was said about our many women and children who had been captured and sold into slavery. When we brought up the subject, we were rudely ignored.

We saw Carson and his men destroy our crops, demolish our homesites, and slaughter mercilessly entire herds of horses and flocks of sheep. He said it was not wise to kill the Navajo, but it was all right to starve them. In our fleeing, we evaded their foot soldiers and horsemen, but starvation was not to be escaped; it followed our footsteps like a lean wolf.

We existed on wild berries, piñon nuts, yucca fruit, and other sparse but edible plants. Our little ones cried because of the undesirable change. But soon hunger drove them to eat the strange, raw, unusual food.

Other families whose homes had been desecrated by Kit Carson wandered in sheer despair. They, too, were surviving as well as they could. Their small ones had trails of tears down their hungry, dusty faces. We banded together, helping one another as best we could. Strewn along the way were starving families, some in much worse condition than others.

It seemed that every family carried bad news instead of ya'at'eeh, or good. Then, with cruel strategy, Carson persuaded other Indian trackers to corner the fleeing Navajos. We had no friends among other Indian nations. Finally there was no place left to go. We were slowly being surrounded by soldiers on well-fed horses.

Our children were growing faint from walking. Mothers could no longer take time to nurse tiny, crying infants.

The Great Creator knew in advance to place these creases upon the aged and weathered faces of my people. Tears of pain became rivers flowing in the creases of our suffering, but more for the suffering of helpless women, little ones, and the older ones who quickly perished from miserable exposure.

In sorrow, our sick eyes saw blood oozing from the feet of beloved wives and children. We knew surrender was our only hope. A few more days of such wandering with hollow stomachs and dry mouths would find us all dead.

Some families we met while traveling in the night told us that Kit Carson would feed and clothe us upon our surrender. As we looked at the lean ribs of our precious children, naked and cold, all agreed this was what must be done. The aching exhaustion of our flight had dried several mothers' milk. Small ones were fed with the desperate mothers' saliva placed upon trembling fingers.

Many turned themselves voluntarily over to the strong army of Kit Carson. At last, we thought, our ordeal is over. But when we had gathered at the camp of Kit Carson, we were told to begin an immediate march, which was over three hundred miles, into the higher plains of New Mexico Territory. A tight guard narrowed our trail.

The army had come to fight us, to force our surrender. The supplies they carried were not food and blankets, but bullets and bayonets. We began the Hweldi, "Long Walk," in the same condition we had fled capture in the first place.

Many died from exhaustion, their hearts giving out. But the army relentlessly pushed us on, drove us like cattle. Some tried to escape, but the horsemen soon caught the frightened families, then sternly escorted them back to the main body of suffering people. Not a night or day went by that someone had not lost a loved one to exposure or starvation. There was continual wailing and mourning.

Many beloved clan members closed their eyes for the last time on this trail of tears. We had laughed and sung together only days just past. If they died in the evening, when convenient to army commanders, we were allowed to place them in a shallow grave, to say a few words in supplication to the holy people in their behalf. We began to pray that the soldiers'

horses would tire so that the ones dying continually could be
put on the road to the western sun in proper burial. But the
horses did not tire. They were better cared for than the massive
trail of struggling human beings.

One who was there, my great-grandfather, Hastiin Ts'ini
(the Slender Man), recounted the tragedy that befell my
people. For long years afterward, his memory was clouded with
the pain of one who had seen things and been powerless to
help. These are his words: "Someone's child, only five years of
age, cried from thirst when the sun was high. White film had
formed around her mouth, and when she begged us for the
water we did not have, her dry tongue clave to the roof of her
mouth. How my heart broke.

"There was a soldier on a horse next to us. He looked at us,
took out his government canteen, sloshed it around, then took
a long, cool drink. The thirsty little one, with uplifted, begging hands, went toward him. A cruel, black boot sent her
reeling back into the struggling trail of human beings.

"There was no water to clean the stirrup abrasion on her
forehead. We would have to wait until we came to the next
waterhole. And we did not know when that would be, for we
had walked into unfamiliar territory.

"When the night came, we were all pushed into a tight, circular huddle. The intensity of the crying and painful wails over
the loss of loved ones made it impossible to sleep. Thousands of
my people lay dead in the wake of this long walk. We were
hungry, cold, frightened, and dying.

"The soldiers made campfires all around our group. The
blaze of the fire spotlighted our movements. Upon these watch
fires they cooked their evening meals, while the aroma passed
through our midst. It only made the children cry more, and the
parents' hearts ache. Occasionally an unthinking soldier would
throw a scrap or two into the shivering mass."

Most of the soldiers just ate and talked about the enjoyment awaiting them at Fort Sumner. Fort Sumner! A remote,
uninviting place. There, the Navajos were herded onto what
some would call land. It was flat and grassless. There were no

high mountains to climb for prayer, no canyons to vary the view, no plateaus—only a small, trickling stream ran through the area.

We were told to begin farming, and that if we tried to leave, we would be tracked down and slaughtered. "Live peaceably, or else," we were commanded. There were no trees to cut for hogan posts. We were given no implements for farming. We sat on a treeless, barren plain being told to create a miracle, a miracle for which we had learned no magic in our simple ways.

The stronger of my people were corralled into a stockade. They had been seen by soldiers as being capable of arousing others and causing trouble. Here they were kept under constant guard. Many of the people, both those on the desolate farmland and those inside the improvised stockade, died from starvation. Kit Carson expected us to subsist upon his unfilling words only. As usual, we were given the runaround.

We could see the eyes of the negotiators and knew how to recognize a liar, but we kept our mouths shut, hoping that things would at least stay the same and not get worse. We expected no better, but we received worse.

Our scraped and bleeding hands dug sleeping burrows in the ground for our families to escape the hot and cold extremes of a continental climate. Many of my people could be seen building shelters from the unwieldy sagebrush. Others braved the elements, allowing their neighbors to have the best of what was only scantily available. Four years we lived here. Sagebrush was our only source of firewood. After the first winter, it was no more. Every winter claimed more lives. Only a few blankets arrived—those promised by the invisible government.

We at least received government rations. Sometimes we received flour and coffee beans. We did not how to use this strange food. Our families tried to choke it down dry. They ate the dry flour, often infested with maggots and mice pellets, by licking the white dust from their fingers. We tried to mix the flour with other unsavory rations. We did not like the taste of the alien food, but we understood we must have nourishment.

Flour and coffee beans were boiled together for stew. The dirty water was thrown out each time. Some were confused about why the beans would not cook.

In a short time, it was apparent that we would all perish. We were not farmers. In our condition, it was difficult to imagine we had a Mother Earth, for why were we treated in such a way? Many suffered agonizing deaths, slow starvation, and just giving up the will to live. The soldiers used our women as they saw fit. But despite our suffering, we at least retained our identity as the People.

Finally a treaty was made wherein our people would be allowed to return to their homeland if they agreed to stay within certain boundaries that the white man would name. Parts of our own land were given to more submissive tribes of the area and also to white settlers. In going home, we could no longer roam at will, as in the past. And during our journey, the hunger-ravaged people ate almost anything—rats, mice, lizards, snakes, and other creatures and edible plants—in order to survive. But, we were going home as hunters and not as farmers. The ear of the Great Spirit had turned our way.

From Fort Sumner, my people came with pained pace, weakened from famine and fear; yet fearlessly they came to their traditional homeland. Seized with acute homesickness, the stronger and the ablest hurried, while the weaker struggled step by step, their hearts aimed for the sacred land, the home of holy dreams and visions, of birth and being. Hope was here manifest in its purity. Mile by mile their faith increased as they drew ever closer.

Northeastern Arizona. Fort Defiance. My people received clothing, scant supplies, and animals, but now they were free from the surveillance of soldiers, free from suspicion; now there was a chance to regain some self-respect. Torturously they trudged over mountain and valley, through pain to promise, as feet cracked and worn finally felt the earth place of our fathers. Old men prayed, remembering; surviving women wept; and some, bent with age, stooped to place a parched kiss upon the broken but beloved land. In this human drama stood my great-grandparents with their dear ones and friends, enveloped within the embrace of the four sacred mountains. For them, as it had been for others who returned, the wait had been much longer than the walk.

But the tragedy was not ended. The old hogans were collapsed to the dust. No yellow corn was there to furnish sacred pollen to bless the dawn. Mother Earth only cried for their plight, but she was the mother that would bless their way again. So upon this land, and in their souls, they began anew.

1

SON OF
DONKEY MAN
AND RED WOMAN

The traditional homeland of my great-grandparents is now known as Four Corners, the only spot in the United States where four states join—Arizona, Colorado, New Mexico, and Utah. Somewhere southeast of this now-famous point, they ended the Long Walk to begin life once again.

No cities, towns, or highways, not even a buckboard road, broke the horizon for the eyes of my great-grandparents. Shortly, within several months, the San Juan River at Shiprock, New Mexico, became the site of a government agency serving all the Navajos of that region. Fort Defiance had been the service area; now Shiprock Agency was closer. In this area lived my great-grandparents, Hastiin Ts'ini and his beloved companion, who remains nameless. My great-grandparents lived humbly, but I respect and love them through the traditional legacy they left, full of wisdom, life, and love. For me, it is as familiar voices from the dust. We are what we think and do. When I think and do honorably, I know the names of my great ancestors. Their lives in the living were their names. God grant me the same honorable living.

My grandparents died before I was born, but I do have the names of three of them. My paternal grandfather is Hastiin

Jaaneez, meaning Donkey Man. This title came of respect because he was the only Navajo for miles around who had a donkey. The small donkey was useful in herding sheep, hauling
water, or bringing *chizh,* or firewood, on its back. Hastiin At-
sidii (the Silversmith Man) was another name given to him.

Asdzaa Adika'i (Woman Playing Cards) was my paternal
grandmother. She liked to play cards and was one of the very
few people of the area who could. Somehow this woman of no
formal education had learned to recognize the different symbols on the cards and their different combinations and had
learned to play card games. It says something of her great intel-
ligence.

My maternal grandfather was Hastiin Abani (Buckskin
Man). It has been said that he wore buckskin clothing, and
many of his belongings were of buckskin. I do not know my
maternal grandmother's name, although I know her clan
name. The clan name is very important as it identifies one with
a very large family group, an idea that is hard for someone of
the modern nuclear family to grasp. All the members of a clan
have close family feelings. So this binds me to my maternal
grandmother, even though I may not know her actual name.
This grandmother died when my mother was ten years old. My
mother was born about 1906.

Mother's life was harsh and difficult. Her family depended
entirely upon the forces of nature to provide a livelihood. Back
then, there was no other consideration except to live off the
land. The Navajos cared for the sheep just as meticulously as
they cared for their own lives. Without the sheep, starvation
would have overtaken the early Navajo families.

In this setting, Mother came into the world. Her parents
died when she was but a baby, so she was reared by her elder sister. When just beginning to walk, Mother was out learning
how to herd sheep. Since there were no other children in the
home, great responsibility fell upon my mother. Once when
the flock was very large, it was divided, and Mother became responsible for half of it. She was still only a young girl. She
herded sheep until she was grown.

Even after marriage, she had to herd sheep. When her husband ran off, she was left with the total burden of rearing a family, as well as caring for the large herd. With one child barely walking, another in her arms, and one more cradle-boarded on her back, Mother herded sheep under the relentless desert sun. In addition to caring for the sheep, she also chopped firewood, hauled water, and did all the household cleaning and chores.

My mother loved her elder sister and appreciated all she had done for her. My aunt's name is Hastiin Abani Yee Bitsi (Daughter of Buckskin Man). The hogan of my aunt and uncle, Man Who Halts, was the only home Mother ever had. In this respected place I lived and grew. From its humble entrance, in many mornings, I walked into the east whence rose Father Sun. From that doorway were my comings and goings into what wisdom's path would yield.

My parents are full-blooded Navajos. My father was born about 1899. Pete Lee was the English name given him during World War I as he served America briefly in the army. He was sent home because of medical difficulties. He was losing his hearing, in addition to not being able to understand English.

Hastiin Jaaneez Yee Biye is my father's Navajo name. You can see why the army just called him Pete. They could not even spell his name, much less pronounce it. Son of Donkey Man is the English meaning of the Navajo name. Asdzaa Lichii (Red Woman) is my mother's name. When she was grown, she received the name Mae Lee. But there were other Mae Lees in the Shiprock area, so she received the initial K, making her name Mae K. Lee.

The Navajos have a unique kin relationship called the clan. My father was of the *Kin Yaa Aanii,* or Under the Flat-Roofed House People clan, and Mother was of the *To dich'iinii* or Bitter Water clan. My clan name is traced through my mother, for the clan system is matrilineal. But my father's clan is important too. A Navajo is born into his mother's clan, but born for his father's clan.

The clan takes in all blood kin but is not restricted to biological ties only. It may bind Navajos who are not biologically related or reared in the same locale, or even people who may have seen each other only once.

Because of this unique clan relationship, each Navajo is related to many families throughout the reservation and is quickly made welcome in their homes. Navajos will always go out of their way to do a favor or show preference to a clan relative, even one they have never met before. Upon greeting a stranger, the first question a Navajo asks is, "To which clan do you belong?" When I am asked this question, I say I am of the Bitter Water clan. Also, all fellow clan members are called brothers and sisters. This is very confusing to non-Indians. We look upon the clan brother or sister with the same love as an immediate family member.

One important principle of the clan system is to limit marriage choices. A Navajo must never marry within his own clan or his father's clan. The old, traditional Navajos are very strict in this regard, and as far as I know, there have been very few violations of this restriction. A Navajo who marries within his or her own clan is thought to be mentally unstable. The traditional way of selecting marriage partners is for the father and mother to go wife hunting for their son. The son usually doesn't have any choice in the matter. I am thankful that this was not done in my behalf, for the eternal companion who lives with me, whom I deeply cherish, is my heart's own choice.

Neither of my parents had a formal education. The bedrock of their education was Navajo culture. There were few schools then, and even they were small and inaccessible to many. Too, Navajo life saw no need for such. The way of *Dineh,* the People, was education enough. Children were to care for the sheep herds. My parents were both experts in caring for large sheep herds. In those days the flocks were quite large.

The Navajo began to prosper after the Treaty of 1868. Mother Earth was kind. The green grass grew tall under good rain. Upon her face our sheep and horses increased to bring prosperity. The Navajos worked hard to oversee this increase. By 1920, almost every family was blessed with large herds. In peace of thanksgiving, one's eyes could feel good to see such herds; the People and Mother Earth were flowing together. It felt right. My own father tells humbly of these good times, of how the gentle rains in blessing came to green the waiting blade of grass, of pure fallings of white snow that signaled the time for winter storytelling. The time was good then. It was the time of running water that not only nourished the beautiful land but also cleansed the mind and heart of the People, giving life to all.

Can you envision the woolly, fat sheep and healthy horses in your mind? You can barely see the sun-highlighted back of the sheep because the tender grass is so tall. See the stallion's shadowed chest ripple as he moves toward the dusk. Beauty is plenteous.

Then Washington's new livestock policies came like a bolt of lightning. The government's ill-planned livestock reduction plan mirrored the Long Walk because of its lengthy and devastating economic upheaval. This, along with the Great Depression, came like a two-edged sword upon the Navajos.

What happened to the bounty the Navajos once enjoyed? The Great Depression. Widespread were its effects as it made its way from the national economy to touch even Navajo pastoral life. Then drought came; the rains ceased their pleasing of the earth. Quickly our livestock stripped the prairies and the hills of vegetation. Poverty, death, and starvation had come upon the Navajo like the unheard wind; the earlier times were gone and forgotten. Where were the kind gods of the Navajo? What had the Navajo done to displease them? Most Navajos thought only the reservation suffered, because of their geographical isolation and lack of Anglo cultural understanding.

In place of moisture came Washington's directions. The Bureau of Indian Affairs commissioner systematically reduced all grazing livestock equal to rangeland capacity. Entire herds were taken away, or shot and then left to rot in front of the pained Navajo eye. Here was a people who would eat rabbit or prairie dog rather than prized sheep. And now the sheep were shot and lay bloated in the sun. Even our prized horses were slaughtered. The Indian commissioner soon joined Kit Carson in the oppressor's hall of infamy, as the old ones viewed it.

Possession of livestock was our standard of wealth. Many of

our people were thrown into abject poverty and could barely stand to face their family and friends. One had to find out just how far his heart and strength could endure. This was a Long Walk into our souls, a walk burdened not with physical trial so much, but more with the agonizing question of "Why?"

As the horse was prestigious, it did not matter that he greatly outgrazed other animals. The slaughter and removal of our thousands of horses hit hard in the solar plexus of Navajo manhood. To the Navajos, it was ruthless aggression.

Both my father and mother have painfully recounted their story to me. Their stories of the reduction are bitter and bewildering. Their own livestock were dealt this destruction. Surviving animals were mere flesh and bones; and these were regulated by the commission through permit. Our herds were not allowed to increase for many years until someone else thought the capacity of the land was right.

"Why is this thing happening?" asked the old ones. "The gods must be angry. This is why our sheep starve. The living of the white man's way has caused these things. This is why. We have displeased the gods in turning from the Navajo way." The rains refused to come. The gods would not be appeased.

During this time, however, Navajos treated kindly non-Indian families and hobos who crisscrossed our land on their way to California, the land of better opportunity. From these migrants, some caught a partial understanding of what must have been occurring outside the reservation. The depression favored only those who helped create it.

These conditions prevailed during the first marriages of my parents. Perhaps the starvation and poverty collected its due— their first marriages dissolved.

Times were hard for all people. My parents met and married in hard times. My father had four children, and my mother, who twice before had married, had four children. Two of her four had died. All told, they had seventeen children. I am the second child of their last marriage. I was born in a dark, depressed time that covered this promised land. Mother and Father were married in a traditional Navajo ceremony. This took place in a hogan and is a sacred thing. As they cleansed their hands with life water and then dipped their fingers into the corn mush, their cultural upbringing brought to their minds the oneness of their married selves with the earth and the endless universe.

After their marriage, my parents began living with my aunt and uncle. My parents had nothing. They were dependent upon the loving Daughter of Buckskin Man and my respectable uncle, Man Who Halts, for everything. My aunt and uncle had but little, but what they had, they shared. This is the way of my people. The depression still hung like a dark cloud. The family sheep were few. My father and uncle found little work. Daughter of Buckskin Man and Mother wove rugs and sold corn-bread, which brought in little. But the Navajo has learned to be thankful for small things, and for this his heart has been blessed to be large. All my family owned was just two wild dogs. But some families were so poor they didn't even have a dog!

Because Daughter of Buckskin Man and Man Who Halts were aged, all of us children, my brothers and sisters and I, did the herding. This small herd seemed like great wealth to us. Perhaps people today look upon furs, jewelry, boats, and beautiful homes in a similar way. But we Navajos have a relationship with our prized flocks and herds that really cannot be expressed in words. They live with us and are fed by the same Mother Earth. Only reluctantly would we use sheep as food. My uncle, Man Who Halts, had a few horses, which pleased his kind eye and made his heart happy. He could talk to them. They would listen. And I observed, my uncle was a gentleman of nature.

Oh, how I wish I could tell you how the beautiful desert smells just after the summer rain, how the scent of sagebrush rises toward the heavens to give thanks, how happy nature springs alive with gratitude, and how my mother, Red Woman, looks upon nature's face as she enjoys this blessing upon the land. This simple thing is beautiful to those who live and die upon the desert. In beauty such as this, though life was hard, I was born.

Just a few hundred yards north of the Colorado/New

Mexico border, the traveler scarcely notices the little two-track dirt road that turns off the highway to the east. A short distance from the highway this little road enters a small canyon that climbs and curves like a bow, southward to the New Mexico side, then northward again into Colorado. After about ten miles of rough travel along a wash, the road abruptly comes out on top of a high mesa, which rises about a thousand feet above the highway. There on the mesa was our winter home.

Usually the Navajos will have a winter home at a lower elevation and a summer home in the cool pines of the nearby mountains. These seasonal moves lead many to believe that my people are nomadic. This is not true. They occupy the same homes and grazing areas each year. Our seasonal moves are no different than those of people who travel south to Florida for the winter.

However, our family grazing arrangement was backward compared to that of most Navajos. The higher mesa country was still low enough to be free of snow most of the winter, and it provided the best winter grazing. Our summer range and hogan were on the land just west of the highway, slightly south of the state line. An advantage of this lower summer range was that we could graze our sheep near the highway. This allowed us to make a few dollars from the tourists who would stop to take a picture of us with our sheep.

From a distance our hogan looked like a brown beehive, for it was a rounded, mud-plastered log home. A blanket covered its door, which was on the east side. There were no windows. It had one small room with a dirt floor. In the middle of the dried mud roof was a hole for the chimney. To walk into the hogan is like walking into an almost lightless basement. But it was home, especially during the winter, when stories could be told around the central heating system, an old oil drum converted into a stove.

A few cracked and unmatched dishes and old smoke-stained pots were stacked high on crudely made crateboard shelves. There were sheepskins, old blankets, and quilts folded and piled against the wall to lay out at night for sleeping. There were no chairs. Most of us sat on the floor. The pipe that reached from the stove through the open smoke hole was made of a piece of eight-inch corrugated culvert pipe that my father had found along the highway. Before I was born there was no stove, just a hollowed-out place in the center of the floor for a small fire.

Clothes were hung on nails or pegs driven into the hogan walls. A few old boxes held additional clothing and were stacked on the north side of the hogan. Also hanging from the walls of the hogan were ropes, bridles, saddles, and other equipment used in working sheep and horses. When my father was home, he took care of the equipment, as well as taking the responsibility for building corrals and fences and hauling firewood and water. Our water came from a small reservoir or pond we had made. This pond was also used by our animals. We relied completely on rain to fill it.

Surrounding our winter hogan was our mesa-top grazing area, covered with cedar and piñon trees. To the east was a village of Ute families who shared our grazing area. Eventually these families moved down to Towaoc, Colorado, during the early 1950s when the Ute tribe received Indian Claims money

The Lee family summer hogan

from the government for building homes. After they moved, the entire mesa top was left to us, even though we were technically living on the Ute reservation.

A lot of our time was spent at the winter hogan on the mesa rather than at the summer home below. The winter hogan was where I spent most of my early years. To the north of this hogan, the sheep corral was nestled under a nearby cliff. It held the family herd of sheep and goats. The corral was made of brush and branches that we had matted together to construct a fence. Outside in front was the family wagon, which belonged to my aunt and uncle. This buckboard wagon was used to haul wood, wool, and water, and to make trips to the trading post. The ever-present woodpile of cedar and piñon was stacked near our hogan. This was our only source of fuel for cooking and heating.

This seemingly barren and forlorn place even today is the home of my heart, the sweetness of my youth. As one drives north on U.S. Highway 666 from Shiprock, New Mexico, toward Cortez, Colorado, the terrain, although hilly and with broken mesa, is virtually treeless. But it is not without life, for the abundance, the thriving life of the living desert, surrounds the periphery of human view. Only the distant mountain ranges far to the north and the tops of the higher eastern mesas are forested.

Twenty miles from Shiprock, the highway passes into Colorado. The only indication of any change is the man-made state markers. The border line, known only to engineers and surveyors, also divides the Navajos to the south and the Utes to the north. But in actuality, the two people have defined their own territorial separation that takes into account the natural terrain. This is far easier than worrying about some imaginary line that can't be seen.

Around the outside of our hogan there was only bare, red dirt. There were no shade trees, no fenced-in yard, no ornamental bushes, and no softness. Sheepskins, blankets, and skirts were hung out to air in the sun on cedar poles. Pathways led in every direction from our hogan. One led to the water hole about two miles away. Another led to the hills where the grass grew tallest. Still another led to the sheep corral. One led down to our summer home, and another led to the Ute village to the east. In the olden days Navajos were constantly at war with the Utes, but when I was small we were living in peace with them.

To my people, the hogan is not just a place to eat and sleep; it occupies a special place in a sacred world. The first hogan, according to the traditions of my people, was built by the holy people. Navajo mythology and traditions prescribe certain positions for people and objects within the hogan. When someone dies, the body must be removed through a hole broken in the wall to the north, and then the hogan must be rebuilt in a different location.

A new hogan is often consecrated with a blessing or a ceremonial song. Sacred corn pollen is usually sprinkled along the base of the hogan posts both inside and out. It was my uncle, along with my father, who built our winter and summer hogans. My father, being part medicine man, usually gave the blessing on the hogans when they were built.

During the first nine years of my life, we moved back and forth between our winter hogan and the summer hogan. About the only variation in our life-style was when we left to do migrant work.

$$\underline{2}$$

A BRUSH WITH DEATH

T his son was twice born, for not only was I subject to my
mother's labor, but into a tumultuous time I came. The
sounds of war had seized upon Mother Earth, the groan-
ing of man and darkness of death shadowed the entire human
race.

During March of 1943, all the earth was agonizing under
the contraction of death. The Second World War had em-
broiled practically every nation, and indirectly all were affected. During this springtime of my youth, the favor began to
turn toward the Allies. In the west, the last of the German resistance in North Africa was rooted out while preparations for
the invasion of Sicily and Italy were underway. The expanding
power had just been halted in the east; the Japanese rising sun
had proved to be but a bright eastern star that had its zenith
momentarily in this night of history. It hovered over the harbor of this youthful America that for only a little over a century
and a half had been swaddled in constitutional freedom. Allied
Pacific victory from island to island was just beginning.

During the concluding months of the Pacific campaign, a
group of Navajo Marines conducted Allied radio communica-
tions in the Navajo language. The code was never broken by
the Japanese. Not only is the language in its inflection, intona-

tion, and origin most complex, but beyond that, my people can communicate in a sublime, poetic manner. The Allies may well have been helped a great deal by this handful of courageous Native Americans. This, of course, does not disparage any who gave their service and even their lives for this great land. For the giving of life unto belief is the greatest form of poetry God has bestowed upon mankind. It finds its greatest metaphor in free agency.

Although the war was seemingly far away from our reservation home, we felt its effects. Though the depression and dire drought of the thirties had dissipated, prosperity knew not my people. Now commodity shortages and war-related travel restrictions hampered our progress. Too many Navajo young men were away fighting.

Though the memory of this nation's ideas of manifest destiny still burned in the minds of many Native Americans—ideas wherein massive rights and lands were accumulated in favor of American political policy but hurting the American Indian—my people held themselves in valiant patriotism.

My father had served in World War I for one year before receiving his medical discharge. He was losing his hearing and did not understand English. He was physically unacceptable to serve in the war, but his patriotism was still strong. His full effort was now turned to our support. Gone for months at a time, he worked laboriously in railroad gangs, herded sheep in Colorado, and sought whatever employment would benefit his family. He was not afraid to work, and to work hard. During his absences, Mother; my aunt, Daughter of Buckskin Man; and my uncle, Man Who Halts, bound our family together. Because my father was hundreds of miles away from home working on a railroad, he was not at home when I was born.

Being heavy with child, my beloved mother left our hogan, entering the crisp, cutting, morning air on March 23, 1943. Just when the child would come, she was not certain. Glancing back over her left shoulder toward the sheepcote by the cliff, she noticed something different about the day. Something would happen. She was not sure exactly what to think about this feeling. She had felt this way many times before, and whenever she did, something usually occurred.

She then turned toward her right and began the arduous journey down the mesa. The buckboard trail was to the east. This was a possible route, but on foot it was much too long as it spiraled down the Masada-like mesa. Her decision was to walk to the edge of the mesa and then climb down, almost straight down, with groping fingers and feeling feet. Not only did her swollen abdomen make things awkward, but a tattered shawl draped around her shoulders was filled with Navajo corn bread. The purpose of her trip was to walk the thirty miles to Towaoc, Colorado, to sell this bread in order to buy the much-needed commodities for her family. She hoped to catch a ride once she had made it down the escarpment of the mesa and to the highway.

Perhaps her Ute friends at Towaoc would purchase the blue corn bread. So that morning she began the thirty-mile journey to the Southern Ute Agency at Towaoc, Colorado. If fortunate, she would have to walk only half the distance.

Just before attempting the descent from the high mesa top down into the deep canyon below, she paused and said to herself, "It is a long way off—the highway. I have no choice but to go. My children depend upon me. There is a strange feeling inside me. It is as though I would be sick. And if I should fall trying to go down this mesa, my child inside could die. I must be careful. It is too bad we have no horse. Even a donkey to ride down the other way would be better."

With that last thought, she put her hand against one of the huge boulders that acted as a natural sentinel at the trail's head. As she hoisted the weight of her body three feet down to the trail, she pushed the rock with the muscles of her hand. As she let go, she braced herself against a waiting rock below with her other hand. The jar took her breath away. She waited there momentarily to catch her breath. She had to repeat this procedure all the way down. When she reached the base of the canyon, she had to walk several miles on a soft, sandy canyon floor. Just before midday, she reached the highway.

A sympathetic driver gave her a ride for twenty miles, as far as the Towaoc turnoff. She then walked several miles west to the small Ute community near the base of Sleeping Ute Mountain. From house to house she silently walked. The load of bread on her back lightened as she went. When her shawl was completely empty, the contractions of childbirth suddenly began.

This is what she had sensed earlier. The feeling this child gave of wanting to come into the world was different than earlier births. She sensed something different. It was in the midday of spring lambing time. The sun was at its highest, overshadowing the village of Towaoc.

Anxiously she made her way in agony to the small, rundown village clinic. Within minutes, she was delivered of a son. I had taken my first breath. I had come into earthly existence. The crowded government clinic afforded only a cold floor where my mother lay for the needed recuperation. But rest was rare. In the clinic, there was no room; it was crowded, small, and uncomfortable. She determined to return home the same day. I was born a Navajo on a different reservation, on a Ute reservation.

Still weak with searing pain, my brave mother carefully swaddled her little one in the same shawl she so selflessly had unburdened of bread. She turned once again into the cold, windy March day. The previous journey was reversed, except now and again she rested as dizziness overcame her.

"Many times, my son," she later told me, "I sat alongside the road from Towaoc. I could not take many steps at a time. Blood dripped down my legs. The pain I cannot describe to you. But I had you in my arms. It was worth it. When you cried from hunger, I forgot the pain. Carefully I would unwrap the old shawl and bring you close to my bosom. While you filled with milk, my heart was pleased. No matter the pain—I had a son."

After hitchhiking to our turnoff, she again began the ten-mile hike up the soft, sandy canyon floor. Her legs ached. The weariness was indescribable.

Much later, she was looking up the same mesa escarpment

she had descended earlier that day. The coyotes had begun their wailing. Desert nightlife was coming alive. She wanted desperately to be inside the warm hogan. Several times she thought she would pass out. Only her firm determination kept her going. Her strength was spent. She had not eaten all day. The weight of the infant had increased tremendously. The mesa trail wound to the top through gigantic boulders and oversized slab-rock fragments. The fragments were upended in the side of the mesa; some were vertical and others were horizontal, but all made the passage along the trail formidable, especially for the tender mother and child. Once again, she grasped the sandpaper-like surface of the rock. As pain hit, she doubled over. But she did not cry. Instead of worrying about herself, she checked the precious bundle in her arms to make sure everything was all right.

Only able to climb and grope in the darkness for short distances, Mother stopped every twenty or so feet just to rest. So exhausted was she that almost every time she stopped, she fell asleep. Not wanting to do that for fear of not waking so she could care for her helpless infant, she rested only momentarily

First level of the mesa climbed by George P. Lee's mother. Two other levels, out of camera range, rise above this one

each time. Each time she also stiffly aroused and struggled another few feet. Between the upheaved slabs of rock, she was forced to contort her body in order to pass between. But she was not concerned about the piercing pain that enveloped her whole body. She was concerned only about the small bundle. This she kept safe. The last length of her struggle to reach home is an ordeal difficult to imagine. It took her long into the cold night to make it. Even more incredible was the fact that both my mother and I lived through it.

For a man to write of what women experience in childbirth is futile. The severe pain and subsequent exhaustion are more than debilitating. If a person were to walk across hot coals barefooted, or lay upon a mat of sharp spikes, there would still be no comparison. Though the feet may burn or the body be pierced, yet the searing pain of childbirth creases the memory with sharpness. And yet, somehow in the divine purposes of God, the sorrow of birth grows into effulgent love, and the symbol of pain, the child, becomes the object of the mother's affection.

"Son," my mother told me many times, "when you were born I could think of nothing else. I wanted to get you home to show your aunt. I knew all the children would be happy. I knew your father was going to have joy. I wondered when you would have your first smile. That would be a good time. We would invite some friends over to eat then. Our traditions are good. The Great Spirit has watched over our home."

Mother is still as interested in her family as ever. It is her great joy to have children and grandchildren relish her cooking—I can tell by the way she looks when I tell her I appreciate what she has cooked. It seems such a simple thing to cook. But her whole soul is in it, and I am her son. When she cooks for me, it tastes good. I wish I had the words with which to honor my mother. She is the stalwart of my life. From her example, I have learned to never give up.

Mother was strong and soon recovered after my birth. Over the next few years she gave birth to seven more children. I hold my mother in highest reverence for going through the depths of travail to give me life and to keep me alive after I was born.

It was not long until my father was notified of my birth. He hurried home to proudly greet his new son.

I saw my first year of life almost entirely from a Navajo cradleboard, which consisted of two hand-carved juniper boards for the back, with a curved board over the front to cover my head. Snugly wrapped in a warm blanket, I was laced tightly into the cradleboard, face up.

I was unwrapped only for changing, feeding, and bathing. The rest of the day and night, only my head and eyes could move. In this manner I was carried from place to place and set upright when awake, watching my mother and the rest of the busy world around me. While sleeping, I was usually laid flat.

Perhaps muscle development was slow during this first year, but my sense of belonging, of being loved and wanted, grew quickly. Fastened snugly to my cradleboard, I soon learned my world would respond to my every demand, whether it be for food, a change, or simply to be played with or entertained. With so many caring family members in our household, there was no chance for a child to be lonely or unloved.

Near my first birthday, I was released from the cradleboard. Quickly I learned to crawl, and then walk. I was small but agile. And, as was generally the case with Indian babies, I was thin from not having enough to eat. My first areas of investigation were on the hogan's dirt floor and the surrounding, hard-packed earth outside. My memories also include playing about our campsite in the furrows of Colorado bean fields when my parents found seasonal work.

Life in the hogan at this time was extremely primitive compared to modern standards. In our humble home, we had no running water, no indoor toilets, no electricity. It was completely devoid of modern conveniences. When it rained, one of the family members walked a mile or two to reach a mesa that had pockets of trapped rain water. The person would collect the water in a container and haul it home on his back. Survival was our constant concern.

My parents tried their best to keep the dirt floor swept. Other than that, they could do little to keep things clean. Lack of water made bathing a rarity. We were always dirty, but never

by choice. There was no way to wash clothing, so we wore
what we had on until it was so caked with dirt and grime that it
had to be thrown away. To ease this problem, little boys were
allowed to run around naked. What little clothing we did have
was ragged and usually secondhand or even thirdhand if it
withstood the test of rough poverty.

Lice were everywhere—in our hair, on our clothes, and on
our bodies. I remember my trousers being so caked with lice
that I could scrape them away from the seams with my fingernails. And I wish I could say those fingernails were clean be-
forehand, but they weren't. Lice caused itching most of the
time, making life uncomfortable, but we became numb to it
after a while.

The saddest part of being poor was our lack of understanding about basic sanitation. That there might be a connection
between our deplorable living conditions and the ever-present
sickness and disease never occurred to any of us. Even had we
known, though, the lack of decent water made a cleaner standard of living almost impossible. The invisible bars of poverty
were strong and solid. We survived from one day to the next.

I can clearly remember my father strapping my elder
brother and me into an old saddle astride a gentle horse. It
scared me to death, for I was only two years old. But through
the patience and kindness of a loving father, I learned to ride
with skill when I was not much bigger than a toddler.

As was customary with Navajos, my parents were in no
hurry to give me a name. I was just referred to as *Awee,* or baby.
In time, I was given the name of Ashkii Yazhi (Little Boy).
This name continued with me until I began school. Tradition-
ally, a baby was given a nickname and a sacred name. Ashkii
Yazhi was my nickname; my sacred name Ashkii Hoyani (Boy
Who Is Well Behaved and Good).

Though the heaviness of hunger and hardship frequented
our home, and though poverty's stern fist knocked continually,
in our struggle as a family we always seemed to be happy. I always felt wanted and needed as a member of my family. That
was of great importance. My poor mother, despite our poverty,

always said her children were the greatest riches life could possibly give.

There were numerous times, too many to want to remember, when racial prejudice was added to poverty. The feelings of inadequacy were inescapable. Prejudice stung more than once when we migrated to small towns looking for work. My parents were sometimes denied services by white merchants.

Oh, how it hurt to see my father and mother turn so peacefully away from this. I know their hearts were pained, not for themselves only, but to have their precious family see such humiliation and social injustice. But this, too, like the lice, we became numb to. My parents did not teach us to return unkindness for unkindness.

Training in the ways of my people began early. Before three years of age, I was sent out with the older children to herd sheep. As I tagged along, I learned. Sometimes my three-year-old mind did not want to face the cold, but I went because my parents urged me to go. Above all, I had respect for their wishes.

My father always rose early and got us children up early too. He would say, "The sun must not see you sleeping! It is time to run, my beloved children. You must run to greet the sun!"

And then out into the cool dawn we would run, eager to please a father we loved so much. We ran, often in races, a mile or more. To the east, we hurried to greet the rising sun. This was sure to make our minds clear and our bodies strong.

If there was sufficient snow on the ground, we would take snow baths. We did not like these. Only when our mother became quite stern would we strip off our clothes to go out and sit in a snowbank, where she scrubbed us with icy snow. Despite our cries of protest, she kept at it until we were rash-red all over. Only then were we allowed to reenter the hogan. As we grew older, mother did not have to scrub us; we took snow baths on our own. But before we went back into the warmth of the mud-insulated hogan, we ran a mile or two toward the east in a foot of snow. And we were naked when we ran. We usually ran as quickly as possible. Once in the hogan, we bundled up in blankets and drank hot coffee to warm us. Tears from the cold snow bath were soon gone as we watched the pot of prairie-dog stew bubble on the stove. Mother then began to slap frybread dough back and forth before gently laying it into the deep grease of a hot frying pan. I could tell by the way she worked that she cared for us. This was no chore, and she did not complain, for we were her little ones, her beloved family.

My father had an uncanny way of being able to smell the aroma of stew in the air. He always knew by his sensitivity when it was time to eat. Then he would come in and sit on the ground beside the stove. Mother would fill a bowl of stew, lay a piece of frybread across the top, and set it beside him. There were no spoons or forks; we ate by dipping the frybread into the warm stew. The only utensils we knew for a long time were our fingers. The stew was usually rabbit, prairie dog, or mutton. We lived off the land to survive.

When times were really hard, we would kill one of our prized horses for food. We did not want to eat horsemeat, but we did need to satisfy the hunger pangs that plagued our bodies.

We learned to play with desert animals as we grew. They were our only toys. Because of our attachment to the things of nature, we did not like to kill anything. My brothers and I used to catch the tails of rattlesnakes just for fun after our dogs had weakened them by shaking them. We never hurt them. One had to be quite brave and quick to do such a thing. It was fun. There was a lot of laughing in seeing a brother jerk back in fright during a close call. When we did catch one, we would dangle it in the air while someone else caught it just behind the triangular head. Then we would gently stretch it out full length to see who had caught the longest one. These were better than store-bought toys; they never wore out and were in plentiful supply. Chasing lizards, prairie dogs, cottontails, and lambs were other favorite pastimes. One cannot approach a relationship with animals in such a way and not feel some guilt in having to kill them for food, although man is justified in doing so.

As we ate, we ate in silence, for a meal was of Mother

Earth, and our attention was given to joyful gratitude and enjoyment. Mealtime, if properly revered, is most sacred. According to my father, the meal was almost a religious observance, the time being used in meditation to the holy people. While we ate, we sat crosslegged around a soiled, torn piece of oilcloth spread on the dirt floor. This was our best tablecloth.

If there was food, we would eat when we were hungry or when company came, no matter the time of day. We did not eat according to a set time or group cultural standard. The arrival of visitors was always a good time to stir up the fire and prepare a meal. It was a standard Navajo courtesy to feed visitors, and no guest would think of refusing a meal. Even in times of hunger, our guests were welcome to share what little we had. We were taught to give our last bread to a guest, whether Indian or non-Indian.

My father and mother loved us above their very lives, though their love did not appear in outward affection. For the depth of their love, I will be forever thankful. My parents had little comprehension of the honors and awards that were reserved for me later in life, even of my Church callings. The only thing that mattered to them was that I honored my sacred name, Boy Who Is Well Behaved and Good. As well, my successes had something to do, they felt, with an earlier event. Their humble pride was shown in telling and retelling to friends and relatives of the time I supposedly died. They were so proud and yet humble to tell this story, and they spoke of it in quiet reverence. They felt that the holy people had preserved my life for a wise and divine purpose. I have heard my father, in deepest humility, tell one trusted enough to hear: "When my son, George, was near four or five years of age, he became extremely ill. My own heart became ill with him, and I hurt inside. When this illness would not leave, my wife and I decided to contact a good hand trembler to diagnose the cause for sickness in my little son. We did it with the intent to know which traditional ceremony would be just the right one. This we did. After the trembler left, we knew which medicine man could do this particular ceremony.

"A medicine man would come soon to sing over my little

one, to lay him upon a sand painting. This 'sing' had no power, for the son of my love worsened. Something must have gone wrong. Finally, we went to the Anglo doctor at the public health service in Shiprock. We would see if the Anglo doctor could help. He put an X-ray machine on my son and then told us there was nothing wrong. I knew there was, but those doctors would not listen and turned a deaf ear to my pleading. With tears in my eyes, I walked out of the hospital with my son in my arms, dejected, with hopelessness carved on my face, not knowing what to do next.

"The next day, my son had not improved. Both my wife and I worried and were afraid to discuss what tomorrow was to bring. The second day he grew worse, and so did we, his parents. He had not eaten in a week. That evening, I saw a blueness come upon my dying son. As I checked him over, his heart had no life.

"My own heart felt as if it would end; the pain was piercing. I wondered if my strength could hold, even to pray. I poured my own heart unto the Great Spirit above so that my son would revive. I cannot describe the pain I felt each time I looked down upon the small body that was so still.

"As I prayed, I took out the medicine bag and gently placed the corn pollen upon the tip of my son's tongue, on his head, and tenderly all over his body. As my hand went over his body my prayers increased in pain. 'My little one, my little one, how I love you. Do not leave us. Oh, Great Spirit, hear the words of my prayer!'

"With the special prayer feather, I chanted the sacred songs and touched my bag as the ritual had been taught to me. Also, I made a sand painting upon the floor and took the little body into my arms. All I wanted to do was hold him there, but I knew I must place him on the sand painting. Upon the dirt floor painting, I reluctantly left him. While he was there, I continued to chant and pray for him, but my tears choked the words as I would look at him and feel the love that had been alive between us.

"By the third hour, I was weak from appealing to the gods for the life of my son. I could no longer distinguish between tears or perspiration. All the rest of the family were crying just as hard. Grief had entered our lives."

With finality, my father, drenched in tears of love, turned to the rest of the family and told them that the Great Spirit had taken me, that my soul was traveling the road toward the setting sun.

Acting decisively, my father said he was going to build a casket for the burial. The casket was crude because of poverty; the wood was weathered and found about the hogan. He asked the visiting neighbors to go several hundred yards from the hogan to dig a small grave. My mother began to dress me in the best clothes reserved for special occasions. The sacred corn pollen anointing was left on my body. It was now past midnight.

The preparations made, I was carried to the gravesite. My father performed a last ritual over me. Tearfully, after using all his strength again, he gave up, his heart completely broken. With what little energy his kneeling body still possessed, he carefully, but still so lovingly, lifted his limp son into the crude box, his tears moistening both himself and his son into oneness. In pain he closed the lid. The box was lowered into the dry grave. Dirt was ready to cover what would become only a memory.

Again my father cried out, sobbing and chanting the prayers of the Navajo for the dead. Only this time, he asked that my spirit would be able to walk peacefully toward the western sun and not turn back to haunt the family.

In darkness, where tears were hidden but yet felt, the family who had been through so much already stood with shoulders sagging in mourning despair. The night could grow no darker.

The first shovelful of dirt hit the top of the pine box. Then all stood quiet, listening. Where was that strange sound coming from? Within seconds it was repeated. Then almost everyone at once realized that a knocking sound was coming from the wooden casket in the grave. All were quiet. Thoughts merged with the night's fearful darkness. Evil spirits were banging within the box!

Navajo custom had taught a great fear of death and dark-

ness. Someone ventured an opinion that maybe I was all right
and not really dead. But how could such a thing be? Impossible! They all had seen him dead! My parents had to make a decision. For a few moments, their minds tumbled over this turn
of events.

"Is this our son, George, or is it an evil spirit?" they wondered. Their fear was almost paralyzing. They needed to decide
whether to bury me or to lift me back up. To a Navajo, having
anything to do with evil spirits was inviting tragic conse-
quences. With this in mind, they would be taking a dreadful
chance in bringing the casket back up to see if I were still alive.

They silently thought about this for a few moments, discussed it, and finally came to a decision: They would bring the
casket back up and check inside to see if I were still alive.

When the little group finally wrestled the box to the top,
then pried open the lid, they saw I was alive. Immediately a
most exhilarating joy and peace thrilled their whole beings.
They could not contain themselves. I was the most beautiful
sight they had ever seen. Because of the prior sickness, my
body needed nourishment. I asked for a soda pop to drink.
Then my father wept upon my neck a good while. His tears
brought new life and new energy.

Even though I tried to cry, the tears would not come.
There was not moisture enough in my body. My heart wept
profusely, though my eyes did not.

My dear mother held me close, so close to her motherly
bosom while she wept. I wish I could describe the mixture of
sorrow and happiness her tears then contained. Her embrace
upon me was desperate, but not so desperate as was her soul in
gratitude. Having no material possessions to speak of, Mother's
children were the focus of all her divine attention. So, when I
say she wept and held me, it is an understatement.

My mother later told me that following this experience,
there was a change in my personality. Somehow I was more
obedient, submissive, and teachable. Too, I cannot help but
feel that two grateful parents were made more conscious of my
life. My parents felt there was something special about me. I
was treated as a special son, one who had come from a dark pit

into life again. However, my parents love all my brothers and sisters, and I was not really treated better than the rest.

When I herded sheep, I didn't play around as much as before. My parents sent me out with the sheep more often than the others because they knew I would do a good job. I had become much more serious about things. My parents expressed often their faith and confidence that I would do what I was supposed to do. They almost couldn't believe what had happened, and they were so glad that they had made the decision to bring me out of the grave.

My becoming more serious at this time gave birth to a determination to achieve. I began to think more about how precious life is and about what my purpose on earth might be. I became more attentive to my father and uncle as they taught me the Navajo way.

Because of this experience, my appreciation for life grew. And in future years this incident gave me a desire to improve my family's economic condition, to improve their lives along with my own. As I grew older, I thought about building a beautiful home for my family. I began setting little goals for myself, my family, and even my Navajo people. I wanted the best for all of us.

I often wonder about my loving father as he stood drenched with tears. I wonder how he must have felt to have had his prayers answered. I have learned of his tremendous faith and his special relationship with the Spirit of God.

3

THE NAVAJO WAY

As I sat upon the pile of ceremonial shawls, I couldn't help but remember the story of how the Navajos began. We came to the surface of the land from several levels far beneath the earth's surface. Just thinking of the earth caused me to watch the deft hand strokes of the medicine man as he made sand images upon the earthen floor. The bright array of colors connected in my conscious thought. Black, red, blue, and now this world, yellow, representing the levels *Dineh*, my people, had passed through to arrive upon the earth's surface. My father's interpretation of the legend was that five-fingered people (earth people) came from beneath the earth through much water. The medicine man was using these promising colors in the sand painting on the floor. This sacred sing was for me, for something in the outside world had brought a terrible sickness upon me. This was the way of my people. And I believed it.

Aunts, uncles, and clan family swarmed into our desert hogan. Its beehive shape was most fitting and natural for the coming Navajos. Even though I may have never before seen some of the clan members in attendance, it was their right, their place, to come and to belong.

Of course, my own family was there—Mother, Father, and

the rest. The expressions in their soft eyes told me they were happy and full of faith for my future, especially my immediate recovery. All eyes were upon me, and alternately, upon the powerful, working medicine man. Meanwhile, more relatives arrived. Sitting crosslegged, everybody managed to honey-comb themselves into comfortable positions.

I saw my eldest brother, Joe, and my other brothers sitting there. Joe had been through a ceremony before. I was glad to see them there; it gave me added assurance, along with the glances of my loving parents. All had come to give comfort and compassion. I knew I would get well. There was no doubt.

Adjusting my sitting position on the shawl pile, I thought of how my parents had first sought a hand trembler. This man's work was precursory to the actual sing itself. There are about two weeks between the two, time enough for adequate prepara-tion on the part of all—medicine man, relatives, and the pa-tient. The hand trembler had diagnosed the problem and pre-scribed the proper ceremony. Only one particular sing would work.

I had submitted silently as the sacred corn pollen was salved upon me by the trembler. All the while, his low chant and prayer had filled our hogan. This ritual prayer had filled me with hope for a cure. With the same pollen, he had anointed his bronze arm, then began to listen. The hogan had been ut-terly silent. Soon his arm had shook, his hand had moved a certain way. He had been in communication with the holy people. The diagnosis was then complete.

"Son of Donkey Man, a witch has shot your son with some foreign object," he had said. "You must have the Shooting Way ceremony. This witching object must be sucked out. If not, he may die, certainly he will grow much worse. An evil man is seeking revenge against you and has chosen to harm your son to accomplish his evil designs."

Father had listened intently and said, "My son, we will go get a strong medicine man, one who is close to the Great Spirit. We know of a good one, one who can sing well and who is very knowledgeable. The holy people hear him. He has the power to make you well. I could sing over you, but it is a taboo for a medicine man to perform a ceremony over his own son or daughter.

"Red Woman, you must go to the trading post. Talk with the trader and pawn your jewelry. Alert the relatives. Get what little food you can. Maybe the clan relatives can help if we fall short of money or food.

"My children, your brother is very sick, you must help us out and get things fixed up. Go ask Man Who Halts to select a couple of good, fat sheep. Many of our friends and relatives will come. We must treat them well. All must go right so a spirit of harmony will be here."

Now I sat looking at the medicine man my parents had sought after the hand trembler had given his diagnosis. The figures he was drawing formed colorfully on the floor. They were the holy people, some with square heads, some with round. The images all faced east, the direction of good. In order to accommodate my body, the painting was much larger than what one could see in the trading post for sale.

The images of the sand painting have been passed on orally from father to son. No written pattern exists, and no blueprint—just powerful memory. And though each painting is extremely detailed, the medicine man has stored several hundred in his almost endless mental capacity. Thousands of symbols are ascribed to each painting and every part thereof. The medicine man understands each and every symbolic pattern. When you hear that this knowledge is equal to a doctorate degree from a university, you hear an untruth, for the medicine man's knowledge, in the Navajo culture and wisdom, far surpasses the college doctorate. You see, he also learns just as many songs and chants to accompany the varying ceremonies. If the slightest error in design, word, or singing pitch is committed, the ceremony could fail. How is that for a doctorate examination? And all the examiners—the coming family, friends, and relatives fully expect it not to fail.

As I sat upon the soft shawls contemplating all that was unfolding, some of the meaning was beyond my wisdom, but I had

faith anyway. And my faith blended with the faith of the on-
looking participants. By participating in this sing, they were
also to receive a protection from the evil witchery.

As I sat, I remembered my pain, how it caused difficulty inside my being. But very soon it would be gone. That thought
eased the pain somewhat. But still I wondered what would be
sucked from my body. I was curious and frightened at the same
time.

I looked toward my parents to gain added assurance. They
had not taken their eyes from me because it was my first sing as
the patient. I needed their attention.

The medicine man had almost finished the design. As I
studied the holy people drawn on the floor, the teaching of my
father came to mind: "George, these holy people are very powerful—you must never offend or anger any of them. You must
always tell me if you think you have; then we will do something
about it. They can protect us if we pray to them in the right
manner."

I was glad the movements of the medicine man were
smooth and flowing. This relaxed me somewhat. At the same
time, I felt that he could understand my thoughts. Though he
was very powerful, the feelings emanating from him were tender. The anticipation of the release of pain was what made me
nervous. Pain, no matter how brief, seems a constant companion. At the time, it seemed endless.

The medicine man would not totally involve me until he
had detected the harmony of nature, including the condition
of my own being. The familiar smell of the earthly hogan and
the burning cedar in the stove put my heart at ease. I had
walked among the cedars many times. They were my friends.
My knowledge of the Navajo cultural use and sanctity of the
cedar tree reverenced my silence further.

The hogan had been blessed continually through its entire
construction. It was constructed of cedar posts. Humble as it
was, the hogan was a temple to us. Not only sings but marriages
were performed there.

The pile of woven shawls was the right place in nature for
me now. The positive thought that my pain would soon be

gone only made the pain a greater reality. Time to think abruptly ended. Then, suddenly, the sand painting was complete.

Sensing my needs, the medicine man moved slowly toward me. The power pulsating from him drew my attention directly to him. Somehow his closeness made fear flee. His attention was completely focused upon me. I knew he could see right through me. My parents had told me of his special gift of discernment. I surely believed it now.

A low, masculine, hollow chant began to flow from the recess of his throat. The other singers were also singing in time with him. The beauty of their clear voices bolstered my faith. The ceremony had begun.

While I was still sitting on the shawls, the medicine man helped me remove my clothes. I was so attentive that I forgot any embarrassment at being disrobed in the presence of onlookers. When the medicine man was so close that I could hear him catch his breath in the chant, my attention could go nowhere else. I had not been told about the removal of clothing before. However, my shyness was not as great as the unbearable pain. I just wanted to be relieved by having the witching object removed. No one in the hogan laughed or made light of my nakedness. The ceremony is considered sacred in all its aspects. The human form is but a part of a harmonious universe. Do we laugh or make light of a beautiful green tree, river, lake, or mountain?

After all my clothes and jewelry were removed, the medicine man helped me onto the finished sand painting. As my body touched the sacred figures, I felt a chill of expectation. The medicine man was careful to stay close to me. The singing heightened beauty, harmony, and life with nature. I could barely distinguish one voice from another as harmony began to fill the perfection of the world around. Only occasionally would someone interrupt his singing to clear his throat, but someone was always singing through another's pause. When they reached a fervent pitch, it sounded like busy bees flying near the ceiling of the hogan.

My body received rubbings of corn pollen. Some was

placed upon my tongue. Sacred anointings of herbal water
were placed upon me. Also, I was guided to sip some of the
water. The taste was acrid. The drink was then passed around
to the others, who in turn sipped it and rubbed their bodies
with it.

The medicine man drew sacred symbols upon various parts
of my body. Later, I would be instructed not to wash them off
until four days were past.

The singing started to crescendo, float, and soar, and the
area where the witching object had entered became inflamed
with excruciating pain. My face was pinched and wrinkled in
penetrating, searing, indescribable pain! The chanting became only a whir, a powerful pinnacle of perfected voice, harmonious beyond mortal comprehension. My mind had reached
the threshold of blacking out.

Just below the surface of my skin, somewhere unknown to
me, the medicine man saw, or sensed, the cruel witching object in my side. With his mouth he sucked hard to pull it out.
When the medicine man emptied his mouth, he revealed an
arrowhead in pus mingled with blood. Thus, the fiery dart of
the adversary had been quenched. It was like new life to be free
of the pain at last.

Through all this, the presence of my family sustained me.
The medicine man was with me throughout the process. I contrast him with the Anglo doctor who occasionally steps into a
lonely hospital room to mark a chart and put a cold stethoscope
on the chest. The medicine man works many grueling hours,
in both comforting and healing. He is a good counselor and
therapist for ailments Anglo doctors know little about.

I got dressed and sat back on the colorful pile of shawls,
pondering the experience. I watched the medicine man as he
used a feathered stick to erase the sand painting from the floor.
Its purpose had been served, and he erased it in the reverse
order it was made. The honored medicine man signaled that
the ceremony was complete.

My relatives made their way out of the eastern entrance of
the hogan. The patient was cured. They had seen the trouble
removed with their own eyes. Faith had become knowledge.

As a youth, I saw such healings performed time and time again. The faith of my people is seldom slack. Their faith, humility, spirit, and strength are at times unsurpassed.

I tell this story to let you see how deeply thrust I was as a youth into Navajo cultural thought and ways. As a boy, I was taught the way of my people, the traditions, superstitions, taboos, and all that encompasses the Navajo religion, which is deeply interwoven with everyday life. My father and uncle taught me. A system that has only sporadic times or places for religion confuses a Navajo. To us, religion is constant. Prayers, directions, and restrictions are part of every waking moment. I do appreciate my culture, even now, for I am Navajo. Of course, my views are now altered as my life has progressed beyond the days of my childhood.

Religious practice had only one meeting place really: the heart. Our hearts were enlarged by our harmonious surroundings. Religion lived in every Navajo, in the family and in the land. I flourished in the Navajo way, and I desired to learn all about it from my father and uncle.

I can recall many times when my brothers, sisters, and I stayed up late into the night lying on our sheepskins, or just sprawled out on the hogan's dirt floor, listening to stories about my people. We huddled around the warm stove, listening to stories retold only after the first snow had fallen. We had no television, movies, magazines, or books. Our entertainment and our education were the oral traditions told in the beautiful poetry of the Navajo language.

After the arrival of *Dineh,* or the people, into this present world, many traditions and rituals were set up to govern our lives. These were taught to the young by the older generations. It is said the older generations received these traditions from the holy people.

Holy people are spirits, both good and evil, who live either in a spirit world or on Mother Earth. They travel about on rainbows, lightning, whirlwinds, and even the rays of the sun. They taught my people long ago how to survive when a great flood drove them into the present world. A good spirit has power and authority over an evil spirit. An evil spirit can bring harm to a Navajo if he is out of harmony with the holy people or Mother Earth.

Whenever any of us boys had our hair trimmed at home, our parents were meticulous about making sure that all the trimmings were plucked from the ground. So, upon my hands and knees, I developed good eyesight while painstakingly picking up every last hair that might have dropped to the ground. We never received haircuts while the wind blew or when time would not allow us to gather the fallen hair.

My parents had taught us well about the wolfmen, or skin-walkers. Skinwalkers are earth people who have alliance with bad or evil spirits. Had any strands of our hair been found by them, they could work their evil magic upon us. So not a hair of our heads would fall to the ground unnoticed.

The skinwalkers concealed themselves with the dark cloak of night, when they lurked about doing their dirty business. During the day, they either stayed in their hogans, or, if they did come out, they looked just like the rest of us. Even though they may have seemed like anyone else during the day, inside they were ravenous wolves.

As a child, whenever I misbehaved, one of the adults in the family told me to be more obedient or a skinwalker, the *yee naaldlooshii*, would come looking for me. I generally tried to stay in line with the wishes of my parents.

Witches, the same ones who can shoot objects into people, are said to have power to run like animals. Sometimes they dress up in the hides of animals, such as the wolf, bear, or coyote. Their hides are literal skins, not having much to do with spirit matter. They are always about on the darkest of nights. And we believed in them to the point of dreadful fear.

Many nights, I did not venture into the night unless it was to look for a stray lamb. I did not whistle for the lamb to come, but imitated its voice; then it recognized me. It's bad to do any whistling—that is what witches listen for.

The skinwalkers and witches paint their bodies and faces, wearing no clothing. Upon all fours they run, wearing masks and causing dogs to bark, horses to neigh, and flocks of sheep to become restless.

As a child, I was pleased to find no coyotes following me. If they were, it meant that I might have lost a sister or brother. Putting turquoise in their tracks is a good remedy. Also, I always kept a sharp eye out for them.

Dogs were good watches, but if they smelled dead meat, they might become distracted. And if a female dog had pups, she might be more worried about them than about us. So, it was always good just to watch carefully.

If we saw a coyote cutting in front of us, we would immediately turn around. If we did not, we were sure to die. Coyotes have been depicted in Navajo lore as sly, mean, greedy, and smart. But this smartness is not accompanied by much wisdom, and his actions usually turn on him somehow. Stories of the sly coyote are usually told only during the winter months. They are quite humorous but are threaded with wisdom and teaching. It is important for a Navajo to learn wisdom early in life.

We avoided death and everything associated with it. We took great precautions in burying the dead. Also, we greatly feared ghosts and the evil spirits of dead people. No matter how good or affectionate people may have been in life, when they died, they could come back as evil spirits to avenge some wrong or neglect.

As in many Indian cultures, we buried our dead with all their earthly belongings. That assured us that their ghosts would not return to haunt us. My brothers, sisters, and I were told that ghosts appeared after dark or just before the death of another family member. We were afraid of the dark. Ghosts could come as a coyote, owl, mouse, whirlwind, or even a human being. Navajos are very careful to shake hands when they meet someone. A ghost's hand cannot be felt, or they will refuse to shake. The Navajos have a special ceremony to exorcise ghosts.

Navajos avoid anything struck by lightning. If someone sees lightning strike a tree, he must be out of harmony with the holy people. A healing ceremony is at once prescribed and the tree is scrupulously avoided thereafter.

Other taboos were that we should never cut a watermelon

with the point of a knife, poke meat with a knife point, comb hair at night, or point at a rainbow with the index finger. A son-in-law was forbidden to look into his mother-in-law's eyes. Even walking down the street or dancing with the opposite sex of the father's clan was prohibited. Also, pregnant women were not to look upon four-legged animals or attend a funeral. These are just a few of the hundreds of taboos that filled the Navajo world.

If one had broken a taboo, the people would perform a ceremony for protection. The ceremony was usually accompanied by an Enemy Way ceremony. Those participating in the ceremony received protection against ailments from breaking similar taboos.

The Enemy Way ceremony is the crowning jewel of Navajo social life. Today it is commonly referred to as the Squaw Dance. Originally, it was very sacred. Nowadays some scoff at its significance because of violent behavior and public drinking. The wiser and more mature medicine men deplore such activity at an Enemy Way ceremony.

As a child, I remember well the many times I attended the Squaw Dances with my family. At first we went in a wagon, but later in an old pick-up truck owned by one of my older brothers. Although I was extremely shy, somewhere in the back of my mind I always hoped that I would be asked to dance. Even now I can picture the bright yellow fire blazing in the darkness, in the center of all the dancing Navajos.

However, I kept in mind the sanctity of the event, as my father had taught me. Such dances are often held for people going into or coming out of military service. This helps the returning servicemen feel better and gives protection to those going out. Anciently the Squaw Dance was a war dance to prepare warriors for war.

To this dance came many Navajos from the surrounding territory. All had set up camp around the huge bonfire. It was a spectacle to behold. Navajo men and women, dressed in their finest jewelry, greeted one another with smiles of surprise and gladness.

The food is usually served at a place other than the ceremonial hogan. That night they had an extra-large summer shade-house constructed. Many hungry folks were attending from miles around. There were several sheep butchered for this particular ceremony. This fact made the occasion even more enjoyable. Lots of people were still coming. It was the third night, the big one. I could sense the feeling of joy in the heated air.

A group of men began to gather to one side of the yellow fire, singing and chanting. Just after midnight, a young Navajo girl chosen for her comeliness and good heart came forth from the ceremonial hogan. In her hands was the sacred, feathered prayer stick. She begin to dance, first with one man, then another. She avoided clan members of her religion. As she danced, other girls came forth to choose partners.

Though I wanted to dance, I stayed out of the firelight. I played hard to get, which is the polite thing to do. Though we men may have stayed in the shadows, the firelight flickered in our eyes. I think some of the women must have been able to detect this, because they would go to great lengths to drag us into the firelight.

This night I really played hard to get. We had to pay these girls to dance. If we didn't they would take something that belonged to us until we did. Though I could have borrowed some money earlier from my mother, I had not. That would prove to the young lady that I really had not wanted to dance. So even before I danced, I had mastered the art of playing hard to get.

I could see the young women eagerly anticipating the money they would receive. The most popular girl made the most money; it was as simple as that. I had really fooled these girls, as none had her eyes on me—except one, named Slim Girl. I crept farther back in the darkness. She still kept her eye on me, though.

Back in the shadows, I supposed she couldn't see my eyes, which were full of expectation. I supposed wrong. She could catch even the slightest flicker of the light in my eyes. Before long, she was asking her friends to help her drag me into the fire's warm glow.

All eyes turned toward me. What could I do? Before I knew

it, they had grabbed me, and I couldn't get loose. I wiggled and squirmed, but Slim Girl and her friends had a tight hold on me. I tried to make it look as though there was no way I could get money to pay them. But I knew that my mother had a few old coins in the bottom of her purse because I'd seen her put them there before we left to come to the Squaw Dance. So my mother lent me some money, and I was able to dance.

All of those experiences were part of Navajo life. As a boy, I spoke only Navajo, except for a few English words I had picked up here and there. I ate as a Navajo, thought as a Navajo, slept as a Navajo, dressed as a Navajo, and behaved as a Navajo. I did not know at that time what the future would bring. New experiences and a vast new world existed beyond anything I had dreamed. My Navajo roots were strong and would provide stability in the years to come.

4

FATHER AND SON

My father and I were close. Because of our bond, he had a great influence on me during my life. As I grew up, I was guided and taught by many fine, helpful men and women. Few of them, however, molded my character as did my father. His spiritual stature was awesome.

This strong influence of my father was something of a departure from Navajo custom. In the Navajo matriarchal society, a man moves near his wife's family upon marriage, and their children are thought to belong to her extended family. Furthermore, usually an uncle, the husband's brother-in-law, has the primary influence on a young boy, even more than the boy's father. This uncle is expected to teach him the Navajo way, to guide and encourage him into adulthood. While my mother's brother was always there and taught me much during my childhood, it was my father who taught me much about the Navajo heritage and the purpose of life.

It was my father who would get us up early in the morning to run. He would take us out to pray. His prayers were sometimes long but were always from his heart. Father was a very spiritual man, close to nature and all of God's creations. His prayers were traditional Navajo prayers, invoking the blessings of the holy people upon his family. As part of the sacred prayer,

41

he would cast yellow corn pollen to each sacred direction. To
these four directions the pollen would scatter lightly upon the
breeze as a symbol of prayerful supplication. My spiritual training, which was to be so important in my later life, came from a
wise father. I have never doubted the existence of a Great
Spirit, a God who watches over all His earthly children. But I
learned to worship something that was impersonal, though sacred, supernatural, and mysterious. Even my father was not
certain of the nature or personality of the Great Spirit.

Father taught me to work hard. Work was expected. In
teaching us to run so that we would be strong and not weary, to
pray so that we would be close to the holy people, and to work
so that we might provide for ourselves, he taught us to assume
adult roles early in our lives.

"My children," he would say, "the world is hard, especially
when you are an Indian. But the Great Creator made you this
way. It is good. You must accept who you are in this great nature He made for us. We are the People. That is the most important thing. The future belongs to the People, the Indian
people.

"Do not forget to pray, and you will be led in the way of
beauty. You must learn these things while you are young. By
the time you are old, it is almost too late. Pay attention to my
words. I know what I speak. I speak from wisdom, from knowledge that the Good Spirit has blessed me with. I am what I am
because of Him. I am your father. It is not my desire to tell you
wrong things."

At times my mother would give him support: "Yes, what
your father says is true. If you learn how to grow up right, to
take responsibility, you can succeed in a marriage and have
good children. All these things will help you prepare. Listen to
your father. My marriage with him has given me beautiful children. This is what life is about.

"Never look upon a naked woman with lustful thoughts. If
you do, you will be out of harmony with deity and nature.
Something bad will come upon you. You might be hurt by fire
some way. That is why I wear this long dress down to my an-

kles; I don't want to expose any part of my body to cause bad thoughts in others."

We were further told that these sacred teachings would temper and refine us to withstand the trials and afflictions in life. They would also bless our own families.

My father was very kind, understanding, and loving. He never considered himself poor. Poverty, always present, was simply a way of life. My father learned to treasure trial and affliction. In fact, at times he was too friendly. When he had a little money, it often wouldn't last long because he gave it to anyone in need. His favorite saying was *Beeso nahoodleelii at'e*, meaning "There will always be money." He said, "Friends you cannot always have, but money will always be around."

My father had his weaknesses, but my love for him prevented me from focusing on those things. And there were times of tension between my mother and father. Their marriage was not perfect. I do not know of a perfect mortal marriage. At times these marital tensions erupted in front of us children. It was painful to hear and see. Most of it came about because my father had a problem with alcohol. Most non-Indians do not understand what the world of an Indian is like, particularly the pain and sorrows therein. I do. It is very easy to forgive my father. I am sorry, though, that my mother had to suffer so much.

Father told me, "Son, I cannot believe that I have allowed myself to become a slave to this bad alcohol. It seems I am helpless to move it away. My son, I hate myself for drinking. I don't like to drink. What can I do to get rid of it?"

Young as I was, I could not figure out why he spoke with me about his problem. I was just a boy, but at times tears would fill his eyes, and in silence he would embrace me. After a while, he would cry on my shoulder and tell me he wanted to get rid of his habit, but he did not know how. I knew he was sincere, but I did not know what to do. I just felt his pain and cried with him.

My father fought this battle with liquor most of his life. He hated it. Also he seemed so helpless, with no one to turn to.

Only I listened in painful love. I knew agony. At times I tried to strengthen and help him by praying in his behalf. Sometimes my simple counsel to him was just not to drink anymore.

He told me that the Navajos did not always have firewater, or alcohol. This was one of the things that the white man and others brought. When he was a young man he did not drink. The Navajo was not much bothered by alcohol then. He missed the old days and talked often about them. He had a hard time understanding what was happening to the Navajo world as times changed.

Through all my father's problems, my mother stuck with him and forgave him. She would tell us with sweet resolve, "Respect your father. You do not know what he is facing out there just to make a living for us. It is hard for him." She tried to counsel with him but gave up after a while.

Of course, my father was always sorry after he had been drinking. There were the sober times when his true heart would seek forgiveness from all. In our pain, we forgave, for there was love in our home. We somehow understood. There were times when my mother thought about leaving Father, but she never did.

"George," she addressed me seriously, "what should I do? There is not another man around as kind and loving as your father. He loves you children as I do."

As I grew older and was able to understand more about marriage, my father confided in me on this subject. He spoke of his first marriage, of course, and I knew the four children of that marriage. Though he loved his first wife very much, he had the feeling even while he was married to her that someday she would be taken away and that there was someone else he was supposed to marry. He felt that his first wife had passed away so that he could marry my mother.

My father lost his first wife at the same time my mother had broken up with her former husband. When my mother's parents were out looking for a man to marry their daughter, they happened to meet my father and were very impressed with him. One reason was that my father's family had a large herd of sheep. To a Navajo, this meant that a family was influential and well-to-do. My mother's parents were happy with him as the choice for their daughter.

Father said, "The first time I met your mother, I knew she was the one. I had a feeling that I had either met her before or knew her from somewhere." Father was not alone in this way of thinking. These special feelings were typical of an older generation who had similar feelings for one another and a sensitivity to things of the spirit. He did not feel right about becoming a full-time practicing medicine man because he did not wish to abuse his spiritual powers and gifts.

My mother never would drink. Though some of the rest of the older family members did, she did not. Not only was she sweet, but her strength was as the mountains. She resisted the temptation time after time. I have learned of her strength in the matter of alcohol. She did bootleg wine on the reservation, however, but only to help provide for hungry children.

I will not be deceptive in speaking of myself or my father. He was not perfect, and neither am I. Even though I occupy a high Church position, still I have many weaknesses and imperfections to overcome. I am only a man. But I am thankful I have heard the better part of my father's and mother's teachings. I pray that my own children will love me enough to overlook my own weaknesses.

During the times my father was sober, he was so compassionate and understanding. Sometimes he would gamble his hard-earned money away in an attempt to make more money to meet the ever-demanding family expenses. But usually he somehow brought home food, clothing, and a little spending money. On other occasions he would become overly generous and could be seen passing out money—ones, fives, tens, and even twenty-dollar bills to friends or anyone who looked in need. When in his right state, he was a benevolent man, kind and sensitive to the needs of others. He was very loving and full of life and had a ready smile for everyone. As our family grew, he also grew with us. Some of his bad habits disappeared. I am very glad that his relationship with my mother improved as well.

After I was eight or nine years old and big enough to be

helpful, I would spend part of each summer helping my father herd sheep for an Anglo Colorado sheep rancher. Over the years, the sheep rancher developed a great confidence and trust in my father's ability to care for his livestock. Herding sheep was no easy task. With the help of good sheepdogs, my father had full responsibility for two thousand sheep in very rugged country high in the Colorado mountains. This summer sheep range, about fifty miles northeast of Cortez, Colorado, was both mountainous and heavily timbered. No one else was in sight for around us miles around. It was just Father there, all alone, except for cougars and bears. It was an isolated, hermit's life.

These mountains saw the summers that warmed the love and strengthened the bond between my father and me. He took me along for companionship. When the sheep were bedded down and the stars glistened overhead, we would talk as we prepared the evening meal. Many things we talked about were never shared beyond the steeps of those glorious mountains. I have the intimacy of my father's heart in my own. He would talk, often far into the night. From his bedroll he would speak, and most attentively I would listen as he unburdened his mind of Navajo lore and of his wise perceptions about the world.

He said, "My son, never believe that these mountains cannot listen to you, for they are alive. If you watch them a long time, you can see that they also have movement. They are sacred. That is why they reach into the heavens. A man may grow close to his Creator up here. As the winds pass through the trees that adorn the mountains, they whisper messages to which all nature listens. You may hear these things if you can be calm enough inside. This nature is not illusion, but often what man does is. You are a part of nature too. Learn to be quiet inside and listen. This way you will always be filled with peace and beauty, for Mother Earth will bring her best forward just for you."

It was as though there was some unwritten direction for him to share these things with me. These were his middle years, but his wisdom was almost ageless.

"I have seen you grow, my son. It is good with me. Your

mind is good. This is a gift and a power. Maybe one day you will record the wisdom of your people as I have given it to you. It would bless the lives of many people."

Raising his hand about five feet off the ground, he would say, "When I was small, the grasses all around were taller than I was. The Great Spirit knows the circumstances of our people. He knows the good and the bad. Rain came in the old days because the Navajos were good. They were in the right way with the earth. There was beauty in all directions. Today we have no rain, no grass, because our harmony is not with our Mother Earth and with the great Creator. The Great Spirit is displeased with five-fingered people on earth."

Often he reminisced of the beautiful life before the coming of the white man when the Great Spirit watched over the people because they were in harmony.

"Before the white man came, my beloved son, our people knew much about the wisdom of the earth and the universe. Our older ones were ancient and honorable. They had close ties with the heavens. But the Anglos came, and their man-made things caused many of our people to falter in the old ways. Our people began to covet what the white man had. The white man is learned, but his knowledge has not brought him to understand Mother Earth. He may own the land and be in control, but only we have the power to understand the spirits within the land. So, on a higher level, it is yet ours. Only an Indian has the power to understand the spirits within Mother Earth and all creations.

"You must be wise in our understanding, which is ancient. We are the firekeepers, and one day our wisdom will flow into oneness again to bring life and light to the world. Do not forget these things. But you must also try to understand what is taking place around you in the white man's world. One day soon, the white man's world will come to an end. You may learn both, but if you will never forget these things, never forget that you are an Indian, you will not become confused. Never forget that when the white man's world ends, the Great Spirit will bring much light, life, and wisdom among His Indian children. The future holds great promise and power for the Indian people."

I learned much from Father about animals. He was naturally sensitive to them. He loved them as smaller brothers and sisters from the Great Spirit. He said, "My son, all living creatures, even the tiniest ones like mosquitos and ants, have souls and personalities, just like people."

At other times he would counsel his children, "Do not even destroy an ant hill. The ants know you. They can hear and understand you. They are just like people. How would you like someone to destroy your home? That is exactly what you do when you destroy their home. It is like someone coming to destroy our hogan. Do not even spit on an anthill, as it is a home for them."

During the summer months when the temperature would rise above a hundred degrees, the rattlesnakes would occasionally crawl into the shade of our hogan. When it was cool at night and warm inside, they would sometimes crawl inside the hogan. In the morning, we would find them stretched out by the fire close to our sleeping spots. Our father taught us not to fear the snakes, but to let them know by talking to them that we were in harmony with them and had respect for their lives.

"Children," Father would instruct, "you can talk to these snakes and they will understand. They are like a person: they have a spirit and can understand. They have feelings." He would further teach, "These snakes have a purpose for being here upon Mother Earth. The Great Spirit made the snake for some wise purpose, just as the five-fingered ones have a purpose."

Whenever we found a rattlesnake inside or around our living area, we would get a stick and gently pick it up. Then, carrying it a few hundred yards from our hogan, we would gently lay it down and talk to it. "We have not harmed you. You have all that great area out there to live in. We have this little place here. We have respected you by not hurting you. Please have respect for us by going your own way, and try not to come back this way again."

An Indian's understanding is that we are here to assist the Great Spirit, to look after and take care of his creations, no matter what they may be, animal or plant. This is an Indian's idea of having dominion over the living things of the earth. Because of my father's love for animals, he also had no fear of them.

Once in the mountains of Colorado, he came face to face with a big black bear near our tent. When I saw him standing there with the huge beast, I became scared and ran away. My first thoughts were to hightail it up a tree, but when I got my wits I looked around. There stood my father. There stood the bear. My father was talking to him as though he were a person. The bear was standing very still on his hind legs. He never took his eyes off my father. He seemed to be listening to all my father had to say. I couldn't hear it all since I had run so far away.

I did manage to hear him say in Navajo, "Please don't bother us, as we don't bother you. We have great love and respect for you. You are a creation of the Great Spirit, as we are. You live your life and let us live our lives. Let us not get in each other's way. You go your way and I will go my way." He said many other things. I was amazed to see the bear get down on all fours, turn around, and lumber off as though that was what he was supposed to do.

That day my father grew larger in the eyes of his respectful son. He lived what he preached. I can still remember him saying, "Don't let an animal see that you are afraid. Let him know that you are his friend. Let him know that you do not fear him and that you are like him, a creation of the Great Spirit. Tell him the Great Spirit wants us all to live in harmony." Though Father's employer gave him a rifle for protection, he never took it out with the flock.

One special gift my father had was what I call crystal gazing. With this gift, my father was able to locate lost items for whoever would come seeking his advice. Many times I have witnessed the exercise of this special, spiritual gift. If someone had lost a purse, sheep, jewelry, goat, saddle, or some personal effect, he would ask my father to use his gift to locate the lost or stolen item.

Once a woman had lost a squash-blossom necklace. My father was able to tell her where it was and even the name of

the person who had it. Not once did my father fail to tell someone the exact location of the missing item. Crystal gazing was
very sacred to my father. He did not use it very much, for he
did not wish to abuse it. He advised those he assisted not to tell
anyone about it if they could avoid it.

A few times while in the mountains, my father left me
alone with the sheep while he went to town to visit some of his
friends. Town usually meant mining villages, situated way up
in the mountains. So it was not the same as when we go to
town today. The forests were dense, and roads of any kind were
indeed scarce.

The Anglo sheep rancher so much respected my father's
herding ability that he let no one else herd his sheep. Occasionally he allowed us to butcher sheep for food. What we did
not use, my father would take into town and sell. The owner
was understanding and let it go. He was very kind. If he had
not been kind, I do not know what my father would have done
for a living.

Early one morning, his back loaded with mutton, Father
left for town. He was to return before dark. I was a small boy
then, about ten years old.

Night came, with all the frightening images that only the
Navajo mind can conjure up, but still my father did not return.
I did not even think of sleep all night. I tried to pray, but
whenever I shut my eyes, all I could see were bears and mountain lions. An owl hooted. The hair stood up on the back of my
neck.

"Little safety this thin tent is," I thought. The owl
screamed again. I quickly fingered the rifle beside me. "Bless
the sheep rancher for giving this to my father," I silently reflected.

The owl really frightened me. An owl nearby meant evil
was approaching. Some Navajos believed that an owl was the
spirit of a dead person coming to haunt. Owls were evil mes-
sengers. All night long they made a mournful sound. The gun
and two sheepdogs helped ease my fear through the deep, but
not silent, night.

In the morning, I fixed a big breakfast, which lifted my

spirits considerably. Still, during the day, I could hear things moving upon every small trail. Clear areas without trees and bushes were most appealing that day. At least those owls had shut up!

I kept looking for my father to come down through the timberline, but he never did. I wondered if I should go into town, but I had to look after the herd. Town was a long way off. Twice that day I saddled our horse and went up the trail quite a ways to try to find him, but both times I turned back without him.

The second night without Father was also sleepless, but for another reason. A threatening thunderstorm crept upon the mountains to release itself in torrential rain. I had tied the horse to a tree with a long rope so that it could move about and graze during the night. Toward the middle of the night, after the worst of the storm was over, I heard a loud noise coming from near where the horse was tied. I thought a bear had attacked the horse. I was too frightened to look and find out.

With all the courage I could muster, I slowly got on my knees and poured out my heart to the Great Spirit. I prayed as I had never prayed before. Somehow a sweet, peaceful feeling came over me, and I was not afraid anymore. I cautiously went out to where the horse was tied and found that it had slipped on the wet grass, rolled down the hill, and choked to death. The horse lay entangled in the rocks and brush below. It was impossible for me to move it, so I just went back to the tent, said a little prayer, and finally went to sleep. Maybe those owls had meant something after all.

The third day without my father was much like the other two, but I did a little stream fishing while the sheep were quiet in order to keep my mind occupied. That night I was still afraid and made a bed in a tall pine tree where nothing could get me. I let the two dogs sleep in the tent.

With the dawn of another lonely day, I determined to follow my father into town even though I knew it would take most of the day to get there. Thinking of my father, I happily fixed a nice breakfast, made a small lunch, and fed the dogs well.

After the sheep seemed to be grazing peacefully, the dogs and I bounded up the trail. The trail led up the mountainside to the top, and then down the other side. The elevation must have been around eleven thousand feet.

Just as I reached the top and was about to hike down the slope, I met my father coming up. He had been drinking for three days, and the effects were still lingering. It amazed me that he was able to stay on the trail and make his way back.

When we met, I was overjoyed and shed tears. I loved my father dearly. It gave me comfort and security to be near him. I didn't ask him where he had been or what he had been doing. He simply told me that he had been having fun with friends, gambling and drinking.

As young as I was, I realized that life got lonely for him with the sheep in the wilds of Colorado. During my three days alone, I felt lonely and afraid. I wasn't angry with my father. I was just so happy to have him back. Deep down I was glad that he had had a little fun, for I felt he deserved relaxation to get his mind away from the isolation of sheepherding.

When I told my father about my experiences, especially about what had happened to the horse, it caused him to think. "Son, it is the Great Spirit telling me I should not have done what I did," he said. "Those owls were telling about the evil I was causing. Some more of that drink is left, but I will only taste a little at a time, I promise. In two days you must return home. Maybe you could use some money to jingle in your pocket—just for your own spending money."

"Father, you do not make very much. I do not wish to spend your money," I would usually say. I told him I would take it home to Mother. She would know what to do with it. Ten or fifteen dollars would go a long way in those days. Though the days of loneliness had really scared me, I was not afraid to travel home alone. Many future summers found me with Father in the mountains. Each summer similar experiences happened.

I will be eternally grateful that my father cared for our family as well as he did all those years. When he first started herding sheep, the pay was very skimpy. When he came home out of the mountains, he would often have to hire someone to bring him and a load of groceries to our hogan, about thirty-five miles away.

Other times he didn't make it with either earnings or groceries. He would get drunk in town, spend his money on anyone in need, and arrive at our hogan penniless. He was too willing to bail friends out of jail, buy food for friends and relatives, or simply to give money to those who asked for it. He just couldn't say no.

Sometimes he would walk the ten miles from the highway up to our mesa-top hogan with two or three sacks of flour, canned goods, and other groceries on his back. He would show up unexpectedly in the middle of the night. The next morning he would send us back down the trail looking for canned goods he might have dropped along the way.

My mother was always amazed at the strength he had, at how he could walk all that way with those groceries. She said at times that my father was well named Son of Donkey Man because he was as strong as a donkey.

When my father wasn't working, he would spend time gambling with the Utes or with friends and relatives in the Towaoc and Shiprock areas. There would be times when we were at the point of starvation and he would have a little luck gambling. He said the blessings of the Great Spirit were with him and had a hand in his winnings.

Despite his faults of drinking and gambling, my father has always been a great man in my eyes. I will always appreciate what he taught me. He was a man of great faith, courage, and humility, and he was a spiritual giant.

5

RESERVATION LIFE

Sheep are extremely important to the Navajo. To really understand the Navajo, one must understand Navajo life in relation to sheep. Sheep were primarily introduced to my people by the Spanish ranchers several centuries ago. Like deer to the Eastern Woodland Indian and buffalo to the Plains people, sheep have been the mainstay of my people, the Navajo. We have depended upon them for food, clothing, bedding, and other useful items.

The main advantage of sheep over deer and buffalo is that sheep are domesticated, which provides a steady support to our life-style. By comparison, the Plains Indians were dealt a staggering blow when the buffalo were slaughtered to near extinction. During warfare against us, Kit Carson succeeded largely because of his systematic destruction of our sheep.

Thankfully, our families were given more sheep by the government following the Long Walk, and despite losses during the Great Depression, sheep have been with us ever since. Sheep were very much a part of my growing-up years. I learned early that tending sheep was a major responsibility. I was up before the sun to take them out to graze, especially in the summer. I had to be out with the sheep before it got too hot.

During breakfast, my aunt outlined the day's routine concerning the sheep. I can still hear her, as we slowly disappeared into the desert horizon with the white sheep, directing us from the hogan's doorway.

"Take them over this way," she would say, indicating the direction with either pursed lips or her thumb. "I feel the grass will be better over that way. Stay close to those little children in case of rattlesnakes, but don't do anything bad to those rattlesnakes. Leave all those potteries and arrowheads alone out there.

"Also, don't take those sheep too far. You may have trouble getting back before dark. When your shadow hits half your height, then start back. Make sure the dogs stay close. Watch out for those sneaky coyotes; they are real tricky," and on and on, until we could hear her only faintly. We heard this almost every trip out, but we expected it from our aunt because she loved us.

Life was lonely watching the sheep. But as I look back, the patience that came from herding was worth it all. Life was good. We had no desire to change. While the sheep grazed, we stood watch. My aunt taught us to tell time by the sun. During the hot summer months, we would herd half a day. In the wintertime, we herded all day. We watched the time carefully. According to the length of our own shadows, we knew when to start back so we would get home exactly at dusk. My elder brothers, Joe and Mike, and my elder sister, Nellie, knew a lot about herding. Joe said more than once, "George, watch those goats! Don't let them get too far away from the sheep. They might lead the sheep astray. They go all over the place, in the crevices, on the edge. Watch out for them; they may hurt themselves.

"The goats think they know it all. See how they always go up and over those barren hills? There is no grass there. If the sheep follow them, they won't get fat. Go, circle around them. Hey, you can't just talk softly to those goats—yell at them! Pick up some sticks and rocks to throw. Bring them back!" I heard him chuckling as he watched me running around frantically.

Each day of herding sheep was a repetition of the previous

one, seven days a week. Even if the weather was stormy, the sheep had to be grazed. The search for good grazing usually took us in a different direction each day. We would take a light lunch with us, such as a piece of corn bread wrapped inside a cloth. Other days we went without food, and we had water to sustain us. We drank water with the sheep at the water hole, always trying to find the clearest place to drink. I have so many fond memories of times when we were out with the sheep. The summer heat was sometimes so unbearable that we had to huddle under a greasewood shrub or in the shade of a rock. It got so hot that the sheep huddled together with lowered head in one another's shadows. They didn't graze then and wouldn't until it cooled down. Sometimes we took them home at noon to cool them under the shade of a hogan.

While herding out in the desert, my brothers or sisters would warn us, "It's time to start the sheep to the water hole— look at the sun." All faces would turn upward to check it out; the group decision was the best. "If we do it now, we'll get home before the sun is down! And nothing bad will happen to us out here!"

Like a horse returning from a long ride to the home corral, the flock knew the time to begin about as well as anyone. In this small exodus, the younger ones would pass first as the oldest ones followed. Near the life-giving water, the younger would break into a run, soon outdistancing the older. When their thirst was quenched, we would round them up and urge them toward home. We were happy to get home. It meant hot mutton stew or roast prairie dog.

Sometimes we were so hot and tired we jumped astride the shoulders of a strong ram and rode home that way. We made sure we got off before our aunt could see us, or we would get a scolding.

If she could have only seen us at other times. We used some of the more vigorous bucks and rams to have a prairie rodeo. What gaiety that was! It broke up the day, and it more often broke our backsides with a hard thud on the ground! Our mare had a foal, and after it had grown some, we rode it.

On the real hot, dry days, we didn't seek shade because the

heat was unbearable even there. At noon on those days we hightailed it for home. Once home, we milked the goats. If Mother had some frybread dough, she rolled it into small balls, like dumplings, and put these into the goat's milk. This was a special treat for us children. In fact, I was raised on warm goat's milk. It was part of our daily food. So was frybread or thick tortillas cooked on hot coals. Vegetables were almost unheard of and seldom had.

Winter was the hardest time to herd because of the snow and cold. We usually had a lot of snow in January and February. This assured us of good grass for our flocks in the spring.

During the winter months, when there was snow on the ground, we could easily track cottontail rabbits and chase them into a hole or into a crack between the rocks. If they were too far back for us to reach with our hands, we got them out with a stick. After sharpening one end of the stick, we wet the point with our mouths. Then we poked the stick into the hole until it touched the rabbit. With a twirl, the wet point would bury itself tightly in the fur. Carefully, we pulled out a fat, frightened rabbit. On a good day, using this method, we could catch several rabbits for supper. Our dogs also helped in rabbit hunting by chasing the rabbits into holes or crevices.

In March, spring moved onto the reservation blowing tumbleweeds before itself. Sometimes we gleefully raced after these natural balls, jumping over the small ones and dodging the big ones. (They have little stickers all over.) Some were much taller than we were.

Another thing my brothers and I did when herding sheep was to hunt for prairie dogs. We sometimes got so involved in hunting that we lost track of time and also of the sheep, unfortunately for us. These childhood hunting forays would be followed by frantic hunts for lost sheep, and if Mother and my aunt found out, some lively scotch-Navajo scoldings.

To lose sheep was very bad. If we lost any, we were sent out that very night to find them, even if it was pitch black, and there was no telling what was out there lurking about! Many times, my brother Joe and I were out in the middle of the night searching, far from home and bleating softly, pleading imitations to invite the sheep to answer or come. We used cedar bark as torches to give a little light in the darkness. As we went in fear, Joe hung onto one of our biggest dogs, and I could cling to Joe. Thus we marched in the middle of the night while noisily imitating sheep.

We saw many beautiful things while we herded sheep. In the summertime, especially during August, heavy thunderstorms deafened the heavens above. The thirsty washes would be filled with torrents of raging, muddy water. A few weeks later, the same washes would be lined with lush, green grass. It was beautiful to behold nature during a desert downpour.

As the awakening sun forsook its cool, eastern cover to stretch high into heaven, the distant mountains would become topped here and there by building tufts of clouds, pure and white. As the heat became more intense, the sheep would huddle together for shade. The far, white clouds quickly spread across the sky as if fleeing from the hot wind now beginning its motion toward windy madness.

Soon the sky's creamy brow would wrinkle with grayness, and within minutes the entire face of heaven would scowl in stern darkness. From the mouth of creation we could hear the guttural thunder and see the serpentine lashings of bent lightning. Preceding winds and violent, blinding dust storms would rush ahead squealing the warning, while prairie shallows gave place to the overbearing shadows above. Lightning would flash, and then angry thunder would roll up and down the valley in abusive wrath. The earth would shake in suppliant response, alerting the living roots about to drink the dregs of unfurling fury.

Then would come the rain hitting hard enough to almost hurt. The droplets would plaster and speckle the sand like a gigantic sparrow's egg, and soon the sand would turn watercolor brown. As the storm's anger began to subside, the rain would lessen but continue for perhaps an hour or more. The soil would become saturated rapidly, and reflecting mirrors of water would sheen its surface, reflecting a calming sky. The prayerful scent of sagebrush then would fill the air in purity.

One day during a storm, Joe asked, "When do you think it will quit raining so hard?"

"Soon enough. Be patient," I responded. We all enjoyed these cloudbursts. It made us happy to see the rain.

"Maybe we can catch some fat prairie dogs," Nellie, my elder sister, said.

"I wish the rain was over now. I'm sure hungry for a fat prairie dog," said Bob, my younger brother.

The reason for the excitement and impatience was that a good downpour meant good prairie dog hunting. Good prairie dog hunting meant a good feast. What better logic is there?

When the downpour slowed some, we rushed into the rain, getting soaked to the skin immediately. It was beautiful! We did not mind the cold and wet. The excitement of the hunt was on! We grabbed shovels, tubs, buckets, cans, and anything else that would hold water during our eager rush for the edge of the washes.

Once we reached an area with a lot of prairie dogs, we began digging ditches to divert the rushing wash water into prairie-dog holes, or we used containers to carry water for pouring down nearby holes. The idea was to flood them out.

After flooding the holes, we stationed ourselves by them ready to capture the gasping prey. We fastened our attention on a hole, looking for bubbles, which meant the prairie dog was coming up for air. Just as soon as its wet head popped out, we grabbed its neck to kill it with a club. After we had clubbed the animals from one hole, we threw them into a pile and hurried to the next hole.

Sometimes a prairie dog would jump out of one hole only to speedily dive into another before we could get him. All of us had fun laughing and screaming while chasing after them.

One time, when I was small, I stood over a hole anxiously waiting to catch and club my first prairie dog. Joe had carefully instructed me on what to do. "Okay now, George, when that thing pops his head up, catch him real quick by the back of the neck. Make sure you do it fast, but get a good hold, because they move fast and can bite. Mother would be upset if you got hurt. Remember, do it all fast!"

Well, of course, I grabbed it by the belly in my excitement. I was proud of my catch for only a split second. Before I knew it, he had latched his sharp teeth all the way through two of my fingers. He was more bulldog than prairie dog! The pain was not immediate; then all of a sudden I was yelling and crying, whooping and hollering!

Finally Joe came running to the rescue. He had to choke that stubborn prairie dog with all his might before its jaws unlocked. Though bleeding profusely, I continued in the excitement of the hunt, but my interest was now in the hitting part, not the catching.

After the water receded, we put all the prairie dogs into a sack and headed for home. As soon as we arrived, the adults began dressing the catch with sharp knives. After splitting the stomach and scraping the insides into a bucket, they put the liver back into the cavity, sewed up the hole, and tossed the animal into the fire to singe all the hair off. In addition to the liver, the cavity was sometimes filled with corn and diced potatoes—Navajo-style dressing.

Most of the time, we were so hungry we just threw the prairie dogs into the fire for cooking, after they had been cleaned. But the best cooking method was to dig a hole next to the fire, fill the hole with prairie dogs, and then cover all this with dirt, ashes, and hot coals. We kept the fire going on top of it. After baking an hour or so in the earthen oven, the little animals were tender and juicy. We peeled back the hairless skin to get at the savory meat, and everyone helped themselves to prairie dog. The animals were so fat, tender, and tasty! The part that pleased me best was the little liver. Mother always told us after the second one to slow down or we would get a bellyache. It seemed that we could never get full of something as delicious as that!

March through April was lambing season. Lambing season was always a beautiful time. We laughed at the young lambs as they bucked and tumbled over one another like playful puppies. We watched them closely, as some had not learned to stay close to the main flock for safety. If not watched continually, young lambs might wander away only to find the waiting mouth of a coyote. Our dogs would often corner or run down a prowling coyote. After the lambs were born, they were separated from the rest of the flock during the day. This way, the ewes could eat instead of chasing their little ones.

On a typical spring morning, my aunt would say, "Put those little lambs in the corral. They are too little to go with the big ones. They just get in the way. Be careful if you have to catch them." I can still hear her laugh as we would slip or fall trying to catch the more lively lambs.

"Get them in there!" If I fell again I could catch the sparkle in her eyes. Sometimes she might even try to act angry at our awkwardness, but we could always read the humor, if not love, in her eyes.

"And stay with them until the older children have the big ones far enough away." She would then turn her watchful eyes to those children driving the older sheep away.

"Make sure to get them way out of here. We do not want them to smell the little ones or they will not eat well. Take them into the wind or you will have a hard time keeping the flock together." Once in a while she would giggle to herself, turn her face into the hogan, and whisper Mother forth to see something funny one of us had done.

Sometimes the lambs were kept in the corral until the flocks returned in the evening. We could hear the bleating for miles around. When the big ones had gone out of smell and sight, the lambs were taken a small distance from the corral to graze.

Naturally, we loved to play with the little lambs. We did this in spite of being told not to touch them too much. According to my aunt, when we handled them too much, the mother couldn't recognize their familiar smell and would refuse to nurse them. I loved the lambs very much, and the little goats. We used to chase after them, hold them against our cheeks, and talk to them.

When the lambing season ended in early May, many white lambs and spindly kids required constant vigil. We took turns looking after them. I took my turn while my brother tended the mature sheep and goats. But most of the time I was sent out to help with the larger herd.

It seemed that the little goats were always causing trouble. They would go all over the place, on top of the hogan, on the wagon, in and out of the corrals, and into the ditches and arroyos. We had fun chasing them and looking after them. The dogs chimed in, too, barking and yapping a broken song. These were fun times!

Lambs were earmarked before their ears got too tough. Earmarks were the means of identifying sheep in case they became mixed with neighboring flocks. The day for earmarking found all of us at the corral to separate lambs and kids from the sheep and goats. Joe and I caught the lambs one by one and took them to my mother or aunt, who waited with a sharp knife.

I grabbed the front legs while Joe wrestled the hind legs to throw a lamb onto its side. Mother would then lightly force her foot onto the lamb's neck in order to grip an ear with her hand. This ear was cut with a V-shaped notch, and the tip of the other was cut completely off. I didn't especially appreciate this part of the work, for I dearly loved the lambs. I didn't like to see them hurt or hear them bleat in pain.

After each had been earmarked, bright blood would drizzle down their sad faces. You could see them lying all around panting, trying to recuperate. I cried inside at such a sight. I felt so sorry for those little lambs. In the evening when the sheep and goats were brought in from grazing, they sniffed at the little ones but were not bothered as much as I had been.

After we finished the lambs, the goats were earmarked. The lambs gave us little trouble, but the kids were harder to catch and made quite a commotion. They were much noisier than the lambs. We chased them in the fresh sheep manure, which is very slippery. I did not have sure hooves like those little, evasive kids—do I need to say more?

Usually near May's decline, it was warm enough to begin shearing wool and mohair. One of us would herd the sheep while the rest stayed near the hogan to help my aunt and my mother shear. The children's job was to throw each sheep down, then tie its legs together. While we went after another one, the adults would start shearing the last one.

Shearing was tedious work and very tiring. The metal handshears we bought from the trading post resembled a large pair of lawn clippers. Every so often we stopped to sharpen them on a rock because the dirty wool quickly dulled the blades. Our hands got very tired and sore; blisters were not uncommon.

Each day a few animals were sheared until all were shorn of their winter growth. After the shearing was completed, Mother and my aunt sorted the wool. They kept what they wanted for personal weaving, which required the best. The rest was tamped into large burlap bags to sell to the trader. These bags were the only trampoline we had. We children got to jump up and down on the wool, through the bag's mouth.

Shortly after shearing, my brother and I went after the loose horses on the prairie. We found them, brought them home, hitched them to the wagon filled with the wool bags, and then drove them to the trading post.

After the bags were weighed by the trader, we were given both cash and trade credit slips with which we purchased supplies for the coming months. We bought staple foods: flour, sugar, coffee, and a few canned goods. The rest we could produce ourselves.

After the springtime excitement of lambing, shearing, and earmarking was over, Mother found time to weave. The sheared wool she had earlier set aside was usually dirty, so she washed it with yucca-root soap. The yucca is a cactus that grows throughout the Southwest. We also used the suds of the yucca root for shampoo.

After the wool had been washed, we hung it on the bushes to dry. When dry, it was soft and fluffy. Mother wanted the wool to be free of lanolin grime so it would take the dye well. Dirty, oily wool does not dye evenly.

After Mother cleaned the wool, she was ready to card. I remember clearly the many times I saw Mother sitting in the hogan's summer shade doing this. The carding tools were nothing more than two pieces of wood with sharp metal teeth on the inside, set in rows like combs. She would take a small handful of newly washed wool, place it between the two combs, and scrape it back and forth until the wool was drawn out light and fluffy. It was then ready to spin.

Mother took the carded wool, twisting it with her fingers until she made a long thread. She then turned her hand spindle, winding the thread onto it. The wool would be spun again and again onto the spindle, wrapped and unwrapped until it was tight and strong. Through many mornings my mother and my aunt would diligently work together, carding and spinning until four or five balls of strong yarn rested on the ground.

Next Mother would dye the wool. She used natural dye by boiling the wool with plants, roots, or berries carefully chosen from the surrounding countryside. Natural dyes are pastel colored and are soft and easy to admire. Only the more bold red and black came from commercial dyes bought at the trading post. Both my mother and aunt had a vast knowledge of useful native plants from which dye could be made. The dyed wool was hung on the bushes to dry again before being rolled up into tight balls preparatory to weaving.

The weaving loom was made of long juniper poles fastened together to form a square. This square constituted the loom frame, which was placed either inside the hogan in winter or outside in the shade during the summer.

It usually took some time to string the loom with the vertical warp of the rug. After that, the weaving went quickly. Many times I would sit by Mother and watch the red, black, orange, yellow, and white threads form a design behind her skillful hands.

The designs that Mother wove into the rug were carried in her head. They were never written down and yet came out with near-perfect symmetry. No two Navajo rugs are exactly alike. Some are completed in a few days; others take weeks to complete. In the old days, the Navajo wove blankets for their own use. The women's old-style dress was a simple dark woolen blanket worn folded, with a hole for the head and with the front and back fastened underneath the arms. Now my people weave rugs for the trader to sell. For personal use, Navajos today wear colorful Pendleton wool shawls machine-made at Pendleton Woolen Mills in Oregon.

After completion, the rug was taken to the trading post. There the trader would inspect it carefully and weigh it on the scales. Pay was based on weight and workmanship. In return, we usually received the usual staples and some cash. At special times the children got candy, oranges, soda pop, or Cracker Jacks.

The summers of herding sheep, and all that went with it, were times of many memories. When school was out, there were more of us at home to take turns with the sheep. When the work was over, we played our hearts out, but the most enjoyable summer activity of all was a trip to the trading post.

6
___

THE TRADING POST

About two miles north of the New Mexico/Colorado border and on the east of U.S. Highway 666 stands the Mancos Creek Colorado Trading Post.

The trading post was only three miles from our summer hogan. The fastest way to get there was on horseback. The next best way was just to run. We usually ran everywhere as children anyway. It was fun. Going to the trading post was like going to the mall, plus a movie, today.

My uncle, Man Who Halts, had an old buckboard wagon we sometimes rode while traveling to the trading post. It seemed to take forever to get the horses hitched, bridled, and given the once-over. As I think about it now, it was worse than waiting for Christmas morning. My brothers and sisters and I had treats on our minds. Treats, treats, treats!

I'll never forget the first trip with my family to the trading post. Father had not yet come out of the mountains for the winter, so he didn't go. Our winter hogan was on a mesa about fifteen miles from the Mancos Trading Post. This particular trip began there.

"Mike, Joe, Nellie," Man Who Halts said, "come help me harness the team. We are going to the trading post today. George, you can help."

About this time there was a great commotion among all of us children. We were going to the trading post! Doubtless, there would be other children there our own age. It would be so much fun to see some of the other families. It was hard not to act too excited. Today was the day for joy!

I remember vividly these wonderful childhood trips to the trading post. I was just a little boy then, but a happy one whenever the words *trading post* were mentioned.

Even though it was winter, there was no snow, except near the tops of distant mountains. The dust still jumped up from the iron wagon-wheel rims and from the clopping of the horses' hooves.

Once Joe, Mike, Nellie, and I and Man Who Halts had hitched the team, children started piling in the back of the wagon from all directions. We were all laughing and teasing, and we were so excited about the simple joys the short trip would bring. We children knew better than to expect purchases for ourselves other than light treats, but we still gained the greatest of joy in the desert trading post just by looking around inside. Our minds were already there, but our bodies seemed slow—at least to us.

"Children, settle down some. Be quiet," my mother urged. "Look after those little ones. If you help us, there might be a soda pop for you." This brought us all quickly into line.

Then Joe and I remembered some further responsibility. We jumped down to help our uncle heft the heavy bags of wool onto the wagon's back. These my aunt would sell. Even as old as Man Who Halts was, I could see excitement about the trip in his eyes. He wasn't fooling anyone. He was like us children. We all loved him. He was a good uncle.

Sometimes he tried to pretend that he was angry with us young ones, but we knew his anger was not real. It wasn't in his heart to be like that. But as children we obeyed him because we knew of his care and love. It was one of those family things that was never spoken of. It was sacred because of that.

Daughter of Buckskin Man, my aunt, was bringing her wool to sell. She was anxious to have it weighed and to receive credit to replenish our food supply.

Perhaps it is difficult for those outside our culture to understand, but when she brought the food home, it was shared with
all. There was no mine this or mine that, or it was my money
that bought it, or whatever. The food was held in common
once it was inside the hogan's door. My mother had the same
attitude about her money when she sold a rug. Red Woman
and Daughter of Buckskin Man were true sisters. There was no
envy between them. Many Navajo families are like that. Sharing was a great part of the older Navajo way of life. It was one of
those inbred traits that somehow painted its unseen beauty
across the souls of the Navajo.

With one last heave, we hoisted the last of the wool sacks
into the wagon. Joe and I barely beat our uncle in, and he had
to run clear to the front driving plank. We knew he was excited. Our whole family was caught up in the air of family enjoyment. It was such a simple but beautiful and fulfilling thing.
We knew that the day ahead would be bright and happy.

One of the team mares had a colt. Wherever the mare
went, the colt was sure to go. The colt pranced along behind
the struggling buckboard while we children bounced around in
the wagon bed. As we bounced, we laughed at the antics of the
following colt. His bay hue contrasted softly with the jade
greasewood shrubbery that grew near the wagon trail. Every
once in a while, the colt would wiggle, kick out his hind feet,
and then run for about fifty yards. When he stopped, it was as
though he were asking himself, "Now why did I do that?" He
was funny.

Mother, our aunt, and our uncle were having so much fun
talking that our laughing didn't even bother them. The trip
was beautiful. It reminded me of the saying of how a Navajo
walks with beauty all around.

But the road was long and dusty. And whenever I thought
about that, it seemed to go on forever. Bumpity bump, bumpity bump, over and over, all the way down the canyon's rocky
road went our wagon full of wool and laughing Navajos, with
the clowning colt following behind. Such a day would be long
remembered.

The older children told me that if we were patient, watching for the right moment to ask, Mother might buy us a piece of candy, a bottle of soda pop, or something else that was sweet. On later visits, the trader called me the Soda Pop Kid. I admit there was nothing better than soda pop to wash down the buckboard dust. The contrast between the reservoir water and soda pop helped us prefer the latter, and soda pop was actually better for us at the time.

Mother brought a rug with her this trip. She was pleased with the work she had done. The weave was tight, the borders were ruler-straight, and the coordination and symmetry of the colored, natural dyes made the rug a work of art.

As we walked through the trading post's front door, I was afraid. The trader was the first white man I'd seen. I stared at him for some time, my eyes peering from behind my mother's full-length Navajo skirt.

My face must have looked lifeless. I didn't know what to expect. I'd heard about white men before. Stories had been handed down about the Long Walk, stories that barbed the Navajo mind with images of Anglo cruelty. Now I was actually seeing one! I was glad to be with my family.

"I wish I were back in the hogan now," I thought, as my foot stubbed on the threshold of the trading post entrance. "What's in this place anyway? The smell is different. Not like our hogan. Well, maybe it's not too bad. All these Navajos don't look too worried. Just in case, I will stick close to Mother."

I clung to my mother's bright, traditional skirt just like a baby opossum on its mother's back. I almost swept her from her feet, I was holding on so tight. I stepped barefooted into someone's tobacco spit. So as I tried to watch out for white men, see the sights while peeking from behind Mother's legs, and do a ballet around spots of tobacco juice, the situation grew awkward.

Inside the store, everything was plain compared to today's standards. The old ceiling beams that stretched the length of the store were hewn by hand; the trees had been taken from the nearby Colorado mountains. Instead of bright wood, they were gray, weathered by age and tobacco smoke. The whitewashed walls were of stucco. In the corners and on the ceiling were long V-shaped, coffee-colored stains running down the wall. At first I thought they were painted on, but then I finally realized that the roof must have some long-standing leaks. The atmosphere was slightly damp. Maybe the dripping moisture from the ceiling to the walls caused this. Whenever the door opened, a fresh breeze ushered in a contrast between inside and outside.

Beneath the antique-roof structure, Ute Indians were socializing. Like the Navajos, they were in no hurry to transact business. One of the main purposes of the trading post was to be a place to enjoy friends, neighbors, and family. It took a long time for the Utes to trade.

The trader waited on one person at a time, as though he needed to be careful. He knew that an Indian could read his heart and discern his honesty.

The Utes laughed and laughed. Then they grew silent for a while until another of their party made a humorous observation. Then they all laughed together. Then the group would think for a while. And on and on it went. The Utes as well as the Navajos loved to speak their language and to listen to its poetic quality.

Over time, the trading post began to become more familiar to me. Future trips found me not as frightened as I was during this first one.

In the early days, the Navajos used the trading post as a center for practically everything. From there, one could catch the news from clan members, friends, and, unfortunately, sometimes from a bill collector. Not only did one receive mail there, but one could leave messages for friends and relatives who would be coming.

Both the Navajos and the Utes met at the Mancos post. Along with the surrounding local news and the news of the government in Washington, tribal affairs and prices for mohair, goats and sheep were discussed at length. Often the location of the next Squaw Dance was announced. Here the Ute people communicated the time of the coming Bear Dance.

In the winter, this was a good warm place. We did not tell

the trader how much we valued the heat or he might have
started to charge for that, too. Because the store was warm, the
talk tended to be lengthy, and, anyway, for most people a trip
to the trading post was not an everyday thing.

During the old days, trading post goods were vastly over-
priced, especially such staples as coffee, sugar, and flour. No
competing store existed nearer than twenty or thirty miles
away.

In partial defense of the early traders, it must have been
costly to transport merchandise the great distance onto the reservation. Also, there are always risks when one is involved in
managing a credit-retail business such as a trading post.

Dealing with the trader was confusing, if not difficult. Desperately needed old-age assistance welfare checks came to the
post office within the trading post. Some Navajos were never
allowed to touch their government checks. The trader usually
held the checks, applying the money toward the Indians' personal debts. As a result, these Navajos never received cash for
purchasing outside the trading-post walls. In these cases, the
trader would not have needed to fear outside competition even
if it had existed. Also, by holding the government welfare
checks, the trader was able to see that his own business interests were ensured. This government system helped the trader
rather than the Indian. Many people did not know if the trader
had been completely honest in his dealings with them. The
Navajos hoped he was. Even if they had sensed that he was
not, it would not have done much good. The Navajos lived on
hope and faith in dealing with a world that was almost completely opposite to their own.

Still clinging to Mother's skirt, I ventured to gaze around.
Shelves, shelves, and shelves upon shelves of food. Why
wasn't it like this at our hogan? Why should all this food be in
one place and not on the plates of hungry people?

I could not understand it. My parents had just spoken
about the helpless Navajo widow who had starved to death in
her hogan. No one had known how to help her. She had given
what little food she had to help her grandchildren.

They had also heard of another clan relative of hers to whom she had given most of her old-age assistance. My parents said she was the kind of person who could not refuse to help anyone. She had been sick for a long time. She lived out, way out, all alone. Her family did not do much, but they always wanted something from her, it seemed. Her skinny dog ran off, too. She had given all her jewelry to others in greater need. Now I looked at all those rows upon rows of food and wondered.

I thought, "How is it that someone can starve with so much available? When I grow up, I will share what I have. That is what my parents have taught me to do. I now can see why. Why is the world set up in such a way?"

No sooner had this last thought come than I was entranced by all the colors on the can labels. I'd never seen such bright colors. They really caught my eye. Reds, browns, blues, yellows—all the colors there could possibly be. Amazing! It was so difficult to understand all the material richness in the trading post! Some of my younger brothers and sisters could not believe it either. I clung tighter to my mother's skirt.

I watched Mother take her picturesque rug toward the counter. She laid it down carefully, but not before it had caught the trader's eye. In this way, she had actually begun the trading process, though the trader may not have known it. After she was sure he had seen the rug being laid down ever so gently, she returned to us and a few friends who had sauntered over to say hello and visit.

Now we would wait until the trader saw fit to nod her forward. It was important not to be impatient. Possibly impatience would give the trader a clue that the rug was woven in haste, just for money. If he sensed that, it could mean less money for the rug.

I looked over at my uncle and my aunt. They were busy looking at a glass case containing red coral rings, silver bracelets, and turquoise. My aunt was looking at something she had pawned, and I had heard the adults discussing something about buying food first. They would not be able to redeem her jewelry, so they were looking at it this one last time.

If people wanted cash, they pawned their silver and turquoise jewelry. Squash-blossom necklaces, intricate bracelets, or a silver concho belt could be pawned at one time. All this merchandise today would be valued at a thousand dollars or more. The pawn back then would be about thirty or forty dollars for the handmade jewelry. (Pawn is the money received on jewelry, rugs, or whatever may have value. Usually it is much less than the items are actually worth.)

I have seen my mother pawn precious jewelry just to feed her children. If she did not redeem it within a certain time, the trader sold the items for double, or even triple, the money Mother had received originally.

The trader finally picked up Mother's rug. That was his way of nodding for her to come. He was playing a game, too, but his was not as crucial as ours may have been. His quick, over-the-counter examination of the rug told Mother two things: first, he was interested in the rug, and second, he was ready to discuss a trade.

As many times before, the trader lifted the rug from the counter and headed for the valuing room. He tried to do this without expression, so as not to give away just how little or much he appreciated the rug's beauty and quality. Mother knew she was to follow him to this room that had a scale for weighing and a clean floor where the rug could be spread for inspection.

In that room the rug was weighed and then checked for squareness, symmetry, and color coordination. Its overall beauty was discussed, and, in his mind, the trader pondered how it would sell to tourists or other rug middlemen from the East who frequented his post looking for topnotch weaving.

Today Mother had a bill that was to be paid, so half the amount the trader offered her would have to be applied toward the bill or no bargain could be struck. Finally they agreed upon an amount. She used the other half from the rug to buy flour, canned goods, coffee, and other items to feed the family.

These goods would find a common place with those my aunt had purchased. We were one family.

The rug and wool money would help us make it through the winter. As Mother ordered food, she asked the trader many times how much money she had left. The trader scratched on his paper with a long slender stick, subtracting the cost of the goods on the counter from the amount of credit on the paper. Then he told her the results.

Like my parents, I knew nothing of reading and writing then. Formal education was not stressed in our home. Scratch, scratch, scratch, the trader would mark on his paper. What his hand etched was mysterious, but somehow it helped him to think. He seemed not to be able to think without first moving the slender stick in his hand. In awe, we all just watched, much as a tourist might come to watch one of our ceremonials. We had not the faintest idea what the figures meant. All we knew was this: when he was finished, we would end up owing him money.

The trader could speak enough Navajo to discuss the purchases back and forth until the balance on the slip of paper was fully spent. At the conclusion, half an hour later, when we had finished buying our food, the trader smiled and threw in some Cracker Jacks, a can of tomatoes and some soda crackers for lunch, and a bottle of soda pop as a gesture of goodwill. This was good diplomacy. Our official business was done, but we lingered as long as possible to visit with friends and relatives, although we wanted to be home before dark.

By late afternoon, we were on our way back up the canyon. The trading post had been so strange that I could not wait to get back to the familiar hogan. It had been enjoyable enough, but the thought of being with the sheep and flocks again became very inviting. I was tired.

Though we tried to avoid it, sometimes we did not get home until way after dark. This was one of those times. When we finally got there, we enjoyed the things we had bought that day. While we children were going through all the new purchases, Mother and Daughter of Buckskin Man fixed supper.

After supper, we children laid back on a pile of sheepskins, curled up our legs, and listened contentedly to my aunt, uncle, and mother talk about the news they had received at the trading post. The fire was warming the hogan. Our little stomachs were satisfied. And with the adults still talking, we stared at the embers and peacefully entered sleep.

7

THE BEAN FIELDS
OF COLORADO

I t was a bright morning in midsummer. Already my parents were up, moving about the hogan. Before the sun had a chance to amble very high in the east, my father was well into preparation for the day. Mother was quietly readying the items we needed for our annual trip into the bean fields of Colorado.

After discussing prospects of where to find work, my parents gathered us together. "My children," called Mother, "come over here. Sit down. Be still and listen to your father. Our money is gone. We hope our food will be enough for today. We are going to Cortez to the bean fields again. We will hope for some work there. We must pray for work, and your father will call upon the holy people for help. Sit down and be quiet. Listen. Pat, stop wiggling around.

"You must be obedient to all we say as your parents, or something bad may happen to you. I hope you are paying good attention."

There was a grave look upon Mother's face. We didn't dare move while she talked with us, especially with a look like that in her eyes. This was one of the times we might have been spanked if we did not listen, especially the older children who had more responsibility.

77

"Father," Joe offered, "my prayers are that we will be left alone this year to work. I have prayed that those same mean men will not be around again to beat you and scare us."

"What should we do if it happens again?" I asked.

"George, what does your sacred name mean? Ashkii Hoyani?" inquired Father. A look of wisdom spread over his countenance, a look of fatherly care and concern.

"Well," I ventured, "it means one who is well behaved and good."

"Then that is your answer, my son. That is what your mother and I expect from you, and from all our children. We have tried to fight back before. It is useless. We will defend ourselves if necessary, but if a fight can be avoided, this is the best."

I had watched my father try to defend our rights against some Anglo ruffians once before. But there were more of them than there were of us, and they tried to physically prove that dirty, lice-ridden Indians had no rights off the reservation.

I could not recognize my father's face after they were done. And we knew better than to try to admit him at the Cortez Hospital, for we had no money. Indian problems such as that one were common, and the hospital policy would view it as just another one.

More than once I have heard the Navajo blamed for beginning a fight. Had we gone to the hospital, we probably would have heard the same thing. Things like that are hard facts. And knowledge of them comes from long experience.

The day after he was injured, my father worked hard in the scorching heat, despite my mother's pleadings. Our pain was so great in seeing him suffer innocently. And then to see him labor in the fields because he loved us and knew we needed the money was almost unbearable.

My father expected all of us to behave well. We were not to invite trouble. Anger was something to bring under control.

My father said, "Since the cars will not pick us up all at once, we will travel by twos. Joe, George, Mike, and the older ones will each travel with a younger brother or sister. It will be safe this way."

He turned to Mother and advised, "You will travel with Lucy, the youngest. It is her first trip. We do not want her to be afraid.

"I will be the last to come, just to make sure that you all make it all right. We will meet at the canyon rim in the sagebrush and trees, the same place as last year."

We left after Mother had finished packing our bundles of clothing, food, and bedding. We were not concerned about being overloaded. Each of us carried some type of essential camping utensil, such as a blackened pot, a skillet, and maybe a plate. Usually we took only a cup or two. If we had only one cup, we shared it. There were no knives, spoons, or forks. We ate with our fingers. Joking about utensil-like fingers sometimes helped us do without.

That night we made it to our destination, all of us, safe and sound. When all were accounted for, we followed one another toward the familiar camping site close by on the canyon rim.

From the familiar campsite, Father would range out daily, going from bean ranch to bean ranch until he had secured employment. Sometimes he could not find work, so he just returned to camp. But then he searched day after day or we just moved on to the next town.

Sometimes Father could find no work anywhere. Every bean ranch would have sent him away sad because no help was needed. When that happened, we would just return home again by hitchhiking. This particular journey had brought us about fifty miles from home. Times such as this were worrisome for my parents because we were usually broke, not knowing where money would come from to buy needed food, even the bare necessities. We would have to seek the aid of clan family or friends. Or maybe we would be at the mercy of the trader for credit. When worst came to worst, the family would travel to Towaoc, going from home to home to ask if we could herd sheep for a Ute family. Then we worked only for food and no cash.

Neither Father nor Mother had employable skills other than herding sheep. So my father never had steady work; he qualified only for seasonal work. Hoeing weeds in the pinto-bean fields, or even the potato fields, near Dove Creek and Cortez, Colorado, was his greatest work achievement. He treated it as such by putting in an honest day's labor for a day's pay. He and Mother could each earn from thirty to fifty cents an hour doing this.

This year several days elapsed before my father found employment. During that time, my brothers and I searched for pop bottles along the highways leading into Cortez. We did not do it for exercise; pop bottles brought five cents apiece. We turned our meager earnings over to an approving mother.

Also, we went begging for bones from market to market. In those days, each store had a butcher shop. Some store people would throw the bones away in front of our eyes instead of soiling their conscience by giving to an Indian. When they did that, we just waited in the alley until the scraps were thrown out. Others were kinder, and we were thankful for whatever we received. Mother would place the bones in clear water, boil them, and then serve us the delicious soup.

We often scavenged the city dump for useful items. A tin can, once properly washed, makes a good drinking cup.

One day, Father came riding into camp in a pickup truck. He had a smile on his face. We all knew what that meant: a job! It was time to lift our hearts in thanks.

After we had all piled into the back of the rancher's truck, we began to talk merrily, and we could see brightness in each other's eyes.

When the rancher let us off at a camping spot near one of his large fields, Father gathered us together and offered a prayer using corn pollen. We all faced east in this prayer of gratitude. Oh, how our hearts and souls had been lifted because another day of hope had been sent to bless our way!

With the name of the employer to back him, Father obtained credit at a willing market. Then he brought food to the camp. I cannot describe the gratitude that filled our hearts.

Later my mother said, "George, tomorrow while your father and I and the children work, you will stay in camp to watch the little ones. You should play with them, too. Remember, they are your brothers and sisters. These babies love you. Make sure to change them if they need it. If you run out of diapers, you may have to let them run naked for a while.

"There is a little food. Make sure to stretch it out. Try to feed them enough so they will not be too hungry after breakfast. Put the rest away in a can. They can have that again for lunch."

I played with my baby brothers and sisters around the campsite and in the beanfield furrows. Dirt clods were our playthings. When a diaper needed changing, I did it. When it was time for the babies to eat, I fed them. My parents had asked these things of me, and I respected them.

My family worked ten-hour days, sometimes for a week, if we were fortunate. As I sat in the shade tending the babies, I could see my parents marching back and forth under the scorching sun, weeding the mile-long pinto-bean fields. The soil was so thick, hot, and deep that it was difficult to walk. My older brothers and sisters walked the same furrows. When I became older, I did the same. My pay was ten cents an hour. Some furrows were so thick with weeds that a person could take only two rows at a time. Other rows had only a few weeds so that three, four, or six rows could be gleaned of weeds at once.

As I watched my family work, I thought how nice it would be when the day was done. Everybody would sit around the fireplace eating a warm bowl of stew and having some golden frybread. The day went faster if I played with the babies.

When the sun sloped just right in the west, I began stirring the fire. Mother would appreciate this after having labored ten long hours under the searing sun.

We had camped right under the juniper trees. In those days, it did not pay the farmers to build migrant housing, since weeding took so little time. There were times when old shacks or run-down barns provided a place to sleep, but since June and July usually brought little rain, if any, we just slept under the sparkling stars.

As we sat around the campfire that evening, Father and Mother were silent. The first day's work must have fatigued them. The older children looked tired, too. But it was a contented type of tiredness, one born of an honest day's work.

After dinner, each of us retrieved a soiled, worn blanket, and, after locating a comfortable spot of ground, nestled ourselves in the blankets to sleep.

In the far distance, a low rumble of thunder sounded, almost blending with my father's peaceful snoring. Sleep then covered my eyes.

I was awakened abruptly by the screaming of my little sister. She kept saying that something had hit her head. Soon I heard things crashing through the trees above and landing everywhere around us. Then I heard the taunting Anglo voices through the disrupted night.

"Hey, you Injuns, get those squaws and papooses out of here. You're not wanted around here. Get your dirty bodies and lice out!" Another rock whistled through the air, just missing my head. I dove to protect my little brothers and sisters. Rocks and beer bottles kept coming, hurled by malicious people who disguised themselves with the mask of night.

Soon, I heard my father's pleading voice: "Please go away. We do not want trouble. I have my little ones here. You have hurt one of them badly. Please stop and go away."

"Oh, shut up, you worthless savage! Bring that squaw of yours over here to us; then maybe we'll leave." Their throaty laughter was vile. Their words were slurred in drunkenness.

I heard my mother trying to silence her weeping at having been threatened so. My own heart was breaking for her. "Why do people do things like this?" I wondered. "What have we done?"

After calling my family every foul Anglo curse word that could be spoken, they finally left, confident, I am sure, of their valor. The next morning we were silent as we prepared breakfast.

I wish I could say such things happened only once. But in almost every town we migrated to, racial prejudice reared its ugly head. Many times, in these small communities, white people would call us names and poke fun at us, asking us where our bows and arrows were and slapping their mouths in a television war whoop. Though we became accustomed to being verbally and physically abused, the pain was always there beneath the scars. We did not think of returning revilings for revilings. It was not part of our culture or our nature. To receive cruel treatment just because we were Indians was painful. How it hurt my parents to be so humiliated, especially in front of their children. Their hearts were pained even more when they were denied services by white storekeepers.

We knew that those who slurred us were culturally deprived regarding human kindness. Because of our sensitive upbringing, if we allowed ourselves to return negative words to those jeering at us, we hurt all the more. We had always been taught by Father to pray positively, even for those who were our enemies. Time after time I have heard my father ask the Great Creator to bless all white people the world over. He prayed for all five-fingered people throughout the earth.

At other times, after working in the bean fields, we would return to camp only to find our things scattered and broken by vandals. It was discouraging.

Sometimes we tried to stand up for our rights, but there were usually too many against us. Many times we just ran away in fear. When it was too bad, we moved from that area.

I think that is why my father preferred to leave his family home whenever he sought work. But for two months or more each summer, this was our life, enduring prejudice, camping, moving from town to town, looking for jobs, and doing hard, back-breaking work.

After I was six years old, I began helping with the bean-field work. This continued until I was in high school and found summer work elsewhere.

We were typical children when we worked. Our dreams were to buy our own cars, bikes, watches, televisions, clothes, or whatever we fancied. We always ended up using our earnings to support the family. We knew that was where the money would go all the time, so our dreams did not really matter. Most of the time our total earnings bought only a pair of shoes or a shirt.

Even as we got older and got separate jobs away from home, we sent most of our money back to Mother. We did this out of respect, duty, and love.

Although my father did not work year round, he worked more than the rest of us in paid employment. While not working or herding sheep, he tried to support our family as a medicine man or hand trembler. Still we were always poor, and not because we used our money foolishly. What Father earned kept us in flour for frybread, but the money seldom stretched beyond that. We had no luxuries in life, and the necessities were extremely poor as well.

My family never had a home, a car, or even a buckboard wagon of their own. Our food was simple, lacking in both quantity and quality. Our clothing was always old, ragged, and dirty. We were, in every way, the poorest of the poor. But we were happy. Our happiness came from being a family and from being able to sustain ourselves and to love each other and care for one another.

Our Navajo heritage was our only wealth. Despite having to venture into a white man's world and be treated worse than dogs, we were Navajo through and through. Deep inside, we had unconditional respect for ourselves. We were true to our Navajo heritage, and this gave us respect for ourselves and a higher understanding of nature and of life.

8

GOVERNMENT
BOARDING SCHOOL

The snoring of the boy in the bunk next to mine was not what kept me awake. I did not even know what time it was, but it seemed that I had been in this place forever. Mother had promised to visit, but just to think of my kind, sweet mother only made my pain worse. No matter how much I tried to get home off my mind, my homesickness only intensified.

Rules. Rules. So many rules. All I could think about was the almost absolute freedom my parents allowed at home. I felt trusted there. Here, we were told how to act, what to do, when to eat, and when to sleep.

Maybe if I were home sitting by the warm stove, Man Who Halts would sense my loneliness and tell me Navajo stories until the night was far spent.

I was so wide awake that my eyes must have looked like two prickly-pear pads. It made me feel worse that after being told to sleep now, I could not. I wanted to be obedient. This must be the nettle on the cactus. I wished sleep would come deeply, as it had for my brother Joe.

The moon's mournful light broke through one of the south windows. It squeezed through a pair of steel-rail bunks and streaked the wall above my head with grated shadows.

The walls were so bare, smooth, and cold. They reminded me of my first frightful experience at the trading post. Those plain walls were similar, except these were completely barren. Perhaps I'd learn to like this boarding school, as I'd come to appreciate the trading post. I doubted it, though.

Sleep. I just wished I could sleep. The days I'd spent with the sheep alone in the Colorado mountains waiting for Father to return could not even begin to compare to the gray loneliness of this barracks dormitory. I felt like crying aloud, only I didn't, because almost everything I had done so far had brought either censure or ridicule.

The stink of the inadequate facilities wafted across the room several times. The big bully a few bunks down, the one who had beat me up earlier that evening, had opened a window near his bed. As he was located on the end opposite the clogged toilets, the occasional wind outside drew the air over me down toward the gaping window.

I thought about getting up to shut it. Then I touched the fresh bruise under my left eye. I didn't get up.

We had all been made to take showers that night. All of us had literally been forced in, two per shower. Some of the older teenage boys made fun of us younger ones. I was just nine years old. Why did I have to get under the water? There was no soap anyway, except for a small, broken bar. It had slipped onto the slimy shower floor and finally come to rest on the circular drain screen. Around the drain, for about an inch or two, green matter had jelled uninvitingly. No one had used the soap. Several months later someone removed it, but they neglected to scrub away the mossy green growth.

In the morning, I'd have to wear those green-colored overalls again. We were all dressed alike, those of us whose parents couldn't afford to buy us new clothes, but the sizes never really fit anyone. In the morning when we lined up for roll call, we would look like a scraggly row of cornstalks, only with black cornsilk on the tops. The green clothes we wore were locked up at night, and the awkward shoes also.

I could feel my eyes beginning to puff and swell now. I wished I was home with my family. My eye started to throb.

The older boys had lined us up after bed check. Military style, the younger ones were commanded to stand at attention. Then the meanest one began: "You all owe us money. We want you to give us money. Who's got some? You'd better not hold out, or it will be real bad for you." He walked in front of the line of young boys, hitting and shoving to prove he meant business.

Very few had any money to give. Those who did not give were harassed and thrown around. One big bully came up to me. After shoving my shoulder with his fist, he harshly asked, "Where's your money?"

I stood frozen in fright. Even Joe couldn't help because the bully was bigger than everyone else. I couldn't even swallow. He saw the fear in my eyes. It only fed his bravado.

"Well," he demanded, "talk!"

"My mother had no money to give me," I said truthfully, hoping to be left unmolested for my honesty.

Things went black. When I got up off the floor, I realized I hadn't seen the menacing fist coming. I wanted to cry but groggily sensed it would just make the situation worse. I didn't dare glance at Joe, or I might cause something to happen to him.

"Next time you get some money, you'd better give it all to me," he threatened. I decided to avoid him thereafter.

As I lay in bed remembering the humiliation, silent streams of tears ran down my cheeks. I knew everyone would look at my face in the morning. There were many bullies like that one, and they all walked around in packs, like mean wolves. None of us dared tell on them to the dormitory attendant. Some had registered complaints before, but nothing was done.

I found out later that the older boys used the extorted money to buy luxury items at Saturday visits to the trading post. The food was bad at the dorm mess hall, so they bought bread, bologna, candy, cookies, and pop. The only thing we could do was stand penniless in the store, watching them gorge themselves on what our money had bought. We wished we could have some. If they saw us watching them eat, they would lick their lips, rub their stomachs, and grin sadistically. Times became better, though, as we learned the ropes of boarding-school survival.

After a while, through constant practice, I became the school marbles champion. To play for keeps, which was generally the case, a large circle would be drawn with a stick or finger on the dusty ground. Then everyone wanting to play put an equal number of marbles in the center of the circle. Each player had a "shooter," a marble that was aimed and shot at those within the circle. The marble was shot by flipping it off the pad of the index finger with a snap of the thumbnail. The idea was to knock as many marbles as possible out of the circle when one's turn came. Those marbles were then won for keeps by the person shooting.

I really had to cinch down my belt, because my pockets usually bulged with marbles. And the good thing about it was this: if I did not have any ready money, usually the bullies would take a few marbles as payment. I didn't worry, because I'd usually have the same marbles back in my pocket in a day or two anyway.

The school did not have much playground equipment, so we usually entertained ourselves during recess by playing marbles or by playing the different forms of tag, which are still common games today in schoolyards.

The government boarding school historically has had one thing in mind for the Indian child—to remove him from the supposedly uncivilized Indian world and teach him to appreciate the white man's way. The Navajo language was to be verbally exterminated. This was government policy for more than several decades.

According to boarding-school policy, the Indian was to be assimilated into mainstream America. Ignored was the thought of Navajo language and culture.

The Navajo way was the whole of our very lives. We had been brought fully by our parents into the Indian culture. Now, in boarding school, the indoctrination was directed to destroy all that our parents had taught us to cherish.

My first year at boarding school was not the most promising experience. I was involved in several fights, not of my own choosing. I received rough initiations from the older boys; they wanted the younger students to know quickly who was in charge. This went on not only one night but many wherein I cried myself to sleep.

In fact, the first day Joe and I arrived and when we were left unsupervised among the older adolescents, we were initiated into the bare reality of boarding school.

As they had done to other incoming children, the older boys lured Joe and me into a dark, isolated room. They led us on with kind words feigned in false friendship. Being naive and trusting, Joe and I went.

Once in the dark room, they beat us badly, telling us that we had better understand who the real bosses were. And, they promised, if we told any teacher or supervisor about getting beat up, our next brutal session with them would be worse than the first!

In this school, we marched everywhere in military fashion. Wherever we went, we were told not to get caught speaking Navajo. If somebody did, the offending mouth was washed out with frothy, lye soup. Mine was washed out several times that first year. When I first arrived there, I knew only a few English words. It was all so new. I was very alone at first, not being able to talk and laugh with the others.

Not only was my mouth washed out with soap, but many times I was forced to stand and stare at a blank wall for hours on end. Or, if we used English improperly, such as incorrect grammar, we had to wear a sign around our necks that said "Dummy." If we broke any dorm rules, we were punished.

Once when I was caught speaking my own beautiful language, I was called stupid because I did not know English. Soap eating and being called stupid were the daily menu around the government boarding school in those days.

All the teachers were Anglos. The government required them to follow rigid policy and procedure sent from Washington to use in all reservation government schools. Part of this policy was regimentation and punishment, including corporal punishment such as spanking with hard, brutal, wooden paddles.

Instruction was stiffly formal. Even the rows of runner chairs were nailed to the floor.

For many years professional requirements were very low for teachers and supervisory personnel. Trained people were just unwilling to live in such isolated places. Commitment was usually toward the dollar and not the Navajo. Also, the teachers who did come were underpaid, so turnover was unusually high.

There was no library. When we were not in the classroom or working, there was no supervision. Often fights and brawls broke out easily because of the sparse supervision.

Normally, though, our day was highly organized, leaving enrollees little time to be on their own. Our routine of bed making, kitchen detail, and cleaning filled the hours before classes began.

We rose before the sun every day, only not to a kind father's voice, but instead to the clanging of some regulated bell. Our whole day was regulated by bells, clear until bedtime.

The kitchen and dining room were poorly equipped. Meals were eaten in silence along unadorned mess tables. The fare was usually government surplus food and lumpy powdered milk. Sometimes after the meals, we were searched to make sure that uneaten, unpalatable food was not taken out. The boarding school matron oversaw us to make sure we cleaned our plates.

Over the years, I have increasingly appreciated the food we were served because, even though it was poor, it was generally far better than the food at home. Many of us, when first brought into the school, were very thin because food was scarce at home. Eating regular dining-hall meals was better than living off the land to survive. Most of us went home in the spring looking much healthier.

When we ate in the mess hall, the older bullies stood at the exit, particularly if the dessert we were having was good. By a predetermined hand-finger signal they had shown us, we automatically knew that in order to escape a beating that evening, the dessert on our plate must be sneaked out and slipped to them. Most of us ate with our heads lowered. But this usually worked only once or twice. They caught us later and told us

Students at Shiprock Boarding School, 1953. George P. Lee is second from left

that on those days of good dessert, we had better look up at them or else!

During the year, our parents made every effort to visit as many times as possible. Mother, especially, visited us once or twice each year. When our parents came to visit, they usually brought some home-cooked food to give us a change from the food we ate at school. I enjoyed this because Mother brought mutton and frybread. I would also beg her for a few pennies, just so I could make my forced contribution that night to the older boys in order to avoid being beaten.

In spite of the negative experiences during that first year, there were also a lot of positive experiences. Despite our teachers' efforts to force us to speak English only, we spoke Navajo much of the time, especially when the supervisors were not listening. Still, we learned a lot of English. Some of us looked forward to the day when we could be reunited with our families. We counted the days until school would be out.

During our second year of boarding school, which repeated many of our first year's experiences, my brother and I decided to run away from the school. Some of our friends had run away but were caught by the Navajo police and brought back. There were stories of others who ran away during the winter months but never made it. They froze to death in their efforts to reach home.

My brother, a few of our friends, and I had a plan to run away while everybody was asleep one night. At the appointed time, we quietly got out of bed and dressed. We then crept down the stairs and out of the dormitory into the cold night. Once outside, we slid quickly through the fence and into the fields. While the others hurried ahead, I had a feeling that what we were doing was not right, so my brother Joe and I turned back. Not long after we had silently crept back inside and gone back to bed, we noticed that the others did not come back.

We were worried about our friends. It was just too cold and dark outside. A few days later, some of them were brought back to the boarding school by the police. A lesson was learned—it was useless to try to run away.

Once while playing on the slippery slide, I had a real bad experience. I had started to climb the steps of the slide. A friend was chasing me, trying to tag me. My head was turned as far to my back as possible. I didn't even look down at the slide plane. I should have. In the middle of the slide, halfway down, there was a break that I didn't see. And in my excitement, even when I did face toward the slide's bottom landing, I couldn't see anything wrong. When there was no weight placed on it, nothing looked wrong anyway.

So I slid down, totally unaware of the unseen break. When I got to the unnoticeable break, my own weight caused the sliding plane to give way. As soon as it did, one of the support rails underneath was thrust up. The sharp railing caught me in the left thigh, entering about midway between my knee and hip. It entered about six inches from the curved exit just below my back pants pocket. At first, I didn't feel anything; then the pain hit me going ninety miles an hour.

The kids just stood around looking. Then, once they broke from their entranced stares, some ran to find Joe. After what seemed like forever, Joe came running to the rescue. Meanwhile, I was stuck on that support pipe like a melting fudgesicle.

When Joe pulled me off, and as I looked at what I had been impaled upon, I saw globules of fat and blood on the exposed metal spike. That almost made me faint. I went into shock.

I was in the hospital six months. Mother visited me there. She wanted to have them release me, to take me home for a healing ceremony, a sing. But I told her I would rather stay in the hospital, and that is what I did. I did not feel like going anywhere, even though they gave me so many shots I couldn't count them all. I didn't like shots very much. But after that, I was even worse about having them.

I do not intend to be too critical of the conditions in the early boarding schools. Perhaps these conditions were not found in every boarding school. They probably did the best they could under difficult circumstances.

I also believe, despite poor salaries, that in some boarding schools there were individual teachers who were dedicated. Some were probably very sensitive to the special needs of the Navajo children. These were teachers who inspired the students with a desire to learn.

I had one teacher who, though lacking in professional preparation, instinctively knew how to develop desirable behavior in us without overcontrolling, punishing, or regimenting. On the other hand, I had another teacher who told us in class that none of us would ever amount to anything, that Indians were all destined to fail in life.

Looking back, I am now very grateful for my experiences in boarding school. In a way, the old-time disciplinary program was effective. The policy of not speaking my own native language was beneficial in that I was forced to learn English, which to this day has been extremely helpful.

The same day that Mr. Bloomfield, the Mormon trader, signed Joe and me up for boarding school, we were also signed up for religion, that is religion other than the Navajo religion.

The Bureau of Indian Affairs superintendent of the boarding school had been to the trading post. He had asked George

Bloomfield, the respected Anglo trader, if he would help the government by persuading local Navajos at Mancos Creek to sign their children up for school. The superintendent knew of George's influence and image of dignity among the people of that area. George consented, and, true to his word, as always, he was shortly out among the people.

"Red Woman," he respectfully questioned, "I'm supposed to check a box here telling which Anglo church your children are to attend on Sundays. What should I do?"

George Bloomfield did not push his own religion. He only spoke about it when invited to do so. The interesting thing is that most everyone always gave an invitation, because it made their hearts feel good to be around him. As I said, and it cannot be said with too much emphasis, this great man was well respected among my people. He was completely fluent in Navajo, even though he was white.

Not really wanting any Anglo religion for her children, Mother sat silently, thinking about what she should say. Father was still in the Colorado mountains tending sheep.

George Bloomfield was patient in waiting for her to answer. The calmness he displayed allowed her to make a good decision.

"Is there a box to check for what religion you are, George?" she respectfully asked. "I think your religion will be the best so far."

Mr. Bloomfield, as Navajo-like as he may have been, could not conceal the feeling of endearment within his heart. Mother also sensed she had pleased him. It was one way for her to say, "Thank you, and we Navajos in this area feel good about your being our trader." He sat quietly until he was sure his emotions were under control.

"They do not have a box for my religion, but I will write it on here. It touches my heart that you would think of me. May the Lord bless your home with peace and harmony forever."

In this manner, I unofficially began to be a member of The Church of Jesus Christ of Latter-day Saints.

When Mr. Bloomfield came to our hogan that day, Mother said something about going to school. In filling out the papers, it was necessary to show English names. Joe got his English name then. George Bloomfield asked Mother if it would be all right to name me after himself. She nodded her approval, and I became George Lee. My younger sister and brother were named Lucy and Pat. Lucy was named after Mrs. Lucy Bloomfield, George's wife.

Mr. Bloomfield said that school started in a week and that if Mother would weave a rug, he would outfit her children with clothes. Even though he did not have the rug at the time, he gave us credit for food and clothes at the trading post.

In the Shiprock Boarding School a few weeks later, I found there were already four George Lees enrolled. Since my birthday was in March, I received the middle name *Patrick*, after St. Patrick's Day.

For my two first English names, I'm indebted to George R. Bloomfield, the kindly Mormon trader. To the United States government, I owe my first taste of formal schooling and my middle name.

To propagate Christianity, various churches were allowed to instruct the children, usually once during the week and again on Sunday morning. The parents would indicate which church they wished their child to attend while filling out enrollment forms.

I shall never forget the Sundays during my two years at the Shiprock Boarding School. Out of the three to four hundred students enrolled, my brother and I were the only ones signed up to attend The Church of Jesus Christ of Latter-day Saints. Although Joe was supposed to attend LDS services, he chose instead to attend another church with his friends. I decided to stick with the Mormons.

I was held back while all my friends marched off two by two to the other church meetings. I wondered why no one else belonged to my church. I endured much ridicule from my friends about the strangeness of the LDS Church. After all my friends had gone, someone from the local LDS branch picked me up for Sunday School.

We met in a small, run-down building downtown. At times I thought about changing my religion to be with my

friends and escape ridicule. Somehow I managed to stay with
the Mormons. I think it was because I had kind, loving, and
understanding Primary and Sunday School teachers. These
good women were special. They nourished within my soul the
first seeds of understanding of this new religion that would
someday bring blessings and direction to my life.

After two years at Shiprock, I went to a different school. I
had done well in the first and second grades at the Shiprock
Boarding School, so I was promoted all the way to fifth grade at
my new school. This was closer to where an eleven-year-old
boy should be.

My new school was in Aztec, New Mexico. Aztec is about
forty-five miles east of Shiprock. Here we attended a regular
public school by day and stayed in a dormitory at night. This
was the first year of a new government education approach
called the Bordertown Program, 1954. With this program, the
Navajo children were taken to surrounding reservation towns,
where they attended regular public schools with non-Indian
children.

This was a totally new experience for me. It was the first
opportunity I had to associate with Anglo children. My
schoolwork at the fifth-grade level was trying, as I had skipped
third and fourth grades. Still, I tried hard and did well in
school that year.

My brother Joe decided to stay home and not go to school
again. The two years at Shiprock were the extent of his formal
education. Again, this time with another boy, I attended the
LDS Church. Kind Church members from Aztec picked us up
each week, taking us to the local ward.

I was baptized into The Church of Jesus Christ of Latter-
day Saints following my year at Aztec, although I had not been
taught the gospel very well. My knowledge and understanding
of Christianity was quite limited compared to my extensive
schooling in Navajo ways and traditions.

I was baptized in the summer of 1954 in Gallup, New
Mexico, by LDS missionaries. George and Lucy Bloomfield,
acting as stake missionaries, made all the arrangements for my
baptism. In fact, they took time from their busy schedule to

provide the transportation to Gallup. Imagine the love they must have had for me, to take me alone for nearly a hundred miles to be baptized and confirmed as a member of their church. They were so proud to baptize one little, dirty, skinny Navajo shepherd boy. I remember it took us all day and way into the night to make the trip and return home. It was a joyous occasion. Later, the Bloomfields were heard to say to others, "If all our years and work among the Indians have netted us just George P. Lee, it was worth it." They labored over twenty years among the Indians of the Southwest. Their love and interest in the First Americans were incomparable.

All in all, the boarding-school experiences thrust me into new and different encounters. Though I had been degraded as a human being, I had found new life in a religion that was to play a major role in my future.

9

GEORGE R. BLOOMFIELD
—A WHITE NAVAJO

The seeds of Mormonism nourished by later Primary and Sunday School teachers were first planted in my heart by the Bloomfields. Not only were they instrumental in signing me up for the Shiprock Government Boarding School, but they also helped me, when I was twelve, to enroll in the Utah Indian Placement Program sponsored by The Church of Jesus Christ of Latter-day Saints.

George and Lucy Bloomfield were special people. They spent most of their lives among the Navajos, and George Bloomfield spoke Navajo fluently, even though he was a white man. Because of that, and because of his honesty and fairness as a trader, he was well respected by most Navajos who knew him, and he was respected by Anglos as well. Before coming to Mancos Creek, Colorado, George and Lucy operated the trading post at Toadlena, New Mexico, on the Navajo Reservation.

I shall never forget one of the first times I saw George Bloomfield. It was inside the trading post after the Bloomfields took it over. I felt the newness all over again and hid behind Mother's skirt. Somehow Mr. Bloomfield noticed me and came over to where we stood. He quietly walked around my mother to where I was half hidden. Squatting down, he looked me straight in the eye and began to talk to me in Navajo. I was greatly surprised at this.

He said in Navajo, "How are you, little boy? What is your name?"

It was as though a Navajo were speaking! Then he put his arm around my shoulders and gave me a squeeze. He told me he was my friend, and he gave me a free soda pop. You cannot imagine what this meant to a timid little child, as I was then.

Hearing a white man speak fluent Navajo was a new experience for me. I thought about it all the way home. Mr. Bloomfield had made a tremendous impression by hugging me and expressing his friendship.

After this special experience, every time I went to the trading post, he would give me a free soda pop. He nicknamed me Ashkii Tolikani, which means "Soda Pop Kid."

When the Bloomfields moved to Mancos Creek, they resumed missionary efforts among the Ute families that lived close to the trading post. They also went over to the New Mexico side to visit Navajo families living there. Of course, one of these Navajo families was our own.

"Who is that coming up the buckboard trail making all that dust and noise?" my father asked. By that time, all of us ragged-looking children were heading for the hogan door for a better look.

"It sounds like an automobile to me," Mother offered as we all whisked past her skirt on our way out.

Looking down the buckboard trail, I could see the trader's car coming. I rushed back into the hogan. "Father, it's the Bloomfield Mormons again!"

"Quick, son, tell all your brothers and sisters to run over the hill to hide. Tell them the Mormons are coming again. Hurry up before we get caught here and have to listen to more white man's religion!"

We scurried over the hill near our hogan. We must have looked like a bevy of frightened quail. The children's legs really churned the dust, and their black, unkempt hair flowed behind them like wild ponies' manes.

"Shhh!" Mother shushed us with an index finger over the front of her mouth.

As soon as we heard the motor cut off, we listened for footsteps; the Bloomfields would find no one at the hogan. Soon the engine started, and the car putted back out the way it had come.

"Father, why didn't we just stay there?" I asked.

"Because they come to give us another white man's religion. They are all alike. But we have our Navajo way. It is much better, and it has been with us much longer than these white ones have had theirs."

At first we all ran away because the Bloomfields tried to talk religion. Afterward, when their first attempts failed, they began leaving food to get our trust. At first just we children stayed for the Bloomfields' treats and goodies. And by the time Mother and Father got back, most of it would be gone. Then even my parents began staying so they could be included in the treats.

The bumping of the car springs and the motor's dying drone could barely be heard now. In fact, a distant meadowlark sang well above the disappearing sound of the car.

"Let's go," Father said while rising from his hidden position. He slapped his hands together like two chalkboard erasers to remove the dust they had gathered while supporting his squatting stance behind the protective knoll.

The little kids were chugging about as fast back toward the hogan as they had run away from it.

"I wonder if they left anything this time?" one of them shouted back over his shoulder.

"I'll bet they did!" exclaimed Pat, my little brother, as he bent his head down and really poured on the steam.

All of us children reached the hogan door about the same time.

Yes! There was the cardboard box as usual, left on one of our old crates. It contained canned goods, potatoes, apples, candy, and a sack of oranges! We were overjoyed! We could never have afforded such wonderful things ourselves.

As my parents entered the hogan, they looked at each other as if to say, "There is something different about the Bloomfield white people." Then they began to inspect the groceries more closely.

The next time we heard the motor coming toward our hogan, we knew who it was, and we children stayed at the hogan. The time after that, my parents stayed too. The Bloomfields, in their kindness and especially in their diligence, had gained our respect and friendship. Out of these feelings, my parents allowed them to tell us of their religion.

George and Lucy Bloomfield told us about the Book of Mormon, a volume of inspired scripture that called Indians "the Lamanites." It spoke of the migration of the ancestors of my people to this land over a great sea, and of a visit to this land by Jesus Christ.

I watched the Bloomfields closely as they spoke of this Book of Mormon. From all I could detect, they were sincere and fully believed what they were teaching. I was very interested.

They did not always come just to speak of the Book of Mormon. Lucy Bloomfield occasionally brought her portable organ to teach us Primary songs, or she came simply to play games. At other times, she brought sewing materials and taught Mother how to make things from scrap cloth. The Bloomfields came also to listen to stories about the Navajo religion, in which they were very interested.

In late August, following Aztec's school year, my family and I sought work near Cortez, Colorado. There the Bloomfields came to visit us. They had gone southward as far as Shiprock and northward to Dove Creek trying to locate us. They finally found us camped on our familiar canyon rim amidst the sagebrush and junipers, away from everyone and everything in Cortez, Colorado.

We had been there several days without finding work. Our situation was desperate. We had run out of food and were living out of garbage cans. We had scavenged from the city dump and gathered pop bottles to scrape a few cents together.

"Son of Donkey Man," Mr. Bloomfield said huskily, "we

are so happy we have found you. We have such great and exciting news for you!"

Then he noticed our condition. He asked my mother, "Do you have food here for your little ones? When was the last time you ate?" His voice was full of feeling, and he and Lucy looked at each other without saying a word. They acted like Navajos in that way.

Not waiting for my mother to respond, Mr. Bloomfield took what few dollars he had with him, hauled us into town, and used most of his money to buy food for our family.

After we were fed, and when George and Lucy Bloomfield were satisfied we were all full, we sat around the campfire to talk. They gathered all the family, and even the constant wiggling of the little ones did not disturb them. Mr. Bloomfield asked, "Son of Donkey Man, would it be all right with you if we began this conversation with prayer? And if you wish, I will offer it." Father offered no objection. When Mr. Bloomfield had offered the prayer, he began to bear his testimony.

"This church and the Book of Mormon we've been telling you about is true. By the Spirit, we know it is. Jesus Christ is real, and He is looking over your family under the direction of His Father, whom you call the Great Spirit. This same Jesus, the Son of God, has inspired our church leaders to begin a program whereby your children can go live with Anglo families and attend excellent schools in Utah. It is called the 'Indian Placement Program.'"

I still remember how excited he was as we all sat in a circle together. Lucy Bloomfield wept through the testimony of her husband as she looked with fondness at us ragged children.

George and Lucy were certain that I and one of my cousins should take advantage of this opportunity. My close friend and cousin, Roger Lee, who was staying with us at that time, was invited to go too. Roger was a year younger than I was.

After Brother Bloomfield finished his remarks, he turned his soft, moist eyes to my parents for approval. My parents were confused. This placement program was something so new and foreign. They did not know what to say or how to react to Brother Bloomfield's request. They were accustomed to second-class treatment by white people. The idea sounded suspicious: An Indian child living with a white family? And such a family would accept an Indian as their own? Unbelievable. And not only that, but they would buy him clothes and give him food, and love him?

It soon sank into my parents' minds that they would be sending one of their much-loved children hundreds of miles away from home, that he or she would attend a strange school and live with an Anglo Mormon foster family they had never seen. My parents, of course, loved us very much. To send one of us away to Utah meant they placed great faith and confidence in Brother Bloomfield, believing everything he said.

It took a long time for them to give approval. They looked at me with moist eyes and, though unspoken, their love for me was evident. Yet, I knew what their answer would be because of the spirit that was present. Finally, after a lengthy pause, Father and Mother looked at Brother Bloomfield and nodded their heads in approval. Both Roger and I would be going.

The Bloomfields were elated. With tears in their eyes, they walked over and hugged my father and mother. Then they embraced Roger and me.

I will never forget that moment when Brother Bloomfield looked me straight in the eye and said, "Our Heavenly Father loves you very much. He will look after you and guide you, for he knows who you are."

It was a beautiful and happy occasion. For just a few moments, we were full of the Spirit and completely forgot our poverty.

"When will they leave?" asked Mother.

Brother Bloomfield responded, "I'm sorry to have to give you such short notice, but it took Lucy and I so long to find you. The bus leaves from Shiprock in less than two hours."

Reality struck my parents like a hard rock between the eyes. But, true to their word, they upheld their consent.

"These two boys don't have any clothes to wear up to a fine house and school," Mother said, speaking to herself as much as to Bloomfields.

All I had was what was on my back—a frayed pair of worn

Levi's; a dirty, ragged T-shirt; and torn tennis shoes. My hair hung down to my shoulders. Roger did not look any better.

"Don't worry, the Lord will look after your son George," offered the kind trader-missionary. Perhaps he promised it, more than offered.

With that, the Bloomfields hugged my parents, shook hands, and loaded Roger and me into their car. We were bound for Shiprock, forty-five miles or more away!

I cried as we drove southward. It was sad to leave my family with no work, food, or clothing in an inhospitable town, with no relatives or friends to turn to. My only solace was my faith in the Bloomfields. They had spent their lives working among my people and had our interests at heart.

As we drove to Shiprock, I was uncomfortable and restless. My thoughts raced back and forth between concern for the welfare of my family and my journey to a strange land to live among a stranger people. I had many anxieties and apprehensions, but I put my trust in the serene couple sitting in the front seat. I stared at the Bloomfields for a long time, and finally a beautiful feeling of comfort and peace came over me. I settled back for the ride.

We passed my family's summer hogan. I saw a dim, lonely light coming from the open doorway. I thought of my brother, Bob, who had stayed home to look after the sheep while the rest of us searched for work. A flood of memories came that again brought tears. I remembered the times we had herded sheep together, playing with the lambs and dogs. These memories brought sadness to my heart, but when I looked at the Bloomfields, the spirit of peace returned.

After what seemed like hours, we arrived at Shiprock. We went straight to the missionaries' quarters, where Brother Bloomfield put a bowl on our heads and gave us quick haircuts. We were then given a quick bite to eat, and we rushed over to where the bus was waiting. We were the last to board.

Many Indian families had gathered to see their children off to Utah. I thought I was coming to a funeral. The parents, especially the mothers, were weeping and trying to find a way to say good-bye as their beloved children boarded the bus.

Brother Bloomfield reassuringly took us by the hand and helped us into the bus. After he found our seats, he reached into his pocket and put four left-over dollars into my hand. He then embraced me warmly. With tear-filled eyes, he looked at me and said, "Everything will be all right. The Lord will be with you. I will make sure your family is taken care of."

After Brother Bloomfield left, the huge bus slowly began to move out. The sobs increased, and it seemed there was not a dry eye in the entire bus—even the driver was sniffling. I could not stop crying, and I wanted to get out. But something held me back, telling me everything would be all right. Brother Bloomfield's words kept coming back into my mind: "God will be with you, and all will be well."

At that time I really did not know God very well. I had been baptized just that summer and had not been taught the gospel except in Primary and Sunday School classes. I was steeped in Indian tradition and understood little about the gospel and the Church. Like my parents, I put all my faith in the Bloomfields.

As the bus was leaving, one girl my age ran to the front and desperately tried to open the locked doors. She cried bitter tears and beckoned to her parents from the window in pleading Navajo. Only the gentleness of the chaperone was able to soothe her sufficiently. Then she returned to her seat. With my cousin, Roger, beside me, I had a little more security. At least I knew someone. We cried together in silence.

In our tears and heartache of that departure, little did we even imagine the beginning of the beauty that had begun to come into our lives. The new way of our future life was beyond the understanding of our frightened hearts.

As the engine wound into a roar, all outside seemed silent. The waving people, parked pickup trucks, and buckboards slid past the window where I sat. I gripped the seat as my body braced itself. Roger and I looked at each other with tears streaming down our cheeks, and away we went into the night. There was no turning back now.

Through the unspeaking darkness of the August evening, the bus drive from Shiprock to Cortez proceeded more like a funeral dirge than anything else. The sobbing children and their sniffling noses made a fog inside the bus. The windows were clouded up.

All the whimpering produced more of the same. It seemed that the sobs echoed by a circular route according to seat pattern. With each unintentional outburst, a surge of emotion filled the person either in the seat ahead or behind, depending on who was charged and ready. The sobbing movement was similar to an oval-shaped course set with upended dominoes. All it took was one to fall and one to keep up the momentum.

As the bus drove by our hogan, both Roger and I routinely collapsed according to the prevailing inertia. Our home's light only faintly glimmered, which increased our emotion even more. My little brother Bob was in that hogan, all alone. He did not even know we were on the bus. Tears rolled down into my downstretched mouth. Bob. How I would miss him.

Bob was smaller and younger than I was. I had babysat him many times. I had changed his diapers and fed, cared, loved, and played with him, and now I cried for him. The family had left Bob home while the rest of us had gone to Cortez in search of seasonal work. There he slept obediently in our hogan somewhere near, but camouflaged in darkness.

Years later he was without employment skills because he had obediently sacrificed his schooling so that his parents and family could survive. He began to drink. He had no educational opportunity. The door was shut before him. All he could ever do was seasonal work and sheepherding. It breaks my heart to have seen his sacrifice and now to watch life deal with him so roughly.

I quit thinking so much about Bob when the bus began slowing down to enter Cortez.

My family. They were there, somewhere in the darkness, camped on the canyon rim. Had they found employment? My younger brothers and sisters had to scavenge the highways, city dumps, and back-store alleys. I looked around in the bus at the shiny chrome and sleek seat fabric. Guilt swept over me. Back and forth went my mind between the silver chrome and the fire-charred pot my parents used for cooking.

I extended my neck and squinted my eyes harder toward the area where my parents and lovely family must be camped. Roger's head was turtled out just as searchingly as mine. I noticed that a slender trail of moisture snailed down his cheek.

Not wanting to embarrass him by seeing his emotions displayed, I looked out the window, up to the faraway stars. In the dim reflection of the window, I noticed that a couple of tears had fallen from my own clouded eyes. I sniffed and rubbed them off with the back of my hand.

"It was a lot different," whispered I hoarsely, "when they put me at the Shiprock Boarding School, or at Aztec. Things were different about it all. Somehow, just knowing the family was nearer helped. I could feel them closer, anyway."

Roger didn't say a word; his aching had apparently tired him. He had drifted into a surface doze.

"Nine long months. Nine big ones," I grievously pondered. "Nine months away from my family, my people, and our reservation is a long time."

That last thought of aloneness caused me to think about sitting in the back of Brother Bloomfield's car. I thought of that same feeling again, the sweet peace that had come over me then. And to my astonishment, the same feeling now settled all over me once more.

"The Lord will be with you and all will be well" repeated in my mind. Soon, I had joined Roger in what proved to be only fitful sleep. But at least it was sleep. Just before I lost consciousness, I heard the girls in the seats just across the aisle begin a muffled cry. They were the next domino to topple.

Into Utah, we passed through Monticello, Moab, Monotony, Green River, and Price. Just as dawn came, we passed through Spanish Fork Canyon. I looked up over the tall-backed seat. Most of the students were awake, but they appeared mummified, drained of emotion. I slumped back down into the seat. In my despair, my face turned to gaze out the familiar window.

The casual glance soon turned to a stare of wonder.

As morning awoke, the trees were clothed in a gossamer of light, through which the hint of evergreen teased the imagination. The long shadows tapered from tree to tree in a solemn aspiration of modest beauty. I was enthralled by this awakened awareness, by the beauty of Mother Earth, and by how so cleverly she responded to the gentle, waking call of Father Sun.

"George," a reverie of Father's teaching reminded, "in the early morning, the good spirits are about. You can sense it. At this hour, there is really no hour, for the beauty of nature is preparing unmolested to merge with the dawning light.

"Father Sun that comes up is alive; otherwise he could not crawl up the heavenly mountain to shower light upon the reflection of creation, which is a prayer of beginning to court his wife, Mother Earth."

Soon, I felt myself swaying to the right as the bus swung southward into Sanpete County, Utah. On and on we went. On the other side of the bus, the morning light touched the sleeping faces and highlighted the homesick look of the dazed children.

By now, Roger was so tired of crying he did not even want to look at me, so he just stared out the window with glazed and pretending eyes.

Verdant scenery now extended for miles in all directions until the abrupt Wasatch Mountains loomed in the longer perspective. Small farmhouses were spaced upon green pastureland like speckles of whitewash shaken lightly from a flimsy brush. Such simple splendor, so sublime, was almost unreal. I could feel something special about this area, but I couldn't quite pinpoint what it was. My mind was too tired to jostle thoughts.

On the way past Manti, I had noticed an extra large and stately building that sparkled in the predawn light. The temple had seemed alive, like nature. It was like nothing I had ever experienced before, not even a church building.

10

THE HARKERS
—BELOVED SECOND PARENTS

Before the sun moved into midmorning position, our bus arrived in Richfield, Utah. After it stopped, Roger and I hurriedly pugged our noses against the cold window above our seats. More cars than I'd ever before seen in one place were parked around a large building. I thought it strange that there were no buckboard wagons.

With a noise like rumbling thunder, two huge luggage doors swung open on either side of the bus. Immediately, with precise organization, men began unloading boxes, luggage, and trunks from the motionless bus. They reminded me of ants.

Back home, the day would just be starting. Here, at the Richfield Indian Student Placement reception center, all kinds of activity was going on. The sky was clear. It was August, the moon of yellow Utah corn.

Though we could see plainly out the tinted windows, it was dark inside the bus. For someone outside to see us, we had to get near a window, close enough that our mouths would fog the cool pane. Some students realized they could be seen so close to the windows, and heads began to jerk back in startled self-consciousness.

I had never seen so many white men. A short man strode

around giving commands to everyone. He was bald, and I could see a perfect image of the sun reflecting from his head. His suit jacket was draped casually over his scarecrow shoulders. A dark, narrow tie hung loosely from his collar, which was about a size and a half too large. He perspired freely. He must have been the idea man. Later, I was told he was Miles Jensen, the father of the Indian Placement Program.

Several men lifting luggage wore tightly noosed ties, causing loose flesh to hang over their choking shirt collars. As we saw them hoist some of the heavier trunks, their eyes bulged in unbelief as much as in physical stress.

Near the back of the bus, an inquisitive boy carefully slid a window back for a better look. Out into the bright daylight his head popped. He screwed his head around and twitched his nose in uncertainty, like a prairie dog out of its burrow. When his head was all the way out, one of the luggage carriers spied him.

"Hey," he yelled, "what do you guys put in these things anyway, bricks?"

The surprised boy pulled back his head with a snap. His curiosity, at least for the moment, had been satisfied.

Miles Jensen turned his face to peer momentarily into the bus. He had tried to look inside the bus several times. Each time his eyes would grow from a squint into a discerning stare. For some reason, I liked him. Just then, a faint smile slightly creased his face.

After the luggage was finally set in order on the sidewalk parallel to the bus, the exhausted men laid back on the lawn like lunchtime laborers relaxing. It looked as though we were ready to get off. I was wrong. Soon all the students began watching the chaperone to see if anything was going to happen.

The bus's boarding door swung open. Up the hollow-sounding stairs came a shiny head followed by a loosely filled jacket. Miles Jensen. I noticed a rather slim, pointed nose. As though he could not take his eyes away, he looked us over. If ever I've seen a contented smile, it was then. The chaperone's hand impatiently tugged at his sleeve.

As if abruptly awakened, Miles turned to the seated chaperone. "Well, well, it looks like we have a real good bunch of kids," he said. "Well, well, well . . ."

"How long will the kids have to stay on the bus?" asked the chaperone, more for himself than for the children.

"Well, it might be some time yet. We're still waiting for a few more doctors to arrive. I'll let you know when. Just keep the children here for now. It looks like you've done a real good job; everybody's too tired to be homesick."

He turned his attention to us Indians.

"How many of you are hungry?" he asked. When no one answered, he smiled as though that were the expected response.

"Well, well . . ." were the last words I heard as he stepped down into the morning. The wry, wispy smile still barely crinkled his upper lip.

When he had gone, I realized his presence had brought a comfort.

Suddenly he got back on the bus. "Okay, kids, it's time to meet the doctors," he warned as he started walking down the aisle.

"Well, it looks like you are all eager to get started. Welcome to Utah. You can see things are a little different than what you may be used to. Don't worry about seeing the doctors. They'll be nice to you. Everything will be all fixed up soon."

He turned to the chaperone again. "This is a good bunch all right," he said, more to us than the chaperone. He seemed to want things to get off to a positive start. He must have sensed our low spirits.

"There is a nice warm breakfast waiting for you—toast and jelly, eggs, fresh farm milk—something you'll enjoy. When you get off the bus, just follow me right into the auditorium, that big building. Don't worry about what to do; we've got plenty of nice people here to show you." His face seemed to light up as he looked down the aisle at us.

"Don't forget anything now. Check above your seats in the luggage racks," he kindly cautioned. "Follow me. Let's go!"

Miles Jensen was frequently called the Bald Eagle by some

of the students. After all, it was most fitting. In his later years, he was referred to as Grandfather, a title of even greater respect and honor. Many natural parents had come to depend upon his judgment.

Everyone followed Brother Jensen into the Richfield Tabernacle like lonesome puppies. When the aroma of food caught our noses, Roger and I began to feel better. There were so many white people scurrying about. They all seemed so pleased with us. It made me feel special and wanted.

The first thing I learned about Mormons in Utah was that the women sure could cook! Things were not beginning so badly after all—at least until our names were called off to meet the doctors.

The rumor of shots traveled rapidly among the children. We grew very silent as we watched the first few victims leave to be fixed up by some Anglo doctor.

"George P. Lee, Roger Lee," a smiling volunteer called by the exit. Suddenly I wished I had stayed hidden behind the hills when the Bloomfields first started visiting us. I envisioned a long, pointed needle.

Roger and I got up from what had been a good breakfast. Once out in the hall, we were seated in folding chairs by a small room. And there we sat for what seemed like eternity. I listened for any wails of torment to warn of needlework in process. When I didn't hear anything, it was almost worse than the wails would have been.

Fidget, fidget. My mind fidgeted as I sat upon the hard seat of the folding chair next to Roger. My eyes followed everything, but my head never moved. Up and down the hall, volunteers were busily doing something—just what I did not know. Then, a volunteer nurse stepped out of the room adjacent to us.

"George P. Lee, George is it?" she asked. "How are we doing today? Come right on in. The doctor is waiting for you."

Her last words worried me greatly.

I looked at Roger. He wasn't looking at me anymore. "You're on your own," he seemed to say. I meekly rose and followed the nurse.

"Hello," said the cheerful doctor. "Come right on over here and sit on the end of this table."

I fearfully obeyed while my eyes took in the whole room at a glance. I did not see any syringes for shots. I relaxed some.

"I'm from Gunnison, Utah," Dr. Stewart informed me as he placed a cold stethoscope down the front of my shirt onto my quivering skin.

"Breathe deeply," he ordered. Then he slid the round piece of metal over my chest. "Again. Sounds great. Did you come all alone?"

I didn't say a word.

The nurse chimed in, "It looks like he has a brother, or something. Roger Lee is next on the list. Are you related to him, Brother Lee?"

Being called Brother Lee by a white lady shook me up. I found my head nodding in affirmation to her question even before I'd thought.

"Bring him in, then," Dr. Stewart said happily. "I want him to see something."

The nurse was in and out in a jiffy. Roger cowered behind her as she returned.

"Come over here, Roger," the doctor directed.

While Roger was on his way, the doctor picked up a bird-shaped instrument and stuck the beak of it into my left ear.

"Can you believe that?" he asked. "Roger, come here. Take a look."

Roger cautiously approached, put his eye onto the eye-piece, and squinted in.

"You can see clear through to the wall over there, can't you, Roger?"

Roger was confused and put his eye down closer for a better look. I saw the doctor wink at the nurse. He really had us going. He made sure I saw the exaggerated wink.

When I was finished, he checked Roger.

As I sat there, thoughts of home again came to my mind. Everything here smelled and looked different. As I looked at the pile of cotton on the doctor's serving tray, I thought of the sheep back home.

I remembered my aunt as she gave us our instructions for the day. And my mother . . .

The tears were beginning to come. I frantically tried to think of other things. Especially I didn't want to be seen crying in front of these strangers. Before I had a chance to redirect my thoughts, the nurse shocked me back into reality. "Okay, boys," she announced cheerfully, "I guess we're ready for the tuberculin shots now."

We should have made our escape earlier.

The tuberculin shots didn't really hurt at all; they went just barely under the skin. After that, we had lice checks, showers, blood tests, haircuts. I couldn't believe the fistful of lice that was extracted from my hair. I was dizzy with all the newness. There were only a few hundred Indian students at this reception center, the first of its kind; but in the years after that, the number of students grew into thousands.

All of the workers at the reception center had donated their time and travel expense to assist in this gigantic undertaking. So many details had to be worked out, so many obstacles to be overcome. It was a modern-day miracle of donated performance, pioneered in the upper ranks of the Church by Elder Spencer W. Kimball, then an Apostle. All of this had started in an interesting manner.

In the late 1940s, Helen John, a teenage Navajo girl, was taken into a Latter-day Saint home in the Richfield area through the efforts of Golden R. Buchanan. During the first five years of the 1950s, a few selected Navajo children were placed into Mormon homes, somewhat on a trial basis, through the determined efforts of Miles Jensen and Golden Buchanan. Ours was the first group of children who were recruited and transported by bus as part of an official and continuing program sponsored by the Church.

After the medical examinations were over, we were given a sumptuous lunch and then led in play and fun activities designed to keep our attention while the foster parents arrived to take us to our new homes.

After the foster parents had arrived, they attended an

orientation meeting in which they were given advice, direction, and encouragement about being foster parents of an Indian child. Elder Spencer W. Kimball spoke to the gathering of foster parents, and the Indian children were brought in to listen to this great man's wisdom.

Elder Kimball began by telling the audience of his great love for the Lamanite people, the Indians and their cousins. He commended the foster parents for their contribution to the great work. He blessed the congregation and asked the Lord's blessings upon all the missionaries sent to the Lamanite people. He also asked the Lord to help all Church members to be nursing parents to the Lamanites.

Finally, he asked the Lord to bless the Lamanite people, saying that the Lamanites were a great people, intelligent and receptive to things of the Spirit. Elder Kimball said the difference between the Lamanites and those sitting in the audience was opportunity. Through education, employment, and other means, the Church could assist in the development of the Indian people.

These two short excerpts from later talks are representative of his words to the foster parents that day in the Richfield Tabernacle:

> Only in our doing all in our power to restore these people to their heritage can we even approach a justification for having taken their promised land. May the Lord assist us all to see our full duty respecting these people and give us the courage and determination to guarantee that they have the education, culture, security, and all other advantages and luxuries that we enjoy. (*Conference Report,* April 1947, p. 152.)

> If we as a nation and as a people can ever justify our invasions of these Americas, and our conquest of his promised land and the subjugation of the Indian, certainly it will not be by passing by on the other side, as did the superior priest, or the passing by on the other side as did the self-righteous Levite, but by going to the limit as did the Good Samaritan,

in binding up his wounds, pouring in "oil and wine," setting
him on our own beasts, taking him to an inn, paying for his
care and revisiting him. (*Conference Report,* April 1949, p.
106.)

The speech this gentleman gave had an impact upon the
foster parents who were in attendance. More than anything
else others who spoke may have said, his remarks were the most
magnetic, the most filled with love.

After listening to Elder Kimball, we were separated from
the body of foster parents sitting in the chapel area of the tabernacle. The volunteers informed us the time had come to greet
our new families, our Mormon foster parents. A sudden silence
spread over the students.

The foster parents were ushered into the room where we
waited. The name of the child was called; a brief, but bonding,
introduction was made; and then the family, along with the
new addition, retrieved the student's luggage and left for
home.

It was so touching to watch the foster parents as they met
their Lamanite children for the first time. As though the mortal association had been lifelong, many foster parents lovingly
embraced the lonely and frightened Indian child.

Usually the child was nearly petrified by such responses on
the part of tearful, Anglo parents. This affection from white
strangers was new, and they did not know what to do. Nothing
like this was done at home. Back home, the white man and the
Indians related to each other at a distance. Each lived in his
own separate world. To be kissed and hugged by whites was a
new experience for many of the children.

I looked over at Roger. He had been affected by the tender-
ness of the scene, but now, to cover his emotions, he began to
tease me. I could tell Roger was anxious. He finally said, "I
hope that doesn't happen to me."

As each name was called, that individual found it very
difficult to leave whomever he had come with—sister, brother,
relative, or friend. Many just sat there, refusing to move until

those whose names had not been called persuaded them to go. Others cried uncontrollably.

Through the windows, I saw some of the students drive off with their newly acquired foster families. One girl was framed in the car's rear window. I will never forget the picture of her sobbing into the palms of her hands.

My own heart sprouted wings and flew into my throat. I began to tighten my neck muscles and clench my teeth. Tears were about to get the best of me.

"Roger Lee," Miles Jensen called as he stood by the exit.

Roger looked at me. I could tell he was fighting to restrain his tears. The feeling came over both of us at once that we would not see each other again for a long time. What if something happened to one of us in the meantime? My heart would surely shrivel without him near; our bond and love was great.

"Roger Lee," the beckoning voice called once more. I looked away from Roger this time. It was my way of saying he had better go. When I looked up again, it was just in time to see Roger smothered in the arms and kisses of an eagerly affectionate foster mother. It tickled me inside, despite the loneliness. That was the last thing Roger wanted to happen. But as I watched him walk off with this family, I felt good. To see them hug him in happiness comforted me.

As I now look back on that scene, my heart says, "God bless the foster families; bless them with the dews of heaven, with the precious things of the earth, both above and beneath." Nowhere outside The Church of Jesus Christ of Latter-day Saints are there so many white people so willing to give of themselves and offer to the less fortunate the material blessings accumulated in a more dominant Anglo society.

The scene was similar to that in the Book of Mormon, when the Nephites and Lamanites were united. After a visit among them from the resurrected Savior, fighting was done away with and peace reigned throughout the land as the two cultures became one.

And now, in 1955, in Richfield, Utah, the scene was repeated. The wretched condition of Indian children did not prevent the motherly embrace of most foster mothers and a kind handshake from foster fathers. Cultural differences were momentarily forgotten, and who can say that the Lord's attention was not focused there that beautiful day.

After Roger left, I wept in my loneliness. Most of the children were now gone. Alone and forlorn, I sat in the lounge area. Did I have a foster family? Was I so unimportant that they had forgotten me? I cried again, for I did not want to be deprived of a foster family. After all the lonely waiting, I did actually look forward to meeting my foster family. I didn't want to be left alone any longer.

A volunteer came toward me with two adults and a child.

"George," the volunteer said, "this is your foster family, Brother and Sister Glen Harker. And this little one is your new brother, Michael."

Joan Harker embraced me and tenderly placed a kiss on my tearstained cheek. I just looked at the floor. A flood of emotion swept through me. I had never been kissed before. It was embarrassing.

Then my foster father hugged me and talked with me. With the double dose of outward affection, I don't remember a thing he said.

It was my little foster brother, Michael, who quickly brought me back to reality. He was a real talker, and though he was young, his urgent chattering put me at ease.

On the way to Orem, where the Harkers lived, I didn't say a word. From Richfield to Orem was about a three-hour drive. I noticed the landscape and thought about it. The leafy sage, so green-silver, lay under the blue dawn beneath the scattered puffs of dark mountain oak. Here and there golden flowers bloomed in brilliant contrast to the sage, like dazzling fireworks.

"Hey, George, where is your war paint?" asked little Michael. "Don't you have any bows and arrows?"

I barely heard my new foster brother talking. By now I was thinking of my family on the canyon rim near Cortez. Had my father found work? I began to feel a swell of tears as I thought about them. I knew I was hundreds of miles away from my family and reservation. I felt uncomfortable and lonely.

Again Michael broke the silence. He had a high, squeaky voice that jumped up and down longer and faster than a kangaroo rat: "Hey! How come you've got shoes on? Where are those moccasins Indians are supposed to wear? You're not supposed to have on a shirt or pants either. Where are your feathers? Are you really an Indian?"

I just stared out the window and thought of home. I wondered what Nellie, Mike, Joe, and the rest of my brothers and sisters were doing.

A few miles and much more chattering later, we entered the city limits of Provo, Utah. "Glen, stop by J.C. Penney. I think we need to get George a few school clothes," my foster mother urged her husband. We spent several hours shopping. All the stores with all the wonderful things inside were enough to make me exhausted just looking.

By the time we had walked out of the first store, I thought I must be richer than the wealthiest Navajo on the reservation. I wore my new pants out of the store. They were a size too big to compensate for shrinkage and so I would not outgrow them too fast. The cuffs rubbed together as I walked. I lowered my head to hide from the stares of people, who I was sure were looking toward the sound. I tried to walk a little more bowlegged so the sound would not be so loud.

In one store, the Harkers thought it would be nice to dress me as a cowboy. They purchased western shirts, pants, a big ten-gallon hat, sharp-toed boots, spurs, and two silver six-shooter cap pistols with the Hop-a-Long Cassidy holsters. Michael convinced his parents I should wear the outfit home. I did not know it was popular to play cowboys and Indians among the white kids.

Ready to go home, my foster parents and I strode into the setting sun toward the car. The holsters flapped noisily against my thighs, mingling with the scraping of the pant cuffs. When we finally got into the car, I was relieved.

The motor started, and we pulled out into a much busier

world than I had ever imagined. But inside the car, as usual, Michael made sure it was just as busy. "Wow! George, can I play with your guns when we get home? You look like a real cowboy. I didn't know Indians could look like cowboys. Are you sure you're an Indian? Mom, is he really an Indian?"

I turned my head to look out the window; I could turn it only part way because the brim of the Hoss Cartwright hat hit the window. Since clothing boxes filled the other side of the back seat, little Michael was jammed next to me. It didn't bother him, though. His eyes were fixed on my new six-shooters. Once in a while he would cautiously feel one of them. He was eager for action.

Soon we were home in Orem. As we pulled into the drive-way, the place looked like a mansion! I know now that it was a moderate home by today's standards, but to me, fresh off the reservation, it was overwhelming.

"Here is your new home, George," announced Glen Harker kindly. "We hope you'll like it. It's not much, but what we have, we'll share with you."

"I wonder where Brent is," said Sister Harker. Brent was her younger brother about my age.

I had just opened the car door and placed my spurred boot on the driveway, when the front door of the Harker home was flung open. It was Brent, Joan Harker's brother. His freckled face was covered with layers of multicolored war paint. An Indian war bonnet sat on his head. He carried a skinny bow in one hand and an arrow tipped with a red-rubber suction cup in the other. He looked like an Indian in full regalia. Somehow I felt ambushed.

Brent's eyes were bright in playful expectation, but his sister, Joan, my foster mother, soon ended his warlike dream. She said, "Brent, George is tired. There are many things I need to show him." He obeyed his sister. He trailed us into the house looking me over very carefully. I could tell Brent had never met a real live Indian before.

Joan showed me around their home. (I had not yet believed it was going to be mine, too.) When we walked into the kitchen, it was a miniature Disneyland. All the appliances—

stove, refrigerator, toaster, and electric mixer—were new and strange.

As we turned from room to room, I was overwhelmed at the hugeness of all I saw. Furniture was everywhere. The house was neat and tidy.

Passing by the bathroom, I saw a large tub. I must have stared for some time. Michael rushed in to turn the tap. A flood of water gushed out. "See, George, all you have to do to get a bath is this."

When Michael saw my surprise, he turned on both taps of the wash basin. "The 'H' means hot. The 'C' means cold. When you turn them off, make sure they don't drip, and don't scrunch them down too tight or it'll ruin the little black washers. Then you'll get talked to by Dad." He looked at his parents with pride because he'd remembered so well all they had said.

I later enjoyed getting used to regular showers and baths. At home we seldom bathed, because water was precious and hard to get. Drinking and cooking were of higher priority than bathing.

The drinking water in Utah was very good. It came from mountain reservoirs nearby and was pure and clear. At home we got our drinking water from a manmade pond that was used by our livestock, in addition to other desert animals. At times the water was so muddy and murky, it looked like dark chocolate. When it cleared, we could see squiggly bacteria and black, leggy bugs swimming around, but that mattered little; it was all we had. We would just look at the wiggly bugs for a moment, and then down the hatch it went.

The front screen door banged shut; Brent left with the word that he'd see me again tomorrow. Everyone but me hollered "Bye" over their shoulders and down the hall.

I thought of my own home, with no running water, no bathroom or toilet, no appliances, and only one or two crates for furniture. The contrast was unbelievable.

Then I thought of other things I did at home. Rounding up the horses in order to get water and firewood was fatiguingly difficult. Though the horses were hobbled, they could still range many miles from our hogan. And whenever we needed them, they were never close by. Since there were no reservation fences back then, the horse could be just about anywhere. Many times Joe, Bob, or I tiredly climbed high mesas to look over the vast prairie searching for the horses. They might be four or five miles away.

Then back down the mesa we climbed and headed in the direction of the horses. We tried to stay downwind of them; otherwise, they could smell us. They knew we did not come around just to say hello. It meant work for them whenever we appeared.

Once safely downwind, and close enough to drive them, we made our presence known. At times, if they were giddy, we had to chase them on foot. Our aim was to corner them in a dead-end canyon. Often it was the canyon of the mesa we had used for sighting, four or five miles back.

Going shopping was also a struggle because of the long distance to the trading post or to town. It was a struggle to take a bath, even a traditional Indian sweat bath requiring little water. Our Indian way of life was simply one of hard work and struggle to survive.

"Just wait until you see your room," Michael said. "It's real neat, and we've fixed it up just for you. And it has the softest bed of all!"

I had to get used to that bed. It was my own bed, with pillow, sheets, blankets, and bedspread. Back home there were no such items. We considered ourselves lucky just to roll up in a worn sheepskin or a dirty blanket.

Joan Harker showed me where she would patiently and neatly fold and keep my new clothes. She showed me the rest of the room as well.

My new clothing was especially nice. Back home I wore the same shirt and pants for weeks at a time. Here I would change clothes every other day. Shoes at home were rare, and when we did have them, they had to last a long time. In the Harker home, I always had two or three pairs, including a pair of sneakers for playing.

"I hope you'll feel at home in your own room, George,"

Joan said with sweet concern. "Feel free to change around anything in here you'd like. It's your room, after all."

I thought back to the time when all of my brothers and sisters would have to squeeze onto the hogan floor just to find a
place to sleep. Now, I looked over at the single bed, so nicely
made with a large fluffy pillow at its head. My own room in
Utah was bigger than the whole hogan back home. Nellie,
Mike, Joe, Bob, Pat, Clifford, Lucy, and I, and our parents,
and whatever relatives might be visiting would all sleep in the
hogan. And now I had this big room all to myself. When that
thought hit me, I became homesick. If no one would be sleeping near me, maybe a skinwalker would jump in the window.
Right then, I wished I were back on the canyon rim with my
own family. This was all too new and definitely too strange.

Later that night, before I went to bed, I checked in the
closet, looked under the bed, and made sure the window was
locked. The dogs in the neighborhood started barking. Back
home, that meant a skinwalker might be near. I had trouble
sleeping that first night.

"Come on!" Michael urged, tugging at my elbow. "Come
see all my toys!"

We walked down the hall. Michael ran ahead of me into
his room and flung open his closet door.

"See, here are my clothes. If you were littler, I'd let you
wear some. That shirt there is my favorite one, but Mom says I
have to wear them all. Over here are my toys. You can play
with them. Do you like to play cars? And here are some Tinker
Toys. They're real fun, but some of the parts are gone."

At home we were accustomed to eating our meals while
seated on the floor. We had few plates, cups, or utensils. We
each had five chopsticks—our fingers. I gained some experience with dishes, hard chairs, and benches at the boarding
school, but it wasn't until I came to Utah that I really sat at a
nice table on a soft chair with sparkling clean dishes in front of
me.

I didn't go out with Michael as often as he would have liked
during those early weeks. I was still too shy and timid, feeling
so out of place. My foster mother later informed me that I

hardly said anything for the first two months, not even a hello or thank you.

Conversation at mealtime seemed strange. Back home, when our family ate, hardly anyone spoke. We had been taught that one does not engage in conversation while eating. I was taught that this was the way of the holy people, and, thus, it became the way of the Navajos.

The blessing on the food and prayers were not so strange, because I had been taught by my father at an early age to be grateful to the Great Spirit for our possessions and for our food. Particularly at mealtime, we were to offer up thanksgiving.

I had to get used to eating three good meals every day. Also, the enjoyment of dessert after our noon and evening meals was like a trading-post trip every day. I had never before eaten many of the foods that Joan Harker prepared, and some of them did not agree with me. Once I came down with little bumps all over my body—hives, I subsequently learned.

In the evening, after supper, Michael took my hand and begged me to come into the living room to watch television. When I first saw television, I was amazed to see what I thought was a little movie house. Television was the real miracle of my placement experience. The other things that were new to me, such as the appliances, furniture, carpets, and lamps, though different and exciting to see, were not as special as television. Only after much persuasion by Michael and after gaining some courage did I come out and watch television with the family. Mike climbed on my lap and talked away while watching the program. For the longest time, I didn't turn on the television myself. I was afraid to touch it for fear I might break something.

The first few days in the Harkers' home, I hibernated in my room (with the light on to ward off skinwalkers) and came out only at mealtime or when I had to use the bathroom. I found it difficult to believe all this was happening.

My foster mother was kind, understanding, and patient with me from the beginning. She helped me to feel wanted, needed, accepted, and especially loved. She treated me as a real son. She was and still is so sweet and beautiful. At that time I didn't know she was barely twenty years of age.

At first, I did not know how to react to all the love and affection every member of the family was giving me. Those days alone in my room, I thought about that often. At other times I cried in the solitude of my room as I thought about my family back home. By now there would be ceremonial sings starting at home, with their related Squaw Dances. I thought of jumping in the buckboard with my family. Then we would be on our way to the sing. Only now, when I sat alone in this room, my heart was not singing. I longed for home, sheep, unruly goats, skinny herd dogs, and happiness.

Joan could hear me sniffling in my room at times. Gently she knocked on the door, then entered and sat on the edge of the bed.

"George, I know how hard it must be. It breaks my heart to see you crying like this. I wish I knew what to do to bring you out of it."

I would not respond. But her words comforted me. Often

George with Glen Harker, his foster father

George with Joan Harker, his
foster mother

she continued just talking and consoling me until I finally cried myself to sleep. Without really knowing it, I was growing to love her. Her kindness came to me in many ways. Although she was young, Joan Harker was nonetheless an affectionate, compassionate, and effective mother.

One of my biggest adjustments was getting used to time schedules. The Indian way of life really did not have much structure. We were not used to planning, meetings, and appointments, and time was not broken into minutes and hours, eight-hour days, or forty-hour weeks. We lived by the sun: when it was up, we were up. Also, we were concerned about surviving today and not worried about setting goals for the next day or the future. What we would find to eat each day was of primary concern. Now I had to learn to live by a schedule. I quickly found out what a clock was for.

Also, there were new territorial restrictions. Back home we had all kinds of space in which to roam, play, and herd sheep. All of a sudden, I found myself in a home with houses on all sides. There was not much space, and I felt crowded in. My new home was fenced. I had to get used to a small play area.

Back home our closest neighbor was several miles away. We seldom had visitors. Usually when someone came, it was a passing relative. In Orem, it seemed we always had visitors, or that we were going places to visit others.

Also, at home we did not communicate verbally very much. Even among family members, we spoke only when there was something important to say. In Utah, however, there was constant talking.

Having to be neat and tidy was something new, as was having a clean towel to use. At home we used the same old rag for weeks at a time. I had never owned a toothbrush before, and now brushing was required daily.

To a Navajo, there was no such silly thing as brushing teeth. Fortunately, we didn't have a lot of sweets in our Navajo diet. When I was young, I saw many old Navajos with beautiful teeth because they did not eat much sugar. Today this is no longer the case due to the great popularity of soda pop and other sweets.

Suddenly I had all the clothes I needed. In fact, I was so proud of my clothes that I once put on three or four shirts together along with several pairs of pants to show my foster family.

Now I had all the food I needed. We had the luxuries of running water and electricity. There was no need to haul water or chop wood. I did not have to take a snow bath in the early hours of the morning or go round up the horses. Neither did I need to go out with the herd each day and fight the scorching sun in the summer or the bitter cold in the winter.

However, my homesickness lingered. One way I found help in adjusting to my new home was through prayer. Late at night, after the lights were out and all were asleep, I quietly slipped out from under the covers and knelt beside the bed to pray. There were many occasions when a special feeling came over me, prompting me to pray.

I had never really prayed at home, although I had watched my father pray to the holy people many times. While attending Primary classes in Shiprock and Aztec, and also while being taught by the Bloomfields, I learned a little about prayer, but for a long time I was too unsure of myself to pray. I really didn't know how to approach the Lord during those first weeks in Utah, but I did my best to communicate with a God I only vaguely understood. My foster parents encouraged me to pray each night and morning.

Most of my prayers were short and simple. I prayed mostly for strength and courage in adjusting to my new home and environment. I prayed for my natural family as well as the courage to express appreciation and gratitude to the Harkers. There were many occasions when I felt bad that I did not have the words to thank them for all they were doing for me.

With time, I gradually began to come out of my shell. The Harkers were patient. Slowly I gained confidence to bless the food, then to say family prayer, and finally even to carry on a conversation. Right from the start I was treated as a family member and given the same love and affection everyone else received. I was never treated as a guest. Everything that was available to the family was also available to me.

My foster mother gave me an outline of duties and chores. This I appreciated, because I wanted to help and so return a portion of what I had received. This included love and affection.

From the very beginning, my foster father, Glen, taught many important things that I immediately perceived as being right and truthful. He also exemplified those things he verbally taught.

I recall many hours he spent counseling, coaching, and advising me. Also, this great man spoke to me of love, especially the love that waited in the family's heart for me. His heart was as true as those high qualities he frequently mentioned. Whenever I needed help, he was by my side.

I had never known a man who held more love, respect, and esteem for his wife than did Glen Harker. Love, comfort, and happiness for Joan, his lovely wife, were constant in his thoughts and actions toward her.

Though Glen was an honest, hard worker, he always placed his wife first, and then the other family members above work. But he enjoyed work and robustly moved toward whatever task was at hand.

Glen enjoyed hunting, not necessarily for the sport of killing, but because it helped supplement the family food supply. Beyond this, he really just relished being out of doors. As my own background had included hunting and being out free in the fresh air of Mother Earth, I, too, enjoyed hunting with Glen, Grandpa Harker, and the others who went occasionally.

I began to grow close to the extended families of both Glen and Joan Harker. Both Grandpa Harker and Grandpa Terry were interested in fishing and hunting. I liked them the first time I saw them. As I had never grown up around a grandfather on the reservation, these two men became important to me. Even though I already knew a lot about hunting and fishing, I learned some new tricks from my two wonderful foster grandpas. It was neat to have two grandpas.

Just a few weeks after I had arrived in the Harker home, Glen mentioned going to Rock Springs, Wyoming.

"George, you ever been to hunt antelope?" asked Glen.

"No."

"Well, I think you'll like this. We're going with Grandpa Harker to Rock Springs to hunt antelope—pronghorn antelope. The drive up, you'll like, too. It's really pretty scenery this time of the year. And it's relaxing."

I didn't say much. But inside I was very excited. Brent would go too. Even though he seemed strange, there was something that attracted me to him. After a while we became fast friends.

Before I knew it, we were all in the packed pickup truck headed toward Wyoming. As Glen had said, the scenery was beautiful. The towering Wasatch Mountains were splashed with patches of yellow, orange, amber, and red.

We talked man talk all the way up, not vile words or stories of cruelty, but talk of beauty and past family hunts. I listened and laughed inside.

When we reached our destination, we piled out of the crowded truck. I felt right at home. We began to set up camp.

Even though we had camped differently on the canyon rims back on the reservation, especially with much less equipment, I was able to pitch in more naturally than in the Harkers' house. Glen would always notice, or Grandpa Harker, when I did something that pleased them.

It was fun to sit around the campfire at night. We sometimes sang and sometimes told stories. Always we ended the night with a prayer of thanks for all around us and for the family back in Orem. The prayers also mentioned my own family back on the reservation.

The first morning we were up early. After breakfast, with red vests and hats donned, we set out to hunt antelope. I was enjoying myself immensely. At times I felt like jumping and running just to get all the energy out.

We had walked some time with no prospects in sight, not even a clue on the ground. Then I saw some white dots in the far distance. Antelope rumps.

"Glen," I pointed, "look way over there."

He squinted and so did the others. But I could tell by the way they were squinting that they could not see anything. But eventually, using binoculars, they saw what I was pointing out.

"Well, I'll be . . . Here, Dad, have a look. There's a whole herd on that knoll. And some bucks, too!" He handed the binoculars to Grandpa Harker, and from him they went round to the others.

"George," announced Glen proudly, "we are going to name you Hawkeye!" Everyone smiled approvingly, and I smiled, too, for I was proud of the new name, not only because it made me feel good about being an Indian, but because it boosted my fondness for Grandpa, Glen, and the rest. Time after time I would be first to spot game without the aid of binoculars. You can imagine how many times this was brought up around the campfire later that night.

I went to bed that evening with very tender feelings in my heart for my new family. I wanted God to bless them all. Glen was taking the form of a father in my eyes and greatly so in my heart. It was a wonderful trip.

Grandpa Harker and Glen owned a hardware business. At

every opportunity, Glen took me to his store. He gave me jobs to do and had me run errands. Always, he seemed proud to introduce me to customers and friends coming into the store. He proudly put his arm around me and said, "This is our Indian son, George." However, as proud as Glen and Joan were to have me, I don't think they could ever beat the admiration of little Michael. Little Michael, little Michael, how I grew to love him, too.

We spent a lot of time visiting Michael's grandparents. Both sets of grandparents lived nearby. I soon was more than made welcome as part of this extended family of grandparents, aunts, uncles, and cousins. Perhaps one reason I fit in so comfortably was because of my upbringing within the Navajo clan system. I later learned to really appreciate the similarity between the Mormons and the Navajos in placing great value on extended family relationships.

Within the extended foster family, I found a special friend—Brent, Joan's younger brother, whom I met when I first arrived in Orem. He was my age, and, together with Michael, he made a real difference in my placement adjustment. He was always kind and understanding, never saying or doing anything to hurt my feelings. Brent also took pride in introducing me to his friends. Although I did not feel like playing cowboys and Indians with Brent for the first few weeks after I arrived, I soon learned to enjoy playing with him. I was always the cowboy. He liked being the Indian. Terry Balser was another great friend.

In time, I became closely acquainted with Glen and Joan's families and became used to having a Grandpa Harker and Grandpa Terry. Grandpa Harker was a real fisherman, and Grandpa Terry was quite a hunter.

Grandma Harker and Grandma Terry were also special to me. I will never forget the Saturdays I spent in their homes. To me, Grandma Harker was the best cookie maker in the whole world, and Grandma Terry always had something good to eat, often out of her own garden.

At Glen's hardware store, Grandpa Harker and I made a lot of deliveries. We delivered appliances and furniture all over

Utah County. Always happy and jolly, Grandpa loved hard work. It was from Grandpa Harker that I learned a few things about repair while working on televisions, washers, dryers, and other appliances. Glen always paid me for my work at the store, even during my first year on placement. I learned to pay tithing and to support the missionary program of my ward.

As weeks turned into months, I became more secure and comfortable with the new families who had come into my life. My days of withdrawing into my room and of not speaking were brought to an end by the many patient, loving people. At first, I was very conscious I was an Indian and that these people were whites; but in time, this feeling fled. As the months went by, the persistent thoughts and feelings about my natural family and Indian ways slowly gave way to thoughts of my new family and the new life-style. There was little time for loneliness and homesickness. I involved myself completely in the activities of my new family.

Looking back, I am amazed that I had such an opportunity. There I was, a little, skinny, ragged Navajo boy, fresh off the reservation, immersed in Indian traditions and superstitions, and coming from circumstances that demanded a constant struggle to survive.

Subconsciously, I was still aware that I was an Indian and that I still had an Indian family back home on the reservation. I often took time to think about my natural family, especially on the rare occasions when I received a letter from them.

It did not take me long to learn that the more I thought about the reservation, the more lonely and homesick I became. I then made up my mind that I was going to take the best of what was offered, that I was going to keep my mind on activities with my foster family. I decided to do my best to be a good example and to leave a good impression on my new family.

Being quite sensitive to the feelings of others, I did not want to hurt them in any way, and I did my best to do whatever they asked. I learned many things in my foster home, and one of the lessons I remember most was when my foster mother taught me the little magic words *please* and *thank you*. She was very particular about table manners, and I will be forever grateful to her for teaching me.

Because of my upbringing, I had a hard time expressing love and affection, and since I wanted to show my appreciation to the Harkers in some manner, I did it by asking to help. I asked Sister Harker if she needed help washing the dishes, scrubbing the kitchen floor, or vacuuming the carpets.

In time, I became even more self-motivated. One day as I sat in my room thinking, I decided to always be one step ahead of my foster parents. I made up my mind during that first year in the Harker home that I would never have to be reminded to do such chores as making my bed or picking up my clothes. I made sure everything was in order in my bedroom before I went to school. I always tried to do what was expected of me before being asked.

Whenever I saw that the lawn needed mowing, I asked if I could cut the grass, or I simply did it. When I saw that the garage needed cleaning, or that the car needed washing, I did these jobs without being told. Being sensitive as I was, I did not want my foster parents being stern or angry with me for not doing what I was supposed to have done.

One of the great characteristics of my people, the Navajos, is our adaptability. This adaptability, I suppose, comes from centuries of sustaining ourselves in a hard, unyielding environment. I must have had some of this adaptability in my blood, too. It was not many months before I made a complete adjustment to life with the Harker family in Orem, Utah, so different from the wretched existence of the little camp I had earlier left on the canyon rim near Cortez, Colorado.

11

"WHERE IS YOUR WAR PAINT?"

Several weeks after I arrived in Utah, school began. I'm really thankful that school started then, for until that time my heart nearly broke from homesickness. Now, caseworkers for the Indian Placement Program like to time the busses much closer to the start of school in order to help the Indian students reduce their homesickness. In fact, to arrive a day late would be much better than coming even three or four days early. So, even though I did not know it at that time, the start of school was a good thing.

I'll never forget the first day I attended the Geneva Elementary School in Orem, Utah. I had not really overcome my shyness. I was very timid.

I knew I wouldn't have any friends that first day. Even Brent, Joan Harker's brother, went to another school. And my chattering companion, Michael, was too young for school. I could have done with some of his chattering that day. But alone I went and in silence I walked on my way to school.

Since I was in one of the first groups of Indian students to come onto the placement program, I was the only Indian child in my elementary school, possibly the only one in that whole area.

As I walked that morning, my stride was reluctant, full of

apprehension and anxiety. Even my first trip to the trading post had not scared me as much as this. At least then my mother was with me. I thought about my own family several times during my long walk to school that day.

Besides the Harker family and the Bloomfields, my only contact with other Anglos had been either neutral or negative. And I supposed out of the many white kids at the new school, some were bound to be negative. Maybe there would be bullies like at the boarding school. Luckily, I had a few pennies in my pocket for the extortion payoff. I hoped I wouldn't get beat up that day. I remembered how all those dorm bullies had lured Joe and me into a dark room and then beat us badly.

"I wish Joe were here now," I thought. "I don't know if I can make it alone. What in the world landed me here anyway?" I'd already seen things that would be reason enough for several ceremonial sings.

My mind contemplated the strangeness of the broad-leafed maple trees that shaded the sidewalk. Orem smelled different than the desert. It seemed to have a combination of many unusual smells, like grass, tin cans, asphalt, lilacs, and coal.

"Oh well, the only way through all this is out the other side." So I went, so I walked, and so I thought.

As I meekly ambled onto the school yard, it seemed that all eyes focused on me. Kids came from everywhere, from the bushes and shrubs, from around every corner, from right out of the school's brick walls, or so it seemed! Before I realized it, I had a large following. I was surrounded by all these white kids. I finally knew how General Custer must have felt! When I moved, they moved. Green, blue, brown, and gray eyes were looking at me. Tassled or petitely fashioned above these curious eyes was brown, black, red, and blonde hair. I remembered looking at all the rows of brightly colored cans at the trading post. Now I saw the same array of wonderful color, but that still didn't relieve my anxiety.

One little girl spoke up. "Who are you? Are you one of the Indians the bishop said was coming? Are you what an Indian looks like?"

Another inquired, "Where are your moccasins?"

The group squeezed in closer.

Someone else said, "Say, where's your bow? And your arrows?"

Another boy said, "Where's your war paint?"

One little boy blurted out, "Yeah, I thought you Indians carried a spirit with you."

The group laughed, and a freckled-faced girl with glasses turned to him and said curtly, "You mean spear, silly." She then turned to me: "So, where is your spear?"

All that day the interrogation continued. Every time a question was put to me, I blushed red all over. For the first time, I became a true redskin.

What was happening to me was something I had not expected. Most of the kids had never seen a real live Indian. The only Indians they had seen were at the movies or on television, either attacking wagon trains or being chased by the cavalry. As the questions continued, I just looked at the ground, not knowing what to say. Thoughts of home entered my mind. I thought of my family and the people on my Navajo reservation. A swell of tears began to form in my eyes.

After what seemed an eternity, the crowd of children dispersed, and I was able to enter the building. There, I was soon directed to my classroom, where I quietly entered and sat way in the back.

The teacher entered a few minutes later and went straight to his desk. There was a moment's pause. He looked up to see me sitting in the back of the room. He continued to look at me while he thought things over. My presence in the back of the classroom puzzled him. Finally he got up, walked casually back, and offered his hand.

"I'm your teacher, Mr. Wayne. What is your name?"

"George."

"George who?"

"George Lee," I said, leaving the P out to avoid talking as much as possible.

"I see. You must be one of the Indian 'replacement' students I've heard about. Who is your foster family?"

"Glen Harker."

A big smile of recognition spread over his face. "Welcome to our class," he said. "You'll like it in here, and it won't take long for you to get to know the children."

This man was kind to me. I took an immediate liking to him.

I looked out the window. Most of the children were still out on the playground. The field was so green and beautiful—a stark contrast to the barren dirt playgrounds of the New Mexico schools I had attended. Boys were eagerly playing outside, throwing a ball back and forth. Soon a few girls came into the room, laid their things on their desks, noticed me, took a long look, and then hurried out. Shortly these same girls came back with more girls. They, too, took a long look and then hurried out to tell their friends. I guess those who hadn't seen me earlier were startled to see me in the classroom. Soon word of my presence spread through the entire school. Both interested boys and inquisitive girls were sticking their heads through the door to get a good look at me.

Finally I heard the bell ring, and all the excited children crashed in from the playground. Our room was soon full. The boy sitting next to me introduced himself and was very friendly.

"Okay, everyone, please take your seat," requested Mr. Wayne over the din of children's laughter and excited conversation. Even though the class quieted, heads kept turning back to look at me. I must have been quite a novelty that day; anyway, the situation was completely new to me.

After roll call, Mr. Wayne explained to my classmates who I was. This he did briefly and as courteously as possible. Still, I was embarrassingly uncomfortable. I believe he saw the other children's interest in me and wanted to satisfy their curiosity so the day could begin. The children accepted his introduction, and soon Mr. Wayne was explaining class routine.

The fellow who sat by me was very friendly. In fact, most of the children in the class were. But with the boy who sat next to me, I had made my first friend. His name was Dennis.

When recess came, he waited with me until everyone else went out; then he asked me to play football. I didn't know what to say. I did not know what a football was, but I did agree to join him. As I went with Dennis down the hallway, we met some of his friends, and all of us went out the back door onto a big, grassy playing field. One of the boys had a strange-looking ball under his arm. I learned that it was a football. I had never seen one, even during my previous three years of school.

My friend took the football and placed it in my arms. This surprised me greatly.

"Now," he instructed, "I and four of the other guys will line up across the field down there, and when we give you the signal, you run at us and try to make it to the other end of the field. And we'll try to knock you down or tackle you on the way. Run as hard as you can and try to stay on your feet. Try not to let us catch you."

Deep inside I wanted to tell him I had no desire to play this game, but I wanted to make friends and to make a good impression on all the children. I was very aware that I was far from home. I didn't have any choice but to make friends. Also, I was very sensitive. I didn't want to hurt anyone's feelings, so I made up my mind to do exactly as they asked.

Before I began to run, I noticed quite a few children gathering along the side of the field to watch me. This really made me nervous. Of course, I was well acquainted with running, as I had run with the lambs and the dogs back home. I had also had plenty of experiences in hitting, fighting, and tackling while I was in the government boarding school. There one had to learn how to fight to survive.

Dennis gave me the signal to run. I took off as fast as I could, like a scared jackrabbit. I somehow made it through the five boys, and when I reached the other end of the field, I turned to look back. Behind me I saw the five boys sprawled out laughing on the grass—they hadn't even come near me.

Soon Dennis came over and asked me to do it again. This time he doubled the number of boys on the field so that now ten boys were lined up. As I walked back to the other end of the field, I wondered how I could possibly make it through, but again, at the signal, I took off. I ran as fast as I could. Though some of the boys did get hold of me, somehow I managed to stay on my feet. By twisting and dodging, I made it through all ten boys to the other end of the field.

Again, I looked back; they were sprawled all over the field, laughing and giggling. They were getting a real kick out of the fact that not one of them had been able to tackle me. I was pleased, for friendships were forming.

I apparently had some fans on the sidelines, as I saw quite a few girls and some boys cheering me on. The next recess, I went through the same thing, only this time there seemed to be twenty or more boys trying to stop me. Of course, I didn't make it all the way this time. However, word quickly spread throughout the school that the new little Indian boy was good with a football.

From that time on, I learned to like the game and looked forward to every chance to play with my new friends. No matter which team I was on, I carried the ball. They did this partly to help me learn the game and because they wanted me to feel at home, but also because I had demonstrated some ability in running. In time, I was also introduced to basketball.

I made many friends my first few weeks at school, and I suppose I also made an impression on a number of girls. As the months passed, I noticed my name on their notebooks and sometimes inked in a hidden place on their hand or arm. The girls even went so far as to tell others that they liked me. This part of the Anglo culture was embarrassing and sometimes challenging. At the age of twelve, I really didn't know what it meant to have a girlfriend, because I wanted to be a friend to everyone.

My appreciation for being able to attend school in Utah began in Mr. Wayne's classroom. Not only was he an excellent teacher, but he was also a gentleman. He was a sensitive man, dealing at times with troublesome children. It hurt me to see the behavior of some of the children. At times they were disrespectful. I compared this to the way Navajo youth are taught to respect adults, particularly their parents.

At times spitwads were thrown at Mr. Wayne. This saddened me. Nevertheless, Mr. Wayne showed great love and respect for all the students, even the troublesome ones. He seemed to want to do his best to teach, understanding this to be an important responsibility.

The same group of boys who acted up in class were also my friends. They were the ones who had taught me to play football. And even though I felt bad when they caused trouble, I did not know how to help Mr. Wayne deal with them. I did not know how to approach the subject with them, in or out of the classroom. I was certainly too shy at first to cause trouble myself, and out of loyalty to my friends, I just kept quiet when they were up to mischief.

My first year on placement exposed me to opportunities to develop my artistic ability. I found I could draw and paint. I had always viewed the world in a simple and artistic way, and this showed up in my artwork.

As I expressed my feelings upon drawing paper, the beauty of being Navajo came forth. More and more of my drawings and paintings made their way to the class bulletin board and other places in the school. Others had begun to recognize my artistic aptitude, including my friends. This gave me confidence.

One day Mr. Wayne approached me. He said, "George, your artwork has impressed all of us here at school. Did you realize you had this gift before?"

Silence.

"The Orem American Legion Auxiliary Poppy Poster Contest is underway now. The area includes the whole Utah Valley, from Lehi on the north to Eureka on the south. How about it? Would you like to enter?"

I knew there would be winners and losers. And, I did not want to win if it meant that my friends would lose. Being sensitive, I really didn't want to enter the contest because I didn't want to hurt anyone's feelings. (It had really bothered me when friends spoke of my football ability.) And to be singled out went against the grain of my Navajo cultural upbringing. Yes, it was important to have recognition, but only equal to that of my friends, whom I admired and respected.

"Well, what about it, George?"

It took some time for me to consider the matter, but finally

I was persuaded to enter. Over eighty posters were submitted to be judged by the Lincoln High School art department. I was greatly surprised when I won first place.

I received a lot of publicity over winning the contest. My picture and poster, along with those of the other winners, appeared in the local newspaper. My beautiful foster mother diligently cut out and pasted them in a scrapbook. My poster was judged to be quite unusual: my teacher felt it might even take state and national honors.

My foster family, the Harkers, were very elated and proud of me. They quickly shared the good news with all their family and relatives. Before I realized it, I was showered with hugs, kisses, and congratulations. We had a lot of visits, phone calls, and letters. I was not sure how to handle all this. Nothing like it had ever before happened to me.

Mr. Wayne was as proud as he could be. The other teachers also came in to offer their congratulations. All of my friends and most of the kids at school came to say how happy they were that I won. I was their winner. No one lost after all. All shared the joy together.

However, I still had conflicting feelings. It was difficult to understand why everybody made such a fuss over winning first place. I felt bad that they didn't give the same attention to the other winners. To an Indian, if people have talent or skill, they are to use it to benefit others, bringing recognition not only to themselves but to others as well. I had entered the contest not to win first place, but only because my teacher and friends had encouraged me. When I won, saw my name in the paper, and received a lot of attention, I felt a little sad and a little mixed up because I did not want to outdo anyone or hurt anyone's feelings. I remember feeling out of place with all the publicity and wishing all of us could have been winners.

Again, I was not used to the non-Indian culture where stress was placed on competition, trying to outdo others. My Navajo culture had taught me not to outdo others, especially friends, but to receive recognition and accomplishments for all. The non-Indian aggressive and competitive society was a whole new ball game. My pride in accomplishment came when my thoughts turned to my natural family and I mentally shared this honor with them. I remembered the good feeling of knowing this was an achievement for my family as well as for my people.

Later that year, at the encouragement of my friends and foster family, I entered another art contest sponsored by a local children's television program. Again, I won first prize. My winning picture was shown on television during the program, and I received a miniature twenty-mule team as a prize.

By this time I was getting used to recognition and publicity. It wasn't as overwhelming to me as it was the first time. Little Michael played with that twenty-mule team for a long time.

As far as schoolwork was concerned, my foster parents encouraged me to finish homework before going out to play. This I diligently did. Also, I helped with the chores before joining my friends. Academically I did very well.

My foster parents were a little concerned because of the three grades I had skipped before I came on placement. I hadn't started school until I was nine, and now, at age twelve, I found myself in the sixth grade. The Harkers were worried I would have problems with sixth-grade work; both of them spent time in the evening helping me. However, during the course of the year I consistently brought home excellent grades, and in time the Harkers had confidence in my ability to handle my studies.

Good reading material and literature was always available in the Harker home. I spent a lot of time reading, which I am sure helped me to catch up at school. I specifically spent a lot of time studying the dictionary. During that first year on placement, I decided to do all I could to improve my English vocabulary. I was determined, spending hours and hours going through that book. One of my daily activities was going to this large volume and memorizing words and their definitions. I did it because I wanted to, and the more I worked at it, the more I enjoyed it. I really don't know why I had such a desire to memorize, except that I remember one night as I was saying my prayers, an impression came to my mind to study the dictionary. Glen and Joan encouraged me to do a lot of reading, but they never said anything about the dictionary. However, they greatly encouraged me to read the scriptures.

And I did make the attempt during that first year to read the scriptures, which were provided by the Harkers. I began to get acquainted with the Book of Mormon and the Bible. Glen told me that the Book of Mormon was the record of the Indian people, my people. Of course, being young, I didn't understand much of what he told me. One thing I couldn't figure out was how it could be a history of the Indian people when, as I read it, I couldn't find the word Indian.

I was very active in the Church during my first year on placement. I don't remember ever missing a meeting. I attended Sunday School and sacrament meeting with the family and priesthood meeting with Glen. This year I was given the Aaronic Priesthood and was ordained to the office of a deacon. As a deacon, I passed the sacrament each Sunday and also helped gather fast offerings once a month.

Glen and Joan encouraged me to attend all my meetings, but it was my own decision to comply with their wishes. I made up my mind I wouldn't have them remind me to attend any meetings. I wanted to be a good example to little Michael and to all my friends.

Part of my activity in the Church involved Scouting. This I really enjoyed, along with the other meetings. I actually began looking forward to Sundays. I learned to love Sunday School classes and sacrament meetings. When Glen and Joan couldn't attend, they encouraged me to go without them, as they didn't want me to miss any meetings. Even though I didn't understand all the things that were taught, I still remember having beautiful feelings about spiritual things.

During the year, Glen made a small cement basketball court in the backyard, put up a basket, and encouraged me to practice the game. We spent a lot of days, even cold days, out in the back playing one on one. He must have taught me well because before I went home after the first year, I had learned to play quite well and really enjoyed the game.

Even when Glen wasn't with me, I spent spare time alone

practicing shot after shot. My favorite shot was the set shot. I made up my mind not to leave the court until I made so many shots from five feet, ten feet, fifteen feet, and finally twenty feet out. Sometimes friends from school came over and played a game. Though sometimes fast, always it was most enjoyable.

One thing basketball taught me was that there is positive value in competition. I realized that if I was going to be a good player, I would have to outscore someone, and it really didn't matter if feelings were hurt. This was part of learning to be a good sport. When the game was over, any bad feelings were speedily forgotten. I made up my mind to play as hard as I could and to have fun. If I lost, I would still feel good because I knew I had done my best. It was at this point that I realized that in order to gain success in the dominant society, I would have to compete. I realized in my early youth that if I was going to be successful in life, and in the white man's world, I had to learn to be competitive. I became determined to succeed in everything I did.

As I played more and more at home and school, I competed with boys much bigger than I was and gradually developed the aggressiveness and determination to be one of the best. Every chance I had, I was on the basketball court with friends. Between basketball and football, I learned to love sports, and participating in them helped me win friends and overcome my shyness. I found myself enjoying competition and success not only on the basketball court but in the classroom and church as well.

All in all, as most placement graduates will agree, the first year is really wonderful though difficult, packed full of nice surprises and learning confidence by overcoming obstacles. Being on placement was the most delightful, beautiful, and sweet experience I ever could have had.

I never encountered serious racial prejudice or intolerance. The few times I did encounter prejudice, I learned to ignore it, to think about better things. In fact, at times I forgot I was an Indian, unless my thoughts went back to my reservation family or something reminded me of who I was. When someone reminded me, it was almost never done in a derogatory manner.

Somehow I became completely color-blind to racial differences. To me, color didn't matter. What mattered was that I was somebody. I was important. I was loved. And I was accepted. I was treated kindly, and I perceived everybody in the same light. In other words, I soon forgot that my foster parents were white and I was Indian, that I was supposed to behave differently, to act like an Indian. Even as young as I was, all I wanted was to be a good son, a good friend, and a good person.

Glen and Joan often encouraged me to bear with pride my cultural heritage. They wanted me to take pride in being an Indian, in being a Navajo, and to do everything I could to set a good example for my people. This may come as a surprise to those who think that Mormons bring Indian children on placement to make white people out of them, to teach them to be ashamed of their own people and their culture. This is just not true. Never did the Harkers say anything negative or derogatory about the Indian people, Indian ways, or Indian traditions. Instead, they taught me, even during that first year, to be proud of who I was, to desire an education so I could help my own family and the Indian people. They taught me to stand tall and to never be ashamed of my people or who I was.

Glen was very intelligent and knowledgeable. He seemed to know more about the Indian people and their ways than even I did. The gentle teachings and encouragement of the Harkers gave me special feelings toward my people. They gave me the ambition and incentive to someday return and help my people in a big way.

Overall, it was quite a year for a shy, skinny Navajo boy who only a few months before had come hundreds of miles away from home into a strange community to live with a strange white family and who was so lonely, homesick, and bewildered about what was happening. Somehow, with the help of my foster family and the Lord, I was able to make the transition from my own Indian culture to the Anglo Latter-day Saint way of life without any serious emotional trauma, and without sacrificing my Indian nature.

In May, school began coming to a close, and I began to prepare to return to my natural family on the reservation. I was both excited and apprehensive about the return home. Before school let out, my teacher, Mr. Wayne, took time one day to spend a few moments with me. He expressed his appreciation for the excellent way in which I had performed in his class-room: "George, I remember the first day you sat in the back of this class. You sure were shy then. The change you have made is terrific. I wish I had more boys like you in class."

His last statement put me on top of the world, because I had special feelings toward him, and I valued his judgment and respected him greatly.

Some of the other teachers also gave me some compliments. Most of my friends, along with the teachers, encouraged me to come back the next year.

I stood in awe at the generosity and kindness of all the people I knew. My foster family, friends, and teachers had made the year such a special time.

Before I left school, I wrote down the names and addresses of girls who wanted me to write. At the time, I didn't really think of them as girlfriends, but just as friends, like the boys I knew. I still did not know what it meant to have a girlfriend. I just had a beautiful, special feeling toward all my friends, whether they were boys or girls. I also took with me a number of names and addresses from the boys.

Even though I never was ashamed of being an Indian, somehow because of the delightful experiences I had during my first year on placement, I more or less forgot who I was. I never did totally reject my Indian ways, but it took a return home that summer, and each following summer, to help me realize I was Indian with a Navajo family and home. Once I came to this realization, I simply made up my mind that when I was back home on the reservation, I was going to adjust quickly to life at home and to act accordingly. I tried hard not to dwell on the beautiful experiences I had been through while staying with my foster family, and I made up my mind simply to live the way my natural family did and to accept my family as they were.

The summer vacation was vital; not only did it reorient me toward my own culture, but it also gave my foster parents a short vacation. Over the years, I began to see the wisdom of reuniting with my natural family. The return to placement became more desirable toward the end of the summer and allowed me to share all my beautiful experiences with my family back home.

12

HOMECOMING

Again to sit within the bowels of the leaving bus was sad, but now I was sad at having to leave wonderful people and an especially wonderful experience. I reflected over those precious nine months, and despite my happiness in being able to return home, my eyes grew moist at the thought of Joan, Glen, and little Michael. My heart would have to grow even stouter if I were to make it through the summer. I had not thought of reverse homesickness, had not even realized it existed. But it did.

"Hi, George!" It was Roger.

"Hello! It's good to see you." My heart was leaping now. "Have a seat; I saved it for you."

I remembered having thought, at the reception center, that I'd never see Roger again. But here he was. And he looked good. In fact, he looked real good. To adequately express my joy in seeing him was a feat beyond English words. So I used Navajo: "Ya'at'eeh, Ya'at'eeh, shik'is." And, I smiled a great big smile when I said it.

Roger's face lit up. He promptly plopped into the seat next to me. Immediately his fingers found the reclining seat latch on the end of the armrest. His head was soon parallel to mine. He looked over at me, smiled, and then responded: "I don't believe all this happened. I never did think I'd make it at first. What about you?" Roger looked into my eyes and waited for an answer. I paused as I thought about the contrast in the two cultures.

"Roger, we have no choice but to believe it. It sure helped me feel better about myself. Did you think you were going crazy at first?"

"Yeah," he said simply, while his head shifted on the headrest. The gaze of his eyes stared into something unseen.

It was a beautiful feeling knowing there was another who had experienced the same thing I had. We talked back and forth for some time. The bus, well on its way to New Mexico, was enveloped by the darkness of the night. Somehow, though, the night was not as frightening as before. I was going home taller, heavier, and with a suitcase full of nice clothes. What a contrast to when I first came.

Roger had lived with a family in Monroe, Utah. And according to what he said, he also had an exceptional year. Later, when I said something to him and didn't get an answer, I glanced over. Sleep had taken him. Soon, a doze crept upon me; then I was fast asleep. We slept most of the way home and woke up in Shiprock, New Mexico.

Just as when we left, there were tearful moments when we saw our family waiting for us. But these were tears of joy. It was a touching scene; the many returning Navajo children were embraced by loved ones and went off to their buckboard wagons holding hands with one another. Others were leaving in pickups or cars. A baby brother or sister could sometimes be seen sitting on the returning child's lap. Always there were smiles of gladness.

My own mother and the Bloomfields were waiting for us. I couldn't hold back the tears when I saw them standing there with open arms. It was a beautiful, tearful, happy reunion. To see my reservation Navajo family for the first time after nine long months away from them was indescribable.

It was a touching moment for the Bloomfields. They also could not hold back their tears. I can only imagine how they felt, knowing in their hearts they had planted a seed, an Indian seed.

I soon found myself embracing my mother with moistened eyes. She, too, had tears running down her cheeks. We held each other for the longest time as she broke down and cried. The pounding of her heart told me how much she had missed me. I then embraced my brothers and sisters who were present. My father was still in the Colorado mountains herding sheep.

Brother and Sister Bloomfield stepped forward and embraced me for a long time. A special feeling came over me as I hugged them.

"Oh, George," Lucy Bloomfield cried, "we are so proud of you, so proud! We knew the Lord would watch over you, we just knew it! You look so good."

I wanted so much to express my appreciation for all they had done for my family and me, but I could not find the words. My eyes watered, and I choked up. These two sweet, spiritual giants had labored for many years among my people. As I have looked back on the missionary activities of the Bloomfields, as I have remembered my many experiences with them, I have come to the realization that the Lord raised them up for a divine purpose. Their many missionary accomplishments, and especially their involvement with my family, were by no means accidental.

After our joyous hugs of greeting, the Bloomfields took our family back to our summer home near the highway. It was good to see my aunt, my uncle, and the rest of the family again. What a happy reunion we had! What a chance to speak my native tongue that had gone unused for nine long months! They all looked me over and noted the changes that had occurred.

"Look at George and Roger, everybody. They're kind of fat," Man Who Halts, my uncle, said.

"Yeah," Joe chimed in, "George looks like a fat prairie dog!"

Joe laughed at his own humor. Everyone was caught in mirth, for the homecoming of us two boys had been long awaited.

"George, say that one Navajo word again," Bob said. "You say it kind of funny."

At that everyone broke out in laughter.

This was my family's way of expressing affection and love. Through their teasing and lightheartedness, they were letting me know how much they had missed me and how happy they were that I was home. Of course, I was happy to see them and remained quite anxious to see my father, who was still miles away. The joyous occasion was like that when Joseph, who had been sold into Egypt, greeted his brothers for the first time after many years of separation.

For the first few days after returning home, I was somewhat restless and uncomfortable. I missed my Utah foster family and friends, my room, and all the modern conveniences that were in my foster home. In Utah, it seemed there was always something to do. I was busy and involved. At home, besides herding sheep daily, there was really not much to do. I had a lot of time on my hands. Idleness and boredom can be devastating to a person. Though readjustment to my natural home was difficult, I gained strength from the experience. I was able to view my Navajo culture from a different perspective. Still, I really did have to adjust to this familiar but in many ways new life-style.

Placement had opened my eyes. It was quite a change to go from a modern home to a simple hogan with dirt floors and no running water, electricity, or toilet facilities. On the second day, I opened my suitcase and gave away most of my clothes and shoes to my brothers, for they needed them more than I did.

After a week or so, I was back into the normal swing of things—living, thinking, and behaving as a Navajo. Before I realized it, I was completely immersed in the activities of my family, which included herding sheep every day or going out looking for the horses so water and wood could be hauled. A family tradition was to attend the Ute Bear Dances; these were held in Towaoc, Colorado. At other times we went together to squaw dances, rodeos, or Navajo sings.

Toward the end of June, we went out to look for work as a family. Bob, my younger·brother, stayed behind to help my aunt, Daughter of Buckskin Man, with the sheep. This was our annual family migration, when we would hitchhike into Colorado to look for work in the fields. After several weeks of working the bean fields, I spent time helping my father herd sheep north of Cortez, Colorado. I spent the last half of the summer at home herding sheep and doing what else I could do to help out. I began to apply the principles I had learned on placement.

I figured it was better to concentrate on my involvement with my natural family. Yes, my new friends were important to me, but it hurt my heart to be separated, so I tried not to think about them. When I did this, my summer experience became more meaningful.

A few weeks later I received letters from some of my new friends, but I never answered. I wanted to, and perhaps should have, but we didn't have pencils or paper with which to write. In fact, our home was devoid of any literature—magazines and reading and writing materials—all of which I deemed very precious. As I read their letters, however, many beautiful memories came back to my mind about the placement experience and the wonderful friends I had made.

I did have a copy of the Book of Mormon, which Brother Bloomfield had given me upon my return, and I took time to look through it while out herding sheep. The things that most interested me about the book were those told to me by my foster father, Glen Harker. I didn't remember all that he said, but one thing that stuck in my mind was when he said, "Read this book; it is a record of your people, and a record of all Indian people." Because of this, out of respect for Glen, I developed a desire to read the Book of Mormon and to learn of the message found within its covers. I made several attempts to read a little from it while in Utah, but I really didn't understand very much.

That summer I looked at my new copy and then made up my mind to read it and understand its message. If it really was a record of the Indian people, I needed to know what it said. At first, I just thumbed through it; but as the days went by, feelings came upon me to read it carefully, page by page.

I didn't start at the beginning of the book. One day while I was out with the sheep, I received a direct impression, so I opened the Book of Mormon with intent to read seriously. As I opened the book in the middle, the pages of Third Nephi lay open before me. I felt this was where I should begin reading. I became so interested in these chapters, which told of the Lord Jesus Christ coming to America to visit my ancestors, that I stayed with the pages, reading until the meaning became clear. The story thrilled me to the depths of my soul, and I was determined to fully understand this section before turning to the rest of the book. I was thrilled as I read this passage: "Nevertheless, and notwithstanding it being a small voice it did pierce them that did hear to the center, insomuch that there was no part of their frame that it did not cause to quake; yea, it did pierce them to the very soul, and did cause their hearts to burn." (3 Nephi 11:3.)

And as I continued to read, my whole being was tremendously moved. What I was reading was true, and I knew it was: "And it came to pass, as they understood they cast their eyes up again towards heaven; and behold, they saw a Man descending out of heaven; and he was clothed in a white robe; and he came down and stood in the midst of them; and the eyes of the whole multitude were turned upon him, and they durst not open their mouths." (3 Nephi 11:8.)

What a fascinating story this was! By now I was fully acquainted with television and motion pictures, but all of these marvels paled in my youthful mind as I had unfolded before me, in my imagination, the vivid scene of the Savior coming down from heaven to visit my people. He invited them to come, to feel the prints of the nails in his hands and feet. He prayed for them, blessed them, and taught them for three glorious days. While reading this, I was overwhelmed by the Spirit and found tears trickling down my cheeks. I knew then that what I was reading was being shown to me as true. Though young, it seemed I was much older, and I was given an adult's understanding of these passages.

At this time, I was still largely unacquainted with the Bible, and with Christianity in general. I understood little about the birth, life, mission, death, and resurrection of Jesus Christ. Third Nephi in the Book of Mormon became my first real exposure to the scriptures and to the Savior.

This book became my companion, so to speak, and every time I became bored or idle, I turned to those special pages to read. Any time I had a negative experience or became a little discouraged or depressed, I turned to this chapter, and it gave me surpassing strength and the inspiration, courage, and motivation to continue in what was right.

All through that summer I didn't read any part of this book except Third Nephi. When I read, I had to do so secretly because I didn't want my brothers to see. I knew they would make fun of me if they did. Fortunately, I spent many days alone with the sheep and had all the time I needed to read and study. The more I read, the more I enjoyed and loved this special book.

There were times during that summer, and other summers thereafter, when I had a tremendous desire and urge to pray about what I had read, as well as to pray about some concerns and questions I had about my own Navajo culture. One of the things that I needed an answer for was whether a Navajo medicine man received his powers from God or from some other source. My father, being a medicine man and a hand trembler, had certain spiritual powers that I had witnessed while growing up. He seemed to have the power to make others well when they came to him for help. He seemed to have an ability to communicate with animals. He also seemed to have a certain spiritual gift to help others with emotional, physical, or spiritual problems.

My father took credit for saving my life when, as a child, I apparently died. On another occasion, my father apparently saved the life of my brother Joe when he was seriously injured by a horse. Joe and a couple of neighborhood friends rounded up some wild mustangs. He volunteered to ride and tame the first one they lassoed. Joe was a pretty good bronco rider, but apparently the one they caught was a tough one to ride, because Joe was thrown off immediately. As he was thrown off, his leg got caught in the stirrup, and he was dangling on the side of the horse while the horse kicked him many times on various parts of his body. Also, the horse dragged him for miles until finally the whole saddle came off. Joe was unconscious for many hours when he was brought back to the hogan. My father was home at the time and immediately performed certain rituals or ceremonies, made a sand painting, and did all that he could do to revive Joe. He used the crystal stones to diagnose the damage that was done inside his body.

Joe could not breathe for a long time, and he did not open his eyes for a long time, until after the sand paintings and ceremonies were completed in his behalf. At the end of the ceremony, Joe was able to open his eyes and began to breathe and eat and drink. Before that, he had not eaten or drunk anything, nor did he open his eyes for a long time.

According to my father, Joe's heart and lungs were seriously damaged, and he suffered from internal bleeding and probably would have bled to death if it weren't for my father.

My father was always quick to give credit to the Creator. He always said that the powers came from a great Supreme Being. He told me that the Indian people were naturally very spiritual and very close to Deity, and that before the white man came, the Great Creator had helped them heal one another. They had certain spiritual gifts and powers to help them, and there was really no need for hospitals or medical doctors, for many of the medicine men of the tribes knew which herbs to use as medicine. They took great pride in making spiritual preparations whenever they were called upon to heal a patient.

My father, especially, prepared himself spiritually before he would help make someone well. I remember the many times that he and some of my brothers and I would go to the sweat house, where my father told us about some of the spiritual preparations he needed to make before he could help people heal themselves. I remember that he fasted for days and that he spent a lot of time in the sweat house praying and singing and calling on the powers of heaven to assist him.

I wanted to know, also, where my father received the power to help others locate their lost horses or sheep or jewelry. I was always curious about the crystal stones that my father used to receive supernatural powers and abilities. Many times I saw my father use these crystal stones to assist him as he helped others, but he would never let me look at them, nor would he allow anyone else to see them. He told me many times that unless I became a medicine man, a hand trembler, or both, he would not share his knowledge with me, nor would he allow me to use the crystal stones or know anything about them. The crystal stones were very sacred and had to be kept secret. No one is to see them or use them except one who is trained and learned in their use.

When I was a junior in high school, my father approached me and wanted to know if I was interested in receiving all the knowledge he had. What he was asking me was to be the next medicine man and hand trembler for the family, and I disappointed him very much when I turned him down.

In answer to my many prayers, I received some special feelings and powerful spiritual impressions.

Words cannot describe my profound feelings at the time I was going through these things. They were extraordinary faith-promoting spiritual experiences that I will never forget. Because of these experiences and because of the feelings and impressions that I received, I gained the courage, faith, and strength to move on and to rise above the poverty, illiteracy, weaknesses, and superstitions of my people.

Words cannot describe the sweetness, the warmth, and the tremendous impressions that the Spirit made upon me when I realized that God loved my people—the Indian people; that God loved me as an Indian; and that we had a great future and a great destiny.

After these experiences, I spent many happy days almost walking on air, knowing that God looked favorably upon my people and that they had a glorious, beautiful future ahead of them, even though they were then plagued with poverty, illiteracy, alcoholism, and other problems.

I was sad because of the struggles and hardships that my people were going through with their silent courage. But I was so happy to know that they had a brilliant future ahead of them and that I had learned that their blessings would come in full only after much tribulation. I cannot describe the heartfelt joy and happiness that came to me as my mind was filled with this understanding that the great day of my people—the Indian people—was close at hand and that their great day will not come until after the day of the white man is completed.

I learned that God had blessed my people before the coming of the white man. I learned that they had been blessed with special spiritual gifts to help them overcome spiritual, physical, and emotional illnesses. I learned that these special spiritual powers had been corrupted and abused; therefore, they were gradually withdrawn. I learned that there were very few honest, faithful, humble, righteous, wise, and learned medicine men who had true compassion for their people and others. My father was one of the few. There were many others who professed that they were medicine men, but only to get gain. There were good medicine men as well as bad medicine men among our tribe, just as there are good Mormons and bad Mormons, good Catholics and bad Catholics, and good Protestants and bad Protestants.

I was careful to pray only when I was alone, away from everyone, for I knew if I were discovered by my brothers and sisters, I would receive laughter and derision. Despite my caution, on more than one occasion I was seen while in prayer, and I endured much teasing and torment.

My brothers saw my enthusiasm for the Latter-day Saint religion as only temporary. They tried to involve me in things contrary to placement teaching.

One instance I remember all too well. My older brothers and their friends had been drinking. As they tried to badger me into drinking with them, I persistently refused.

"Come on, George," one said, "have a drink of this liquor.

It will take all those Mormon feelings away. Drink this and you won't need to pray."

Of course, I continued to refuse. I had no desire to drink. I had seen what alcohol did to my father. Still fresh on my mind were his urgent pleadings for help. My inability to help him, I also remembered.

"You'd better drink with us, George, or we might get mad."

I still refused. Then they grabbed me and threw me down. Before long my wrists and ankles were viciously fettered with rope. Though I was indeed fearful, indignation soon took over. I became even more staunch in resisting. But they did not give up either.

I was in the dirt, with them on top. One of them had a liquor bottle in his hand. He and another began trying to force me to take a drink. Still I refused.

"Hey," one of them ordered, "somebody get a stick!"

With this stick they tried to pry my mouth apart, but I clenched my teeth so hard they could not insert the stick in between.

Finally they saw that my mouth was in no way coming open, so they just poured the alcohol all over my face. They laughed as I coughed and sputtered, trying to breathe just through my nose. Some of the foul-tasting liquor did get on my lips and into my mouth. After they got up, I spit, trying to rid my mouth and nasal passages of the bad taste.

"Let's leave the sissy alone. He's not man enough to drink with us anyway. He's no Navajo like us," they said, stumbling away in resignation.

In holding to what I believed, I later underwent similar tests during that first summer home.

Even though my father had given me much religious training in the Navajo way, which included prayer, there was a great difference between our traditional, ritual prayers and the way I was taught in the Harker home. My father's prayers involved the use of *tadidiin*, or corn pollen, which was cast to the east and the other directions as part of prayers, rituals, and chants. These prayers, as I understood them in my youthful mind, were addressed to the traditional gods, the holy people of the Navajo. These holy people were many and were only vaguely defined. Our respect and religious devotion to them were often based upon fear of what might happen if they were angered.

In contrast to this was the relationship to God taught by the Bloomfields and the Harkers. Instead of many gods, I quickly learned there were two—God the Father and God the Son, who worked together for the good and happiness of all men. In later years I was also to learn the place of the Holy Ghost as a member of the Godhead.

I soon learned to have a personal relationship with God the Father. I learned that I could talk to Him as though He were in the room with me; and through the whisperings of the Holy Spirit, I knew He listened and was mindful of me, a lone Indian lad. No longer was God to be feared. I learned to love Him and to feel His closeness and interest.

During that first summer at home, I was pretty much left to myself spiritually, with just my precious scriptures and a bright personal relationship with the Lord to sustain me. Thanks to the help of some wonderful white people, I was beginning to realize who I was—a child of God.

According to my family, I had begun to do strange things that were contrary to our way of life. Besides discovering my reading the Book of Mormon, praying, and resisting alcohol, they began to notice that I no longer drank coffee or cola drinks with them. They remembered how well I had liked coffee before I went on placement, and they also knew I had occasionally used tobacco. Now, I absolutely refused to touch these things. My family had begun to use the hallucinatory cactus bud called peyote, which was beginning to be known among our people to a greater degree. But I refused that also. I refused to use corn pollen as before in our prayers and ceremonies. My parents were a little concerned that I was becoming too much of a *Gaamalii* (Mormon) instead of being a Navajo. I was even called *Gaamalii* by my family for a while.

Peyote is a small, spineless cactus. Most of the plant grows underground, but a grayish-green bud, referred to as the "button," grows above the ground. It is the exposed part of the plant that is cut and ingested.

Now with members of my family practicing peyotism, I heard the differing sides and was able to sustain my own beliefs in the Book of Mormon and the Bible to a greater degree. I compared the peyote church with my own.

Without outside inducement, Joseph Smith knelt in a grove of trees and actually saw God, the Eternal Father, and His Son, Jesus Christ. This happened to Joseph while his mind was clear, while he knelt in sacred prayer. The brilliance of the light that attended burnt the truth so hard into Joseph's breast that he eventually gave his own life so the Book of Mormon could go forth with its message of Christ's ancient visit to the American continent. I have no doubt that this book is the true record of my people, not only of the Navajo, but of all Indian tribes.

My elder sister asked me to go to a peyote church meeting. When I refused, she grew angry. Since she was older and physically heavier than I was, it was easy for her to grab me and start hauling me in the direction of the peyote church meeting. I fought her all the way, but she was able to drag me along despite my protests.

Then I asked a simple prayer for strength. As if someone had been watching and waiting for that prayer, I felt a surge of energy pervade my whole being. I was no longer worried, and as I look back, I know it was the Spirit of God rendering assistance in answer to my prayer of simple faith.

My sister had long black hair that reached clear to her waist. Into her thick hair I purposefully entangled my hand. And when I closed my hand, it felt like a vise-grip being screwed down. I gave her a jerk that brought her off her feet, and then I began swinging her around and around. At just the right moment, I let go. She landed some distance away.

When she got up, dust was all over her and filled the turbulent air. All she could do was stare at my hand in astonishment. And all I could do was stare back, for this unexpected strength from the Spirit was as shocking to me as it was to her. We just stood there a long time staring at each other. Although I, too, was shocked, I realized where the power had come from.

I did not go to the peyote meeting that evening. Later I prayed, giving thanks for the strength the Lord had given me in a time of dire need.

During that summer of 1956, my family noticed that I wasn't as excited and eager to go places with them. Before then, I would never have missed a nearby rodeo, squaw dance, or sing, especially if one of my family was involved. At squaw dances, gangs of boys who had heard I'd gone on placement jumped me. For some reason they wanted to beat me up. Because these boys were bigger and older than most of my family, even my own brothers could not help me. One night I ran many miles, all the way home, in the middle of the night, to escape their wrath. I never did anything to cause the fights, and it hurt me deeply to receive such persecution. I was rejected more by my own people than by the Anglos up in Utah. I pondered this fact deeply.

Whenever Bob, Joe, and I went to town, we had to do so by hitchhiking. At times we did not get started back home until dark. One of these times, as we were standing by the road with our thumbs out, a carload of boys came by, some of the boys with whom I had attended the Shiprock boarding school. They pulled over just a few strides away from where we were standing. They then called me over—just me. As I walked up to the car thinking they would tell us to climb in, one of them said, "Bend down by the window so we can see who you are." As soon as I did, he hit me as hard as he could in the face. Then they sped off laughing.

My father and mother were both happy that I no longer had a taste for coffee and tobacco. And even though my father had a problem with alcohol, on many occasions he had tried to persuade me to shun drinking. My mother was particularly grateful I was so conscientious in helping around the house. I was most willing to look after the sheep, as well as to sweep the dirt floor and haul water and firewood. I had done these things before, but not as willingly. Now, I felt it would be better to help; this would show them my change for the better.

During my first summer home, I had a great desire to attend church services with other Latter-day Saints. I realized this would be difficult if not impossible. We lived twenty miles from the small Church branch in Shiprock. We had no transportation at all. However, in spite of the great distance and the problems in getting there, I was able to go twice. Just to sit in church, to see the kind people, brought peace to my soul.

One Sunday, I arose very early, ate breakfast, and, over the objection of my mother, went to the highway to hitch a ride into Shiprock to attend church. I stood by the highway for several hours before finally catching a ride. By the time I arrived at church, the meetings were over. How disappointed and frustrated I was about traveling all that distance and not being able to attend. I dejectedly went back to the highway and, after some time, caught another ride home.

My second effort to attend church allowed only time to take in the last thirty minutes of the meeting. After church, I was unable to catch a ride home for a long time, so I decided to trot home along the highway. I ran, or jogged, the entire twenty miles. I wanted to get home before dark and didn't want to waste time just standing beside the road in Shiprock.

I reached home just before dark, completely exhausted. I was drenched with sweat and ached acutely in my head and all through my throbbing body. I immediately went into the hogan, lay down on a sheepskin, and fell deeply asleep, not awaking until the next morning. Then I received a lecture from my mother that made plenty of sense: "George, I worried about you all day yesterday. I had a feeling things were not going right for you. I worried over you. It is not good to try to stop cars for rides, not at your age. You are too young to travel like that. Something could happen if no one is with you. I don't like it.

"Church is too far away. Just keep a prayer in your heart. Stay around here; it's better to have you well and alive than risking all that hitchhiking. I don't agree with it. It makes me worry too much."

This was one of her ways to express love. Whenever I could sense her concern coming through, I generally had a warm feeling inside, and I knew that she was really telling me these things for my own good.

"George, don't forget you are a Navajo—we have our own ways and religion. You should get more involved in the Navajo way." This was the only part of her words that didn't make much sense, though other parts did.

I wanted so much to let my parents know that I wasn't completely against the Navajo way. I still had special feelings and respect for all they had taught me, particularly the things that were good, such as reverence for the Creator and respect for His creations. Also, I had complete respect and regard for my father's ability to communicate with animals and for his power to strengthen others physically, spiritually, and mentally. I had a hard time explaining myself throughout that first summer home. I had a desire and deep-felt need to meet with the Mormon people and to worship with them as I had been taught in Utah, but I still lacked the ability to convey these feelings to my family. In many ways, the teachings of the Mormon church coincided with the teachings of my father.

Bless my parents' hearts, this change in my spiritual devotion bothered them, but they allowed me agency in the matter. I continued to study Church materials, reading the Book of Mormon and praying as the Harkers had taught me. The hearts of my parents were good. Yes, my family may have been involved in things that no longer appealed to me, but they were my family, and we loved each other. I also remembered what the Harkers had told me just before I left: "George, we love you," Joan had said with emotion. "You are a good boy. Listen to your parents when you return. Show them by example. Tell them that we love them, and that we are grateful for letting us share in you. But, George, you should not forget that they are your natural parents, your own family."

She wept as she embraced me one last time before I stepped onto the bus. I had listened to her counsel.

I was looking forward with great excitement to returning to the Harker home when school began. As summer's end approached, thoughts of placement began to come more often.

By fall, my parents were completely sold on the placement

program. The greatest reason for this was the change for the
better that they saw in me, so they set aside their mixed feelings about my new religious beliefs. Another reason was because my foster family was able to come for a visit.

The Harkers impressed my parents very much. My parents
realized that these white people were a good family, that they
were beautiful, friendly, and happy. With the Harkers' visit to
our home, my parents no longer had any question about
whether or not I should continue spending the winters with
this family in Utah. The visit bonded the Harkers and my parents.

Also, Glen, Joan, and little Michael were very impressed
with my family, especially with the way my mother was able to
keep the hogan clean. Glen told me later that even though the
floor was dirt, he noticed how clean it was, how it had been
swept, and how things were all in their place throughout the
hogan.

Glen and Joan were always positive and had only good
things to say about my family. I never heard the Harkers say
anything negative about them or about my people. They never
spoke of how poor we were or of the difficult circumstances of
my natural home, but they always seemed to be uplifting and
positive.

When I first saw Glen and Joan driving up the little road to
our hogan, I felt a twinge of embarrassment. What would they
think of me after seeing where I lived? Maybe they would not
want me back, or maybe they would say something bad. But
here they came anyway.

When they stepped out of the car, my fears were relieved.
They were just so happy to see me. My mother could sense that
Joan had taken good care of me just by the way she hugged and
looked me over. Still, it was a little embarrassing for Joan to do
it right in front of my family. However, it still felt as loving as
ever, and it made my day.

Michael, needless to say, chattered to all my amazed family. That little boy just liked people.

Joan Harker fell in love with Mother right away. When
they first met, they hugged and kissed, which was very touch-

ing to me. As I now look back on these experiences, I can't help but realize I was placed in the Harker home for a special reason. It was not an accident that I went to live there.

Despite minor problems, I spent a pleasant and beautiful summer with my family. Before I realized it, we were making preparations to go back to Utah. This time there were three of us: Roger and I were both going, as was my younger brother, Patrick.

Roger was placed with a different family his second year. He went to live with a good family in Alpine, Utah, and Patrick was sent to live with a family in Garland, Utah. During that year on placement, I had a chance to visit both of them, which we really enjoyed. They also made excellent progress and did quite well academically as well as spiritually.

So ended my first summer at home from placement. Not only had I gained strength on placement, but I had grown in character that eventful summer. Next year, I knew, I would come home from placement much wiser about how to better readjust to my own beloved family.

13

LITTLE BIG MAN
—BEING A LEADER

During the summer at home, I had lost a lot of weight because of the scarcity of food and the absence of well-balanced meals. I was somewhat malnourished. I also came back to Utah with very few clothes; the clothing the Harkers had sent home with me, I had given away to my brothers. I did not bring one cent back onto placement. Father didn't have a steady job, and money was very scarce in our home. I also came back to my foster family somewhat darker complexioned because of being out in the hot summer sun with the sheep. Each year I'd come back home in the spring with lighter skin and return to Utah in the fall much darker.

Even though I was anxious to be with my foster family again, I was very nervous. For the first few days I was timid and shy, but it was not long before I was my usual self. This seemed to be the typical pattern each year I came back to them. It just took a little time to get used to the Harkers again, to be comfortable in their home, to come out of my shell and talk to them.

During my second year on the program, I enrolled at Lincoln Junior High School, which at the time was one of the larger schools in the area. I entered as a seventh grader and was still the only Indian in the school. But I didn't view all others

George during his first year at
Lincoln Junior High School

around me as non-Indians. To me, people were people, no
matter who they were. I just wanted to mix with the group
without thinking of racial differences. I didn't want to think of
myself as different from others, that I was from a different culture or race. I was happy to see that most of my old friends from
Geneva Elementary School were attending Lincoln Junior
High.

During the first week or two, there were a lot of school activities to welcome the students, especially the new ones.
There seemed to be a lot of excitement and enthusiasm within
the student body. I was somewhat lost in the midst of all the
people and commotion. I had never seen a school with so many
children.

Warm smiles greeted me everywhere I went. A lot of the
students were glad to have someone who was not of their own
culture for a friend, and they told me so. I encountered a near
absence of racial hostility throughout this and every other year

when I was in Utah. So began my year at Lincoln Junior High
School in Orem, Utah.

Perhaps the most fun activity endorsed by the seventh
grade that year was the Polio Drive Dance. This dance was
planned with charity in mind—the proceeds were to be turned
over to public volunteers and officials to help eliminate polio.
In helping to plan this activity, I began to understand how to
lead and help others in the new society I'd entered while on Indian Student Placement. No price can be placed on such an
experience. I served on several activity planning committees
and gained some valuable leadership training. I found myself
becoming one of the more popular students.

A king and queen were to be chosen to reign over this gala
affair. I was chosen as king, and a lovely and gracious blonde
was chosen as queen. I was glad she received this honor because she served with me on several committees, and I respected her leadership and friendship.

The spirit of the occasion bubbled in the hearts of most
that evening. The boys were spiffed up in suits and ties, and
the girls had fastidiously fashioned their hair. Everyone had
planned and worked long and hard for this momentous event.
The auditorium was draped with crepe-paper streamers. Long,
elegant tables supported crystal punch bowls and plates of gar-
nished food. Beautiful centerpieces embellished smaller sitting
tables in one special section of the dance floor.

Into all this elaborate festivity, the queen and I made a
grand entrance to inaugurate our reign and especially to begin
the dance. After we entered, I noticed everyone watching. In
this capacity I represented a figurehead to help fulfill the childhood dreams and fantasies of those watching, not only the students, but the adults also.

We walked over to a small riser with a floor microphone arranged for the introduction of the king and queen. There, I delivered a short talk to the audience, and then the dance began.

My foster parents had been invited. On one of the sets I
danced with Joan, my foster mother, while Glen danced with
the girl who was chosen as queen. I was not at all uncomfort-

able with the non-Indian queen and danced several times with her myself. In fact, I danced with many girls and enjoyed it very much. I felt that while being king I should dance with as many girls as possible and not be tied down to only one girl.

The dance was a highlight of the year. The evening brought about a unified feeling among my classmates. During the following days, the school corridors were filled with conversation about the eventful evening.

I had many other fine experiences that year. I played intramural basketball, and my teammates chose me as their captain. We managed to do well as a team, winning the tournament held for all seventh-grade teams. On Saturdays, I played on a Little League basketball team. My friends encouraged me to do so, and I also wanted to participate.

I became a carrier for the Provo Daily Herald, delivering papers each day after school and also on weekends. I remember getting up early on Sunday mornings, around 3:00 A.M., to do this. I had a good paper route and learned to enjoy it. Also, the spare change was nice, and I tithed what I earned.

I had a wonderful year at Lincoln Junior High School and went through choice experiences that laid the foundation for the future. This year marked the beginning of many leadership experiences to come my way. It seemed the Lord had plans in mind and wanted me to have such experiences. I will always be grateful for my many friends, the faculty, and others who helped pull me through. Without them, I would never have learned about leadership.

As I entered eighth grade and was on my third year on placement, while walking down the school corridor one day, one of my friends approached me.

"Hey, George. Hi! What are you doing?" Not waiting for much of a response on my part he continued, "Would you mind doing me a big favor? Would you sign this paper right here?"

When he finished the last sentence he handed me a pen and moved toward the wall. There he placed the paper flat, looked at me, moved it down slightly, and then gave the nod to come.

"Just sign right here," he insisted with his left index finger, "right here."

Wanting to make him happy, I immediately walked over and signed the paper. Then I glanced at his face, and it was evident I had pleased him. He was so happy, I didn't bother to ask him about what I had signed. In fact, I didn't think another thing about it.

"Oh, thanks, George. This makes us real, real glad. Thanks!"

And then off he strode, merrily walking down the hall. I was really pleased with myself—until I found out what I had signed.

After a pleasant lunch that day, I began to hear some not-quite-as-pleasant news. Classmates began coming up to congratulate me on something I knew little about.

"Hi, George! Don't worry, you'll do just fine," one said.

And from another, "Stick with it, George, I'm behind you all the way!"

Still another gave me a big clue: "George, you've got my vote." Then reality started to hit. I began to realize what I had signed. And it was much worse, almost, than signing my life away. In signing that piece of paper, I had declared my candidacy for eighth-grade class president. Had I known, I never would have signed that paper. I worried all the rest of the day.

I signed the form because I did not want to hurt my friend's feelings. He did not tell me what the form was for. I thought he was running for some office. I guess he knew I would never run on my own.

By the time I found out what was going on, it was too late to withdraw. I told my friends in a very nice way I would do anything to get out of the race. However, deep down I didn't want to disappoint them and finally decided that if I was one of the finalists in the election, I would go ahead with it. All the time, though, I was really hoping I wouldn't make it.

Later the same day, a group of friends, boys and girls, asked if they could campaign for me. *Campaign?* What did this word mean? Never had I heard it before. I asked what it meant.

One of the group said, "It means we're on your side in this election. It means we try to get everyone to vote for you."

"Yeah," interjected another. "We put up posters in the halls advertising your candidacy, and then convince everybody that you are the man."

"It'll be fun," said yet another. "I can see it now: George P. Lee, eighth-grade class president!"

"I get the picture," I said.

With all that attention coming my way, I was even more bewildered. I wanted fervently not to be a finalist. All the attention was frightening.

Finally I told my friends to do what they wanted, but at the same time, I decided to do everything possible to tell all my friends not to vote for me. You might say my campaign strategy was to do nothing, say nothing, and hope that nothing happened. Nothing would have better pleased me.

In the next few days, it seemed that the momentum of the campaign was shifting toward me. There was nothing I could do to hold back the tide. Everyone echoed to everyone else to vote for the Indian boy who was running for president. My white friends plastered up a lot of posters encouraging students to vote for me, and as much as I wanted to tear them down, I realized I couldn't. I didn't want to hurt the feelings of my friends. I finally decided to face whatever came and to do my best as a candidate.

I can still see the auditorium that day. The bleachers were packed with students. Whenever I dared to look out over the mass of people, my heart flip-flopped in fright. Out of the corner of my eye, I could see the other candidates seated beside me. I wondered if they were as frightened as I was. The rhythm of the audience's conversation came to my reluctant attention, wave after wave. I wished I could faint into another world and wake up someplace else.

The incumbent student-body president announced my name. I gulped. Whether I walked or stumbled to the podium is vague. Suddenly, my ability to move my tongue or open my mouth was gone. I stared down at my gnarled shoestrings. What a lonesome feeling! I thought that I'd have been better off herding on the reservation, talking to sheep and goats. Now, there sat all these people looking at me, waiting for words that wallowed in the mire of my terrified thoughts.

Finally, I began to speak, and all nervousness and fear left me. According to one of my friends, it was the best of all the campaign speeches. It was one of those occasions when a person says a lot but remembers little. I thanked those who voted for me in the primary election. I didn't make any campaign promises, but I did say that I would do my best if elected.

I didn't really have a platform to run on. I didn't even know what a platform was, but I had seen a television western where a hanging platform was built. Perhaps I had a platform after all, and the trap door had just swung open.

My remarks were brief because this was my first experience in speaking before a large Anglo group. When I sat down, I was startled by clapping, even a standing ovation. There was also a lot of whistling and shouting from the audience. I began to feel better, and to grow in confidence. I also started to see that I really could be of benefit to others. If I was of value to friends, then my life felt worthwhile for me as well.

As the campaign days swept by, I watched carefully the efforts of my opponent, a tall blonde girl. Her prior leadership activities aided her eloquent drive for votes. I admired her friendliness and sensitivity to others. I felt she was taller than I was in several ways, not just in physical height. Everywhere she went, she carefully cultivated friendship. She was genuine in her desire to serve others. I learned much from her kind, easy, and friendly manner. Also, a faithful campaign committee demonstrated loyalty to her leadership, and they distributed many posters and handouts. Her example caused me to reflect upon leadership principles. Slowly I developed a desire to acquire abilities like hers.

The candidates for other offices labored as tirelessly as my prime opponent, and each ran a good campaign. I had never before seen so many posters and pictures as those that montaged the walls inside and outside the school. Never before had I seen so much excitement and enthusiasm. The candidates seemed to be everywhere, talking to the students and planning their strategies. I was greatly awed by it all, but I observed and understood the need to learn by participation. Was this one of the reasons for coming on placement?

It was a great learning experience to witness these things. Sometimes I was so caught up in the spirit of the election that I forgot I was one of the candidates. I often had to be jolted back into reality, and reality scared me. But I was growing beyond the impact of the initial exposure. One thought kept recurring in my mind: "If you want to succeed in the white world, you have to compete."

Again, my campaign strategy was simple. Since I didn't know how to campaign, all I wanted to do was say nothing, do nothing, and hope the other candidate won. I didn't encourage any committees or groups to work for me and didn't put out any publicity on my own. You might say that I ran a very low-profile campaign. But I couldn't stop my friends who were campaigning for me. In fact, the more invisible I tried to be, the more the students decided to support me. Apparently, most of the students had mentally cast their ballots before the campaign began, and when the final results were in, I won by a landslide. My opponent, the slender, tall blonde girl, was quick to congratulate me after the election. She was gracious and kind.

I had suddenly won something I hadn't intended to win— the office of eighth-grade class president. Just what that entailed, I didn't know. Who ever heard of Chief Sitting Bull leading the U.S. cavalry? That's just how I felt. Since I'd not been in the Utah school system long enough to observe how a class president should act, I just tried to be myself and to represent my constituents well. I wanted to be a good example. As the responsibility began to rest upon my shoulders, I could see the benefit in being a president. I didn't take long to realize how I could serve those I respected and liked. My friends had placed trust and confidence in me. The least I could do was match their trust by proving my own trustworthiness. My confidence began to grow.

The decision to excel carried over into schoolwork and other aspects of my life. I made up my mind to study hard and to earn good grades. I decided to be a good example among my friends, as well as to my foster family at home. These little decisions for personal excellence contributed greatly to my life in later years. I tried hard to live up to my sacred Navajo name, *Ashkii Hoyani*, The Boy Who Is Well Behaved and Good.

After the election, I attended meetings with all of the student-body officers. We met regularly to discuss ways to promote school spirit and to help each other. The ninth-grade officers pledged to help the seventh-grade and eighth-grade officers until the latter two were able to participate and contribute to the work of the group. Every time we met, there was a spirit of unity among the class officers.

During these meetings, the student-body president surprised me with a new name, one most fitting for an Indian. Right off, he called me Chief, and the name stuck. Every time I raised my hand to make a comment, the president addressed me as Chief. I enjoyed this bit of personal attention. To some native Americans, perhaps this title would be offensive, but I considered it a compliment to me and my people.

Apart from the larger student-body officer meetings, as eighth-grade class officers, we also had meetings. During these separate meetings, there were opportunities to guide fellow eighth-grade class officers through calendaring the year's activities. By now, I'd really started to appreciate the leadership experience, and it was more enriching than frightening.

As president, I received many opportunities to address the entire student body and my eighth-grade classmates. Though it took quite a while to subdue my shy tendencies, the more speeches I delivered, the easier it became. With time, the self-assurance came. Before long, I enjoyed speaking to our audiences and was not afraid to lead out.

My third year with the Harkers was similar to the first two years. When minor problems developed between us, we were able to work them out. During those times, I began to understand my abiding love and appreciation for the Harkers. I determined then that I wanted no other foster home. And I had a good caseworker, Clair Bishop, who helped me through my placement experience.

My little foster brother, Michael, and I grew closer to each other. We did a lot of things together at home. How I grew to love him! I often took time to do the things he wanted to do, to listen to him, to read stories to him, or to watch television with him. Those times will be forever priceless.

I was also able to grow closer to my foster parents, Glen and Joan. We did a lot of things together, such as going on picnics, watching movies, or eating out at the various restaurants in Orem as a family. I again made up my mind that I would do anything I could to please my foster family and be one step ahead in all that was expected of me.

This year and those which followed, as in my first year on placement, I enjoyed occasional weekend deer-hunting trips into the mountains with Glen and his father. We also hunted for pheasant, duck, and quail in the marshes that surrounded nearby Utah Lake. I also did a lot of fishing with Grandpa Harker. I was still known as "Hawkeye."

Every day when I came home from school, I would get my homework out of the way and then do whatever I could to help around the house. I seemed to please my foster parents with my scholastic achievement. This meant a lot to me.

I made a goal to attend all my Sunday School meetings, and I don't think I ever missed one.

I generally continued in leadership and academic growth throughout the year. As school began to draw to a close, everyone started to talk about the election for a student-body president.

The student-body president was elected each year near the conclusion of school. He would then preside over the entire student body during the coming school year. Because I was an eighth grader and was going into ninth grade, my classmates asked me to run for this office.

During the previous summer while I was on the reservation, and occasionally in letters from home during my eighth-grade year, my natural family said how much they needed me and how they wished I would attend a school closer to home. Because of their desires, I honestly thought I wouldn't return to Lincoln Junior High the next year. So, I told my friends I would not be back and politely requested that my name be removed from the ballot. Deep inside, however, I did want to return. I thought I would enjoy being student-body president, even though I did not actively seek the position. As it turned out, my friends hadn't taken no for an answer. When the campaign was completed, I was voted in easily. In a way, I was thankful for the insistence of my friends. I had come to enjoy serving in the presidential capacity.

Another letter from home, along with the approach of summer, intensified my desire to be with my natural family. Finally, I definitely decided I would not be coming on placement again. I sadly informed the school officials of this decision. Another election was held, and a friend of mine was chosen for the office. As I prepared to leave for home, a lot of my friends, teachers, and faculty advisors came to wish me well, telling me they were hoping and praying I would return. Also during my summer at home, many of these same people corresponded with me, encouraging me to come back. I can remember that even my faculty advisor wrote a letter saying that they were all pulling for me to return.

Especially there were letters from my foster family. I had been in the Harker home for three years and was very much a part of the family. Their summertime letters expressed their love and the hope I would prayerfully reconsider my former decision.

How could I refuse?

As it turned out, I did come back. There was much rejoicing in my foster home, as well as among my friends and teachers. I guess my friends were not used to me not being one of their leaders, as they quickly voted me in as ninth-grade class president. Again, I found myself on the student council, and this time I was a little more experienced. I was more sure of myself. I had overcome most of my shyness and had the opportunity to stand before my fellow students many times to express my thoughts and feelings.

There was a special reason I approached my ninth-grade class presidency with interest and enthusiasm. An oft-told American story of motivation is that of the great football coach, Knute Rockne, exhorting his Notre Dame football team to "Win one for the Gipper." (George Gipp was a player who died shortly before a key game.) I too had my "Gipper." I wanted to serve a presidency for a special friend.

During the previous year, while I was serving as eighth-grade class president, I became good friends with the ninth-grade class president. He and I became good friends, in fact great friends. More than any other person, he was the one who welcomed me into the group of student-body officers. He helped me feel comfortable and at home. He often took time from his busy schedule to encourage me, counsel me, and point out some of the things that were expected of a class officer.

Before the school year was out, he became very ill with leukemia and for a long time did not come to school. His absence grieved me. Saddest of all was the day he died. I lost a true friend.

He never really had a chance to complete his term as ninth-grade president. At times we sat together on the school lawn while he spoke of his dreams and aspirations for his class. They were good and righteous dreams. When I came back and was elected as ninth-grade president, I decided to continue his dreams for him. It was my way of honoring one whose friendship will be eternal.

In a way, I was glad I had planned on not coming back and had turned down being student-body president. This way I was able to become the ninth-grade class president to fulfill my friend's dreams. This special young man will always be one of the great influences on my life to serve others cheerfully and to set high ideals and goals. All through that year, I kept him in mind and tried to do my very best in leading my fellow students. This friend taught me best that leadership is colorblind.

During my eighth-grade and ninth-grade years on LDS placement, I was privileged to participate in a unique program. The program caseworker took selected Indian students to several local wards for Sunday speaking engagements. My caseworker, Clair Bishop, initiated the program for Indian students under his supervision. I traveled with this group to nearly all the wards in the Orem-Provo area. For each ward, I prepared a new talk. At first, the thought of speaking to all those Anglo adults jolted me, but after several times, I became more relaxed. This experience helped me prepare for the future. Interestingly enough, I actually grew to enjoy public speaking. The more I gave talks, the more I gained confidence.

Through giving these talks, I became more knowledgeable about the teachings of the Church. I also began developing the ability to express myself better before large groups. My foster parents said I had a photographic memory, for I memorized all my talks. Placement brought out this special gift. My foster parents helped me prepare my talks at first; but later, I did it all on my own. I gave the memorized talks in sacrament meetings. Sometimes when I didn't have time to prepare, I memorized talks out of the scriptures or from books written by Church leaders, giving the talks word for word.

Grandma Harker attended one of these sacrament meetings and listened to me speak. Afterward she told me I spoke just like a seasoned Church official. She didn't know at the

George in the ninth grade

time that the talk I had just given came straight out of a book
written by a well-known Church leader.

The subjects for my talks came from basic information from
the scriptures and from good Church books. Then I labored to
put the message in my own words. While preparing these talks
I developed a deep interest in searching the scriptures, both
the Bible and the Book of Mormon. The more I read, the more
I enjoyed them. My goal was to fit my life into those teachings.

Through the sacrament-meeting talks, I also learned what
it meant to speak by the power of the Spirit. Soon I was able to
just outline talks and to give them as directed by the Holy
Ghost. I also learned to develop thoughts on a certain subject
and expand on these through the power of the Holy Ghost,
speaking from my heart. As I spoke by the Spirit, my mind
turned to memories of how my natural father prayed and taught
by that same spirit.

Also during the ninth grade, through the encouragement
of my foster parents and friends, I got involved in various sports
activities, particularly football and basketball. In fact, the boys
in my class voted me the outstanding basketball player for the
whole ninth grade.

I considered this quite an honor, especially coming from
my friends. I realized how important supportive friends are,
even though at the time I didn't think I deserved the honor.
Nevertheless, I was given this honor and many other honors,
which to this day I regard as blessings.

For whatever the reason, it seems there are always individuals who are frustrated with life and those who generally
have some malice toward others. I ran into one of these persons
while in the ninth grade. Others at school had often referred to
him as a "hood," one of the tough guys. In his leather jacket,
he was leaning against the wall. His slicked-back hair sat atop a
face full of pain and misplaced pride. However, the most unfortunate thing was that the face had angry eyes that had an-
chored themselves right on me.

Other students in the hall saw his discontent, his piercing
gaze, and when he saw others watching, it boosted his artificial

confidence. He scowled at me while his large frame settled in for the offense, just inches in front of my nose.

"Hey, you, Injun, I'm talking to you," he fumed. "I don't think much of you. You're not even a yellow chicken, just a dirty brown one. You shouldn't have come to this school. Who do you think you are coming off that reservation and now holding an office here in my school?"

This was one of those deeply philosophical questions that was beyond my answering. Perhaps he was jealous of the attention I'd received at school. Perhaps he had an undesirable and unfortunate home life. Maybe his life had been full of rejection. I wish that my ears could have been deaf to his next utterance: "You ready to fight me, Injun boy? Or are you really yellow all over?" He was gloating, as some of the girls whispered and giggled while they stood ringside in the hall.

I had been in very few fights, a scuffle now and then with my own brothers, or during the boarding-school years, but all these were never of my own doing. I felt like a dill pickle in a tight, sour predicament.

I did not want to react, but neither did I know how to act, so I just stood there, stupefied, having a hard time understanding what was happening. I thought of the time my father had stood face-to-face with the big bear, and I tried not to show my fear. At least the bear listened to reason, but there was no way this guy was going to drop to all fours and lumber off. The only thing he was ready to drop was a fist upon my poor face.

There he stood, bigger than I was, more muscular, taller, and better built. Surely he could beat me. My own youthful pride would not let me back out, but the example I needed to set nagged me. After a long silence, he spoke again. "Well, you think it over. I think you're yellow," he said as he winked at an admiring girl with thick make-up. Then he walked off, laughing.

When I went to my friends for advice, some advised me to fight and others to forget it.

After several days of fitful worry, I went to this gang leader to negotiate. I wanted to find out if I had done or said anything to offend him. I decided to make it right, to apologize if need be, but he wouldn't listen. He called me a chicken and told me I was scared. I replied that I wasn't afraid (although I really was) and told him I would fight. We agreed on a date and time to meet in back of school to do battle.

All through the day of the scheduled bout, I was really scared. Nerves. I didn't know what to do. Thoughts of fighting with non-Indians in the bean fields of Colorado came back to me. I had never fought a non-Indian one-on-one and didn't know how to develop my strategy. At home we just wrestled and scuffled in the dirt. I had no desire to hit him, or even to hurt his feelings. I struggled with worry all day long and found myself thinking of the fight rather than paying attention in class. I knew he was going to get the best of me because of his size and his hatred.

I said a few silent but fervent prayers during the day, asking the Lord for strength and courage. I asked the Creator to soften the bully's heart. I told the Lord I really didn't want to fight; that if there was any way to escape it, I wanted to know how.

With the ringing of the last bell, which sounded like a trumpet in my ears, the dreaded hour finally arrived. I took a deep breath and made my way down the short hallway and out the back door with a few faithful friends following. Stepping outside, I was surprised to find a large gathering of students. Word had spread, although the news apparently hadn't reached the principal or faculty. I almost wished it had.

After pushing my way through the crowd to the open space in the middle, I expected to find the tough guy, but he wasn't there. A few minutes passed but still he did not show up. Everyone wondered where he was. I didn't request an emissary to look him up either. But a few of his fight-thirsty friends went out looking for him. He could not be found. About twenty minutes later the crowd began to break up and leave for home.

Words will not describe the beautiful feeling that came over me when I found out he had backed down. I was so grateful to my Maker, for I knew He had had a hand in this. All the way home that day I kept thinking about how close I had come to getting into a fight and how very happy I was about the tough guy not showing up. Again, floods of memories came into my mind, the times my father's prayers were answered and the other times my own prayers were answered.

The bully never bothered me after that. In fact, we became good friends. After this incident, he changed for the better, and I found him to be a really nice person.

I think more good came of this incident than bad. Apparently I impressed quite a few students, those who were a little on the bad side, especially those who were part of the bully's gang. The students believed I had the courage to fight even though inside I was afraid. On the other hand, as a class leader, I felt the responsibility to set a good example, to handle problems in a more mature way than beating someone up. Another reason I hadn't wanted to back down was because I wanted to stand up for the Indian people, to show the students that I represented Indian courage and determination.

In my school, as at all schools, the students made fun of teachers, sometimes making derogatory remarks about them. One teacher nearly everybody had a hard time with. They disliked him because of his strict class discipline. In order to get a decent grade in his class, we had to earn it, to really work for it.

One semester I decided to take his class. I wanted to find out for myself why the students did not like him, why it was so hard to get a decent grade from him.

During that class, I learned to greatly love and respect this fine teacher. That he was strict was true. He tolerated no monkey business, and he gave a lot of homework, including preparing a weekly oral book report. There was a little stage at the front of the room on which we stood to give our report.

This teacher wanted us to really learn something rather than just occupy space in the room. He wanted us to think, reason, and make good judgments. If we received an A grade from him, we knew we had really earned it.

Two students in our class received A's; I felt fortunate to have been one of them. I had really learned something. I had studied much and really benefited from having to deliver book reports in front of the class. This gentleman wanted his students to learn self-expression, to become leaders. Some of the students were not ready for this; they wanted the easiest classes. This teacher was one of the best I ever had. I learned to love and respect him for the way he taught.

One sad incident that occurred during my ninth grade year was the death of George R. Bloomfield. He died February 3, 1959, soon after he and his wife, Lucy, had completed a full-time mission among the Navajos. Several weeks later, I received word of his passing in a letter from Mother.

What a shock it was to lose this good man who had had such a profound influence in my life. How I would miss him! Our contact was not just casual; there were times when I worked for the Bloomfields at the Mancos Creek Trading Post. During that time, we grew closer than ever. I really tried my best to be an honest worker, and George Bloomfield did not let it go unnoticed. Many times he complimented me when I did something that especially pleased him.

After his death, I did not forget his wife, Lucy. I frequently drove to Farmington, New Mexico, to visit with her until she also passed away over twenty years later. She lived into her late nineties and was as true and grand a woman as ever walked this earth.

When I heard of Brother Bloomfield's passing, I wrote a long letter to his wife. In my letter I expressed my sorrow at his death and reviewed the changes in my life that had come about because of him and her. I reminded her they had been responsible for my first schooling, and later going on the placement program. I expressed appreciation for their kindness in giving my brother and me rides to and from school, in giving our family soda pop without charge when we came to the store. I put my intimate feelings as best I could into the letter.

Sister Bloomfield told me later that George's funeral was lovely and that over four hundred people attended, many of them Lamanites. Two Navajos, Clyde Beyal and Mary Jumbo, spoke at the funeral, paying tribute to him. Sister Jumbo announced that the Toadlena Indians were keeping a four-day fast of remembrance, one of the ways they demonstrated great love and respect. This fast is a Navajo custom. When a loved one dies, many family members and close relatives go without food during the four days while the deceased person's spirit remains nearby. The fast is to ensure that the deceased's spirit will eventually leave in peace.

Even after the passing of her husband, Sister Bloomfield continued for many years to be involved in Lamanite missionary work. She could always be counted on, with her little portable organ, to bring joy and happiness into the lives of many. George and Lucy planted many gospel seeds among the Lamanites.

All in all, I had marvelous experiences, both educationally and spiritually, during my three years at Lincoln Junior High. I have beautiful memories of these years, and I made such wonderful friends. Toward the end of the school year, I received a letter of commendation from the principal. I include it here as an indication of the opportunities that had come my way during three years of junior high:

Dear George:

We the students and faculty of Lincoln Junior High School, join together and express our thanks to you for the outstanding manner in which you have discharged the duties and responsibilities of leadership as a student body officer in our behalf. As we contemplate the attainments of the year, such as special projects, programs, activities, etc., in which you have been engaged, we are overwhelmed by their magnitude.

Only through persistent effort, unselfish service and genuine concern for your school have these things been made possible. You have rendered a noteworthy service to the school. There should come to you a feeling of satisfaction arising out of these successful accomplishments.

May you continue to accept these opportunities to serve.

Thank you for your inspiration, leadership, and service for they have helped us all along the path we are all traveling.

Sincerely,
Quinn A. Hatch, Principal

A similar letter was also drafted for my natural parents in
New Mexico, but I asked Mr. Hatch to send it to my foster parents because my natural parents did not speak or understand
English. I felt they wouldn't have any idea as to its contents or
understand the accomplishments to which it referred. As it
turned out, the original was sent, as I suggested, to my foster
parents, and a copy was sent to my natural family. The letter to
my two families was quite similar to the one above.

May 27, 1959. I graduated that day from Lincoln Junior
High School. Our graduation theme was "Youth Decides."
And because such a large audience would be attending, the
graduation ceremony was held in the Orem High School
Auditorium.

The printed program contained the phrase "Acceptance of
Diplomas." Under this subheading, the name "George P. Lee"
was printed. I had been selected to give an acceptance speech
for the diplomas in behalf of my classmates. I felt good about
my speech. After the graduation ceremony, we had a reception
and graduation ball at Lincoln Junior High School.

The graduation ball was exhilarating. I had a choice evening with my friends. (I was usually not all that excited about
dating, but I remember having had a date for this affair.) Since
there were no Indian girls in our school, I took a non-Indian
girl to this dance. I danced with her many times. And trying to
set a good example, I also danced with a lot of other girls. After
the dance, many of the students continued on throughout the
night with their celebration. However, I escorted my date
home and returned before midnight.

As I look back on these experiences, I realize that the Lord
had a great hand in all of my accomplishments and successes.
How else could anyone explain how a skinny little Navajo boy,
reared under the poorest of circumstances, unlearned, un-
schooled, and in an unfamiliar culture, could become class
president at one of the largest schools in the state and among
non-Indian classmates, especially at that time! The larger
credit I cannot assume.

Never at any time, amazingly, did I have unduly low self-
image, whether I was on the placement program or whether I

was home on the reservation. In other words, I think I had pretty high self-esteem in the dominant culture as well as in my own native environment, so I was able to function in both.

I am grateful I was not able to see colors in people, that I was able to fit in, that I had the desire to do so. I also had the desire to help others whether they were of my culture or not. As a student leader, I had love and compassion for all. I was ready to help anyone. I was comfortable and happy in a non-Indian culture.

As near as I could, I played the role expected of non-Indians. As I did, my successes came. There were no needless bitter feelings causing me to shy away from new things merely because my cultural sensitivity was challenged. Yes, there were situations that seemed strange to me at first, but I walked forward with faith into the darkness of a foreign culture. It was not dark to the Anglos, but it was to me. After a while, the darkness dissipated, and I was surrounded by beauty. I did not lose my identity, but I gained a better perspective of myself. My mind did not become forked; it became as sharp as a two-edged sword, the sword being life and the edges two differing cultures.

My desire was to conform as expected, realizing that every kingdom is governed by the order thereof, and that to be effective, one operates by the order of the kingdom he is in. I was expected now to be competitive, aggressive, and to accept challenges. And so I was. Lincoln Junior High facilitated my growth in these things.

A day or two after graduation exercises, the familiar rumble of the bus droned in my ears. I was headed back to the reservation for the summer. Ninth grade was over. I had become more mature and was well-rounded enough to better help my natural family. Again, that summer I worked at the Mancos Creek Trading Post. Five dollars a week, my pay, came in handy for helping my parents. It also helped me to understand self-sufficiency.

All during the summer, I anticipated the fall reunion with my foster family and friends. I could think about them now without homesickness, for my two worlds had become as one.

14

THE SWEETNESS AND INNOCENCE OF '62

I n August of 1959, I returned enthusiastically once more to the Utah Indian Student Placement Program and my beloved Harker home. Unlike the year before, when I really planned to stay home on the reservation, this return was exciting.

Though the buses arrived in Utah only a few days before school, I was impatient to enroll and open my books. When school finally started, I was more content, but as I walked through the halls to locate my locker and classrooms, Orem High School suddenly seemed larger than I'd noticed before. Among the teeming students, I felt out of breath and out of place. However, former classmates and friends and I found each other, and once again I felt at home.

The excitement and demonstration of school spirit caught hold of almost everyone. And election time had arrived. My former friends and acquaintances from junior high school again wanted me to be class president, and they nominated me at a student-body assembly.

I was in a dilemma. Most of the tenth-graders knew how difficult it was for me to refuse serving them, but my own thoughts were not to accept the nomination. However, to disappoint my friends would be emotionally painful. But I had committed myself to other goals. The summer on the reservation had found me contemplating what my future placement experience should include. I thought of the Navajo people and remembered the admonition given by a sincere caseworker and others in Utah to gain an education to help myself and my people. Thoughts of my noble ancestors coursed through my mind. I thought of the *Hweldi*, or Long Walk, and of the history of my people in the Book of Mormon.

I also pondered the need for balance in life. Perhaps it would be better for everyone if someone else could give leadership with different emphasis. And I thought it only fair that someone else should have opportunity to hold the office. After all, true leadership means sharing. Also I wanted to be more involved in athletics, particularly basketball and football. I didn't feel I could participate fully in sports and still answer the demands of class president.

As the assembly progressed, I pondered the conflict, realizing the need for decisiveness. When the moment came to address the students in support of my nomination, what to say became clear. I told them perhaps it was time to give the office of president to someone else. Someone else needed an opportunity. I mentioned the unfairness of my holding this class office for such a long time. The time had come for them to nominate another person. Besides, the Navajo culture had taught me to share and to be considerate of others—it was ingrained in my soul.

I then officially declined the nomination, recommending a friend whom I thought very capable. However, I offered my support to serve on committees and to assist in any way possible.

Immediate applause followed my comments. I was pleased the class had followed my recommendation. Another person was nominated, and later, elected. My time was freed for the sports program.

I tried out for the sophomore football-team quarterback. Three friends and I tried out for this same position. Within a few weeks I was chosen. I had become the number-one signal caller. To be selected for this position was exhilarating. I re-

membered the time my elementary-school friends had introduced the game to me—the time all of them had lined up
across the playing field to tackle me had aroused my attention
to this sport. Football had become a favorite recess activity.
Now, four years later, I was the quarterback for the Orem High
School sophomore football team.

A few of my friends wanted me to try out for halfback. This
is the position I had played informally with them for some
time. But because of my junior-high class leadership experiences, I wanted to lead the team as their quarterback. I had
grown accustomed to leadership and had realized the positive
benefits of it. Making decisions had become part of my personality. I enjoyed it. Quarterbacking was a great challenge. I
would have to compensate for my small stature with quick
thinking. I liked this idea.

The daily practice was rugged and difficult. Our team grew
rapidly in spirit. We thought we'd lick the world! Soon it came
time to scrimmage against the junior-varsity team. The clouds
we had been treading on soon dissipated. Instead of wings and
sparkling dew on our boots, we soon discovered the idea of mud
and cleats. The junior-varsity team quickly brought us down to
earth in more ways than one.

The day of the scrimmage, defiant challenges passed our
way from the junior-varsity team through non-team classmates. When we heard what the junior-varsity team was
spreading through the halls, our determination to win grew as
hard as flint.

"Hey, George," a flirtatious girl in a frivolous, frilly dress
said, "I hear the junior-varsity football team is really going to
bloody your noses after school."

This was almost a worse affront than when the bully had
challenged me to fight. I was speechless. In a way, it was nice
to have her attention. In a way, not.

"We'll see," I could only respond.

"I really doubt it, George," she teased, "because your eyes
may be black, too!"

With that, she promptly turned about and sashayed on
down the hall. I stood there for a moment or two trying to

figure out what had just taken place. Somewhere in the midst of my thoughts, I lost track of her flopping ponytail as she merged into the milling students.

Soon, I overheard another conversation. One of the junior-varsity team members almost roared his defiant challenge to one of my sophomore classmates.

"Why, we're not even going to allow one of you pipsqueaks to score a single touchdown. You'd be better off not even coming out on the football field. You know what I mean?"

His mannerisms and boasting had reached a high pitch by his last breath. One of the popular girls passed close by at that moment. He poked his chest out a little more when he spied her out of the corner of his eye. I thought I could put three whiskers on either side of his nose to have a genuine Rock Island walrus. This was going to be a fun game. I would throw the ball just over his head, just out of reach and just to make him mad.

After he had left my teammate, I went over to console my friend. The junior-varsity team members had been bragging like this all week long. Rumors of how they were going to beat us spread quickly among the crowded halls of sandwiched students. I admit to daydreaming of their defeat, even while sitting in some of my favorite classes.

I could envision the grand Statue of Liberty play. There I was, with the football in my golden hand, which was cocked back ready to throw. The opposite team, the junior-varsity braggarts, were fooled by all this, assuming my hand would soon hammer toward an intended, well-covered receiver. So excellent was our fake that the other side had covered both end receivers with several men.

Just at that moment, one of my speedy halfback friends swooped behind me, snatching the ball from my expectant hand. Of course, he ran the play clear to the end zone for a touchdown, the last play of the game, leaving the other team pointless. I did quite well in my daydreams.

The final bell rang. We younger boys, to be honest, had been actually psyched by the boasting of the junior-varsity team. We were afraid, but we were determined to do our best.

As the sophomore starting quarterback, I had long before realized what we were up against: a wall.

Then the game started, and my daydream turned into a nightmare. As I dropped back to pass to one of my receivers, our offensive line broke. Large, extra-large, linemen were on top of me before I knew what had taken place. It was like having three King Kongs on top of the famous Statue of Liberty all at once. They had come at me with their long arms raised high in the air. I couldn't even see a cloud, much less one of my intended receivers. Since I'd eaten school lunch already that day, eating the ball was less than enjoyable. When I attempted to run, I was squashed just over the line of scrimmage.

Before the game was over, some of the sophomore team had bloody noses. I looked over to the sideline. There was that girl who had teased me. Well, at least my eye wasn't black. But my pride had suffered somewhat.

I stayed in during the first half of the game; then another quarterback was sent in. All the sophomore quarterbacks had a chance to play in the game (if you want to call being smeared, playing). They outscored and outplayed us, but we had fun anyway. It taught all of us some hard lessons, and we became a better team by playing them.

A positive result of the defeat was the preparation received for the beginning season. That year we played Lehi, Pleasant Grove, American Fork, Payson, Springville, Spanish Fork, and Provo. Though we won only half of these games, we had fun playing together. We learned much about physical conditioning, discipline, and teamwork.

At the season's conclusion, I discovered I really didn't enjoy football as much as I had thought. In fact, I began to have doubts about being very involved in sports. Still, I had become competitive enough to try out the next year also. However, before I was fully involved, my foster father encountered difficulty in his hardware-store business. Things became so bad that he approached me one day to ask for my help every day after school. He said he really needed me.

He let me decide whether to continue in sports or assist him. Practice after school was really fun. Although it was so enjoyable, I didn't feel right about turning down Glen's request. Right when he had asked for help, I knew what I had to do. In the long run, it would be better to help in the family business. With this in mind, I decided to end my involvement with sports. I decided to devote my after-school time and energy to helping my foster father in the store. From then on, every day after school, I rode my bicycle to the hardware store to help Glen sell, stock, clean, or make deliveries. Grandpa Harker made the deliveries. Sometimes I went with him. I enjoyed that.

I still was an avid participant in intramural football and basketball at school. In elementary and junior-high school, my small size was an advantage; I was hard to catch and too fast to keep up with. As I moved into high school though, my size became more of a disadvantage. My friends grew stronger, larger, and better coordinated. High-school sports were more sophisticated, less rough and tumble. But my enthusiasm was a great asset.

Most of my high-school memories came from football and basketball of the backyard variety. Any available daylight after school and work and on weekends, I spent on the Harkers' back lawn playing football, or on our concrete court shooting baskets with the neighborhood kids.

During my seven years in the Harker home, there were four more children added to the family: Steven, Kerry, Bret, and Jana. I learned to love them dearly, too. Each of these children became as special to me as my own brothers and sisters, and I enjoyed playing with them every chance I got. During my high-school days, I happily babysat for the Harkers whenever they went out. I simply enjoyed children. Oh, how these children enjoyed horsey rides on my back, especially Jana. Steve and Michael became all-American receivers on our back-lawn football team.

Michael and the younger Harker children would gather their friends about them, and I played with them by the hour. Usually I was quarterback for both sides, standing back to throw passes as the children scurried about to receive or defend against my aerial bombs. I tried to end each game with the score tied so that neither team was the loser. These were some of the happiest times of my high-school years. Some of the neighborhood kids my age became my close friends, like Glen Hilton, Roger Ford, Jerald Dixon, Danny Jones, and Paul Christensen.

My job at the store allowed me to make some spending money, some of which I sent home to my natural family. Also, I used part of it to help support a missionary from our Orem ward. But, before all this, 10 percent went to tithing. To this day, my decision to help Glen I have thought to be a good one. The things I learned at the store have stayed with me far beyond anything sports could have imparted.

On weekends, Glen loaded my bicycle carrier with flyers advertising his store. Then I peddled around town distributing advertisements of hardware-store sale items. All day I rode, all over Orem and Provo, delivering the flyers to many, many doorsteps.

About this time, Glen bought property several miles away. At all kinds of odd hours, either in the early morning at 1:00 A.M. or late at night, I often rode my bike over to water the alfalfa and other crops growing on the property. Also, it became my responsibility to feed and water the horses that grazed there. Between helping in the store and doing farm chores, I became more responsible. These things were in addition to helping around the house. I shall always be grateful to Glen, my foster father, for teaching me greater responsibility.

Twice a year, in April and October, the LDS Church held a three-day general conference in Salt Lake City. While a junior in high school, I developed a great desire to attend a session of this conference. I had watched general conference each six months on television and heard many inspired Church leaders speak. Some of these same leaders had come to visit the Orem area. I had even shaken their hands and briefly become acquainted with them. Now I wanted to visit the Tabernacle on Temple Square to hear them speak.

Not only had the desire to attend conference developed from viewing it on television, I also had a special experience during my sophomore year that greatly influenced me. That

year a group of us placement students were ushered into the
office of President David O. McKay, then the prophet and
president of the LDS Church. I shall never forget that special
moment. I had seen him on television, but this was the first
time I saw him face-to-face.

Secretly, I had wanted to meet President McKay. I had
seen his picture so many times in the Church magazines in the
Harker home. To actually be in his presence, to be captured by
his gentle charisma, was beyond my greatest dream. When I
shook his hand, the experience was nearly overwhelming. He
radiated strength and a wonderful, sweet spirit. He was tall,
white haired, handsome, square jawed, and broad shouldered;
he was impressive. Of his spiritual office I gained testimony,
knowing he was truly a prophet of God.

From then on, I had such a burning desire to attend general
conference. Not only did I desire to see and hear President
McKay again, but also I wanted to hear the other leading
Brethren of the Church speak. It would be much different, I
thought, than just listening to them on television.

One of the Brethren who was special to me was Elder
Spencer W. Kimball of the Council of Twelve Apostles. After
the visit with President McKay, we had gone into Elder Kimball's office. The experience was memorable as he hugged and
kissed each of us, then told us how special we were, being of
the house of Israel. He was very gentle, understanding, and
compassionate, as the Savior would have been.

At the time, I didn't realize what being of the house of Israel meant. Elder Kimball related to us the great promises in
store for the Indian nations since they were of the literal seed of
Israel. I had not known these things. It had a considerable influence on me. I could sense his great love for us. He told us we
had great potential, with capability to succeed in life as well as
in the Church. He admonished us to faithfulness on and off the
reservation. I believed all he said, and I mentally began to set
my course in faithfulness. Because of these special spiritual experiences, I became imbued with the desire to attend at least
one general conference one day.

Accordingly, I arose very early on a cool October morning,

slipped quietly out of the house, and hitchhiked the forty miles north to Salt Lake City to attend general conference by myself. As I walked toward the highway, my breath created puffs of fog. From the reservation experience, I knew something about hitchhiking, and this was back when it was safer to catch a ride than it is now. I remembered missing Church in Shiprock, so I was out by the highway early. On the way to Salt Lake, I was worried and concerned about what my foster parents might say, since they were unaware of where I had gone. I left everything in the hands of the Lord. It did not take long to catch a ride. Once I reached Temple Square, I had to stand in a line for what seemed like forever. Finally I was admitted with others into the Tabernacle. Just before the session began at ten o'clock, the last few remaining seats began to fill. I barely squeezed in before the doors were shut. Far to the back, on the top row of the balcony, is where I was finally perched. I was elated just to make it inside. Sitting there listening to the General Authorities gave me such a special spiritual feeling. It was a highlight of my youthful life.

As I looked at all the well-dressed people of the famous Mormon Tabernacle Choir, I thought of sheepherding in the Colorado mountains with my father. Sometimes we wore the same clothes for weeks on end. Now here I sat with a people who, by their own industry, were well clothed. I thought of the many times our family had been persecuted while working the pinto-bean fields of Colorado. If my own family, my own tribe, could have the wonderful opportunities I was having, maybe someday a Lamanite General Authority would sit up by the Tabernacle Choir as one of the leading Church officials. I knew that the gospel would need to be administered over all the earth, so great leaders would need to be raised up from the Lamanite and other cultures. At this time, our Prophet, the Twelve Apostles, and all the General Authorities were American Caucasians.

After a few General Authorities had spoken, again the thought came of a Lamanite General Authority, someone like Samuel, the Lamanite prophet in the Book of Mormon. Somehow, I could feel the presence of Samuel the Lamanite prophet, as well as Lehi, Moroni, Mormon, Nephi, and other great ancient Book of Mormon prophets and leaders near where I was sitting. As my thoughts soared, I could see a Lamanite leader addressing tens of thousands in an unseen audience, watching and listening by way of television and radio.

As I seriously pondered this thought, a special feeling poured over and through me. I wept with tears of joy, for I received a witness of the Spirit that the day would come when someone from the Lamanite nations would sit among the General Authorities, to join them in bearing special witness to the truths of the gospel of Jesus Christ.

At the conference's end, as I exited the Tabernacle, I was greatly inspired and uplifted. I was more fixed in my determination to abide in righteousness and to observe the commandments. To gain knowledge of the gospel and the Church became my aim. I left that day with a special desire and feeling to make available spiritual blessings to my people.

Even as I walked down Salt Lake's State Street to thumb a ride home, the desire to be spiritual and search the scriptures still did not leave. I watched the many glistening cars drive past and thought of the old buckboard wagon creaking down from our summer mesa toward the trading post. I realized that the only way for my people to overcome their afflictions and poverty was to adhere strongly to the spiritual values of the gospel. That the Lamanite would blossom as the rose was profoundly true. More than ever, I resolved to live my life in a way so as to be worthy to help my people grow in righteousness. I knew in my heart that the only way my people would blossom as a rose was through the gospel and through spiritual means. I realized that all the money in the world, all the money from the federal government, could not cause this to happen.

The ride back to Orem was long in arriving. Before I managed to get back, it was dark. In my youthful enthusiasm to attend conference, knowing Joan would have been aghast at the thought of my hitchhiking, I had slipped out that morning without requesting permission. They had worried and tried to locate me all day long. It was much like the time my own mother scolded me for having slipped out of the hogan to go to church in Shiprock. Joan was almost in tears, but she wasn't angry as much as she was frightened for my safety.

I received a well-deserved lecture, but Glen and Joan probably went easy on me. They could see that my experience had affected me profoundly. What could they really do? What could one say when a youth hungers for the word of God that badly?

I was so overjoyed with the conference experience. To never miss another Church meeting became my goal. To be careful in tithing, serving a mission, and doing all things willingly and obediently became as important as life itself. Oh, how I wanted to serve the Lord in whatever way I could! I desired very much to be an instrument in His hands to serve His children, especially His Lamanite children.

Not long after this experience, I felt the need to have a plan for my life. If the Lord had a purpose for me, as I knew He did, I wanted to do all in my power to be useful both to Him and to my fellowman. With this in mind, I sat in my room one day and outlined seven goals for myself.

First, it was my goal to graduate from high school. I was less than two years away from achieving this. I had full confidence that I would achieve this goal. Some of my brothers never went to school, and only one made it beyond high school.

Second, I wanted to serve a mission. I had a special desire at the time to serve a mission among my own people, the Navajos. If the Lord were to call me to another mission, I was willing to go, but still I had a peculiar feeling I would be called to serve among my own people.

Third, I would attend Brigham Young University and graduate after four years. College, I thought, was important, because I wanted someday to return to help my people. With a college degree, I would be better prepared to serve them professionally.

Fourth, when the time came, I did not just want any marriage, but to be married the Lord's way. I wanted to take someone I dearly loved to the temple to be sealed for time and all eternity.

My fifth goal was to earn both a master's and doctor's degree. To be of most service to my people, I had to be trained in the dominant culture in the highest level of qualification.

Sixth, I wanted to eventually return to the Navajo reservation to give a lifetime of service to my people. One of my dreams was to become a tribal chairman, to help make decisions for the Navajos. Along with this was a desire to help all Native Americans, because that is where the greatest needs were.

Last, and most important of all, my seventh goal was to lead my family back to the presence of God. I knew I could do this by keeping all the covenants and commandments and enduring to the end, no matter where I went. Whether on or off the reservation, I was determined to be a good Latter-day Saint. I was determined to accept all Church callings and to do my assignments diligently.

After I had written the seven goals, I knelt by my bedside and asked Heavenly Father to help me achieve them. I kept these goals with me at all times. With them in mind, I was determined to succeed. By now I had learned that in order to succeed in America, in the white man's world, I must compete.

During my junior year, I was one of two student chairmen for a committee of placement students who planned special activities for all Indian students in Utah County. I might add, we always invited all the Indian students, whether on placement or not.

In the fall of 1961, I helped plan a banquet and dance for which our special guest was to be Elder Spencer W. Kimball. Over eighty teenage placement students, from communities stretching from Gunnison south to Lehi north, were invited to attend this event in Orem. I remember well the article in the local paper, headlined "Kimball to Address Indian Students at Banquet Tonight." The article told about the Indian Student Placement Program in Utah and the purpose of the banquet and dance.

A highlight of the evening was the presentation of a scrapbook to Elder Kimball, who had responsibility for the Indian programs of the Church, including the Indian Student Placement Program. This book included a letter of tribute written to him by the placement students, their foster parents, and even a few of the natural parents. Students from a number of tribes were involved.

Clarence R. Bishop, then a director in the placement program, asked me to write a special letter to Elder Kimball in behalf of all the placement students. To do this was a great honor. For several days, I pondered and prayed. Just what I would write was extremely important. The following letter I penned for my fellow students to be presented to Elder Kimball. The letter also reflects my thinking as a seventeen-year-old Indian youth.

Dear Brother Kimball:

Isn't it a wonder how one can remember his past. It seems like it was only yesterday when I was nothing but a little Navajo shepherd boy tending the flock out on the lonely range, or out looking for horses for family use at home, or out thumbing a ride to get someplace. I can still imagine myself, a typical ten-year-old Navajo boy with no cares, worries, or desires, but willing to try anything. I enjoyed my carefree boyhood doing things that any Navajo boy would do. Then one summer the missionaries around that area introduced a program which we now know as the Indian Placement Program.

A lot of changes have taken place since then. For one thing, I am no longer a ten-year-old. I'm reaching an age where I must plan for the future and to start setting high ideals or goals for myself. The road ahead isn't going to be easy.

There is a saying that before a man can be a master, he must be a slave. Nothing can be accomplished unless a person sets goals for himself, goals that are high. Then he or she must work hard for them. Thirdly, comes stick-to-it-iveness. The third one is important. We must stick to or carry out what we set out to do in order to be successful. I have realized these things and have thought much about them.

I am thankful to you, Brother Kimball, and your fellow associates for setting up the Indian Placement Program.

Through this program, I have obtained a new outlook on life, as well as on the Church as a whole, with its many different organizations. Through the gospel, I have learned where I came from, why I am here, and where I am going. The program has offered many opportunities to me and it is up to me to take advantage of these opportunities. I must not, for a minute, take these opportunities for granted, but accept them as real opportunities and a challenge.

I believe that the key to this program is the foster parents. They have a definite role to play in caring for each of us in the program, just as our own natural parents would do. I believe the great reward or payoff is whether we in the program can meet and accept these challenges and opportunities and succeed in everything we do. If we make good, not only will we bring honor to ourselves, but also to our foster families, as well as to our own families on the reservation.

I have accepted and loved them as I would my own family. I try to do everything that is expected of me in helping them. I believe and know the Church to be true and that Joseph Smith was truly a prophet of God, as President David O. McKay now is. I believe and know that Jesus Christ is the Son of the Living God. I know that He is the same Christ who was foreordained to be the Savior of the world, the same Christ who was crucified for our sins whereby we will be resurrected and our sins forgiven because of His sacrifice. He is the same Christ who appeared to the Nephites and the same Christ who will come again during the Millennium to reign.

Again, I say thanks to you, Brother Kimball. Whether you know it or not, you have influenced my life deeply. My great desire is to be found worthy and able to fulfill a mission for the Church.

May the Lord bless you always.

Sincerely,

George P. Lee

Elder Kimball accepted this letter as though it were written by all the placement students. For us, the evening was the highlight of the year. The dinner was enjoyable and the evening delightful, especially since it was spent with one of the Twelve Apostles of the Lord.

Near the end of my junior year at Orem High, Glen and Joan helped me secure a job at the north rim of the Grand Canyon. The opportunity to work was a blessing. It didn't matter whether I made much money; at least I would be keeping busy. As I contemplated the notion, my memory drew back to my first summer off the placement experience. There really had not been that much to do around the hogan. As that summer wore on, the value of being engaged in work became more clear. As the healthy concept of work mentally formed, when I put the thought into action, then my summer softened. I did things for my family and parents. When they asked for someone to volunteer labor, there I was. I've never regretted it since.

Though the Grand Canyon job would not reward me enough to be listed in the Wall Street Journal as a financier, at least it was work. Besides the pay, there were other fringe benefits: the awesome beauty of the canyon, cooler summers, and hiking trips down to the raging Colorado River.

If I did not work at the Grand Canyon employment, what alternatives really were there? Going to my natural home would afford little or no employment, and any pay would surely be meager. Also, I had matured sufficiently to know that it was really idleness and boredom that had snuffed the initiative and spirit of my people.

My summer employer was the Union Pacific Railroad Company, which had operating rights for the resort lodges at the national parks in Southern Utah and at the North Rim of the Grand Canyon in Arizona. The latter area was most easily accessible through Southern Utah. After school let out, at a prearranged time, a group of students, including me, were picked up, then transported the three hundred miles southward to our new jobs.

The Grand Canyon defies description. It stands as a monumental reminder of our nothingness when compared with God's grandeur. As we gaze into its depths, we catch a glimpse

of the eternal supremacy and awesome power of Elohim. And
who shall stand against such majesty? Who shall bring forth
the words to describe the inscription of God so deeply etched
within the simplicity of Mother Earth?

All I can say is that the Grand Canyon is beautiful. And on
its northern rim, at a nearly nine-thousand-foot elevation,
sequestered in the dense pine, was the lodge where I worked.
The lodge was always closed during the winter because of
heavy snow, but during the summer, the sensate climate was
very appealing.

The lodge was located only a few feet from the edge of the
canyon gorge. Nearby were cabin-dormitories where the student workers lived during the summer. There were separate
dormitories—one for the boys, and one for the girls.

Directly across from the dorms, about ten miles away, on
the south rim, perspective-miniatured lodges could be seen
during the day, like little toy houses erected in a fantasyland.
The ink of dark night made the twinkling of distant lights,
those of the southern lodges, to look as though the heavens
had reclined along the canyon. With the immensity of the
canyon width, the shifting of the intervening space caused the
afterlights to glimmer like stars.

My pay was a whopping fifty-eight cents an hour. Though
it was not much compared to today's minimum wage, at least I
had a job. Room and board were included, so I was able to send
money to help my natural family. Also, I sent money to my
bishop in Orem for tithing, and a small amount to my foster
father to place in my mission savings account. Anything left
was scrupulously saved for clothes and school supplies needed
for the oncoming last year of school.

Although this was my first job away from my natural and
foster families, I still had a wonderful time and determined to
return again the next summer. I had fallen in love with the
peace and serenity of the area. And I was awed by the beauty of
the canyon itself and was afforded many opportunities to enjoy
it in quiet meditation. So went the summer between my junior
and senior high-school years.

My senior year in high school was my happiest year on the

placement program. Everything seemed to go smoothly, at my foster home, at church, and at school. Of particular interest were all my classes. I maintained a very high grade-point average. I also entered art contests, both in the Provo and Salt Lake areas. This gave me a sense of self-worth and brought honor to my alma mater, Orem High School.

Like many of my friends, I awaited graduation with eager anticipation. Most of the seven goals I had established during my junior year now seemed within my reach. I looked forward to attending Brigham Young University for a year until I was old enough to serve a mission.

Preceding the graduation exercise was an awards assembly in which several honors were bestowed upon me. The highest honor was being chosen as one of the five finalists from school to receive a special award sponsored by Utah Savings and Loan Association. The finalists were chosen for overall excellence in character, scholarship, leadership, and awareness of others. A scholarship to attend Brigham Young University was eventually awarded the winner. It was an honor and privilege to be among this elite group. However, my greatest joy at this assembly was in watching my classmates and friends receive awards

George with some of his artwork

for excellence, scholarship, leadership, and sports. These were the same people who had become so much a part of my life during the seven years on placement.

Commencement exercises took place on a Thursday evening, May 31, 1962, in the Orem High School auditorium. There were about 325 students in our graduating class. As I proudly walked forward to receive my diploma, I only wished my natural parents could be present. Oh, how I wished they understood the achievements I had made, of being able to come from a traditional Navajo background and from poverty to become a leader among Anglo students. They had no concept of this whatsoever. It was a miracle wrought by the Lord.

The early sixties were filled with happy days of white bobby socks, penny loafers, and saddle oxfords. Hope chests and chastity were still nostalgically cherished. Young brides dreamed of white, flowing wedding gowns with cream-colored rice sprinkled upon bannistered Church steps.

It was a time when marijuana was thought by most to be the name of a Mexican maiden. Throughout the nation, proms known as formals occupied the thoughts of high-school youth.

Classical virtue was the vogue. It was the day of "Lassie," "I Love Lucy," "The Honeymooners" with Ralph Cranston, and "Let's Go to the Hop." Frankie Avalon, Bobby Rydell, Fabian, and Elvis were on the turntables of all broadcasting radios. Saturday matinees, sock hops, and ponytails punctuated this period of American liberality. Ankle-length dresses still covered the consciousness of the nation's youth. But it was also the end of a national era of sweet innocence.

With the excitement of graduation over, a day or two later I was again on my way to the Grand Canyon. A classmate of mine went with me to work. I started out again as a kitchen helper and was determined to do a good job. I had a desire for promotion, which would bring a little more pay. From dishwasher, I gradually worked my way up to being a salad maker, then a cook's right-hand man. Finally, just over a month into my summer employment, I became a cook.

As a cook, I learned to trick-flip pancakes and to crack eggs with one hand. Soon, I found that cooking was really a form of art, and an enjoyable one at that. Dishes in all their variety I made, the hamburger, the omelet, the steak, and the pancake. These were satisfying to create and cook.

During our days off, I, along with others, occasionally hiked down the canyon. This time I had a camera to record the beauty I beheld. Also, I helped to produce skits for the tourists who came in droves—so many that we hardly had time to breathe between productions.

One day in mid-July, I was hard at work in the kitchen. Into my mind came a forceful impression to leave work and return home to my natural family. I felt I should spend some much-needed time there, and then prepare more earnestly for my approaching mission. Where I would get the money to fulfill a mission I did not know. The feeling I had received led me to believe the Lord would provide if I followed the Spirit by returning home. There I felt I would receive an answer.

This homing urge would not leave, so, after a few days of worry, I told my employer of my need to terminate my employment in order to return home. The head chef, not a member of the Church, strongly encouraged me to remain. He and I had developed a close friendship and enjoyed each other's company in the kitchen. He offered to increase my pay if I stayed, but I was too greatly prompted to leave for home.

Coming to a resolution, I informed my employer and friends of my intent to terminate in the middle of July, about two weeks away. The evening before I left, my friends threw a party in my behalf. In their kindness, they fixed a nice box lunch for me to eat on the way. Also, they had all chipped in money for my mission, put it in an inconspicuous envelope, and then placed the envelope in the bottom of my lunch box, expecting me to find it later. They wanted it to be a delightful surprise and did not inform me of what they had done.

Early in the morning after my last day of work, I struck out, hit the highway, and began to hitchhike. It was a long time before I caught a ride. In fact, I must have trudged a good ten miles before I snagged a ride to the Jacob's Lake Junction. From there, one road led northward to Utah, the other east, then south into Arizona. I got off at this junction. Since it was well past noon, I sat down under a shade tree and proceeded to eat the lunch my considerate friends had prepared. I ate a tasty sandwich and a delicious apple and then threw the box, with the remainder of its contents, into a nearby trash can. Some of the lunch was still in the box, the part that covered the money. Though the lunch was good, I was not too hungry, and so I would not have to carry the rest of the food along with my heavy luggage, I tossed it away.

About six months later, while at Brigham Young University, I bumped into one of my friends who had contributed some of the money in the envelope. Upon finding out what I had done, I almost became sick. I felt so bad for my caring friends, knowing the trouble they had taken to collect money for my mission. And then I had just thrown it away. It still bothers me to think about it.

Anxious to get moving, I picked up my luggage and jogged along the edge of the highway heading east. The ride came sooner than before, and three hours later I was in Tuba City, Arizona, a little town on the western boundary of the Navajo reservation. All that area was new and strange to me. Certainly I did not know a soul. Facing me was the Tuba City Junction—two possible routes diverged, each a possible way for reaching home. Home—a kind thought that drew a mental image of the volcanic Shiprock monument.

Tuba City hosted a small service station. At this station, I reviewed a map and realized there were yet many miles to travel. The shorter distance, northeast through Kayenta, was an option. Nevertheless, I opted for the longer route southeast through Window Rock, Arizona, and Gallup, New Mexico. This route would take me through the Hopi reservation. The roads were all paved that way and would be more heavily traveled. That meant easier rides; anyway, I hoped it did.

Having made the decision, I wearily hefted my suitcases and started walking. Still I headed east. I had not had a drink or eaten. I was tired, thirsty, and not yet completely acclimated to the heat of the lower elevation. I agonized in the scorching sun. I thought of the times I had worked the pinto-bean fields in Colorado with my family. The sun bore down then too. That thought carried me forward to my family. It only made the circumstances worse to think of home, of the many significant memories attached to the cozy hogan. After this thought, I noticed my sweating palms. Blisters were beginning to form on the calloused pads at the base of my fingers. A great, depressive loneliness enveloped me.

Darkness was approaching. I was two hundred miles from home. I had never felt so alone in all my life, not even during my three nights alone with the sheep in the overwhelming mountains of Colorado. At least I had the dogs for company and comfort then. Now I was completely alone. After standing for quite a while trying to thumb rides, I started to walk again.

Soon I approached the Hopi village of Moenkopi. Suddenly someone was yelling and whistling from a distance. After collecting my thoughts, I saw a man hollering at me to come over. I sat my luggage by the roadside, not wanting to carry it back and forth, and walked the short distance between us to see what he wanted.

"Are you hungry?" he asked in a friendly, concerned tone.

"Yes," I gladly responded, knowing what he was going to offer. "Very hungry."

What words of charity he had brought forth. I was indeed hungry, also tired, thirsty, a long way from home, and, up till then, friendless.

"Come home and eat with my family. You look like you could use a meal." He said this with smiling kind eyes.

"You won't have to ask me twice!" I said appreciatively.

I retrieved my suitcases and followed the humble Hopi man back to his home. The dinner was delicious; it was everything I expected it would be.

"Where are you going?" he inquired, resting his chin on his hand.

"I'm trying to get home. I'm going through Window Rock and Gallup."

"Why don't you go through Flagstaff? I will take you to Cameron and from there you can catch a bus."

This sensitive man must have caught the idea of my financial state. He did not say anything then, though. I agreed to do

as he suggested; it was the least I could do considering his kind
hospitality. When we reached Cameron, twilight was announced by the evening star. There we discovered no bus
would be leaving until morning. The Hopi man turned to me.

"I'll rent a room for you," he stated, and halfway through
his words handed me enough money for a bus ticket and food.
"Perhaps we may meet again. Good-bye."

Then he left.

Was this really happening to me?

Early the next morning, I was on my way. The actual travel
time to Shiprock was over seven hours. I spent many more
hours waiting in bus stations as I made transfers in Flagstaff and
Gallup. Once I reached Shiprock, hitchhiking the remaining
sixteen miles home would be easy.

Throughout my long day of riding and waiting, I had a lot
of spare time to think. I thought about my whole reason for
existence in that single July day. My whole life flashed before
my mental eyes.

Someone had helped me—a complete stranger, unknown
to me and to my family. He also belonged to another tribe with
whom the Navajos felt uneasy. But there I had been, in his
home, and a recipient of his generosity. Then I remembered
the promise.

A patriarch, a holy man of the Church, laid his hands on
my head to give me a patriarchal blessing. In my blessing, I was
told I was a descendant of Joseph who was sold into Egypt and
of Lehi who led my people from Jerusalem to America. I was
also given a promise that friends would be raised up in time of
need throughout my life to assist me. I was overwhelmed. The
goodness of the Lord burned in my mind. I resolved once again
to keep the commandments and do everything I could to be
found worthy.

In high school, many people had assisted and helped me,
both academically and spiritually. It had been a blessing to
work beside my foster father in the business and at the farm.
While I was on placement, Michael snuggled his way into my
heart, and I grew to love and have an interest in children. This
interest still remains part of me today.

I then reminisced over my three junior-high-school years—about my many friends among both students and faculty who had been raised up to give me valuable experiences in leadership. (Who knows, perhaps I was raised up to bless their lives as well.) At Lincoln Junior High, I learned the skill of effective speaking, as well as the ability to organize and activate others to productive work. I'll never forget the student support I received in junior high; how the students stood behind me, a person of a different race and culture, and elected me again and again as their president. Their generous empathy for me is a pure statement in human kindness, one completely lacking prejudice.

Next my mind raced back through the various experiences I had encountered in my foster home—loving foster parents and their many friends and relatives who I consider my own. I thought of the persistent, childlike kindness of little Michael that coaxed me out of my shell, and of Brent, my foster mother's brother, who was a true friend of my own age. I thought of my teachers and friends at Geneva Elementary School. How the memories of my life flooded my thoughts in sweetness.

Finally, as I neared our summer hogan, I thought of each member of my natural family and how much they meant to me. Their way of life is hard and confusing. While they tried to hold to old ways, the twentieth-century world swirled almost viciously around them. I then vowed to do all within my power to help them.

How? Education was the answer. A mission first, and then I would go to college. I again resolved to gain the necessary university degrees to best serve my family and people.

Darkness now rested upon the beautiful land of *Dineh* as I ran the several hundred yards up the gentle slope to the summer hogan. Yelping and yapping, a frenzied challenge to a forgotten visitor, the family dogs suspiciously greeted me. Several soon began wagging their tails as they recognized my voice. The sentry dogs were followed by bright-eyed children who raced toward me in happy profusion. They grabbed my luggage with slender, dusty arms and began speaking to me as if I'd been gone only a few days. Inside the hogan, Mother sat patiently waiting to greet me. Although her welcome was reserved and polite, as is the way of my people, in her eyes I could sense her joy.

I walked over and embraced her gently, and tears rose in our eyes as mother held son. It was a most joyous occasion. I did the same thing with my little brothers and sisters. I wept because of their destitute condition. Their smiles seemed out of place with the dirty rags that draped their thin bodies. They looked so wretched.

This was home. Regardless of how often I would leave, I knew I would return many times. This was my family, and I was Navajo. Still, I would leave again, after a short time of refreshing, to seek my destiny, a man of two worlds.

15

OF TWO WORLDS

As a snowshoe rabbit changes color with the seasons, from the brown of spring and summer to eventual winter white, so I made the transition from the Navajo culture to that of the Anglo. Every fall found me preparing to leave the reservation for Utah. Late spring found me preparing to return to the reservation. This continued until high-school graduation.

For the return to the reservation, I had to reorient my thinking, behavior, and life-style to function in my native culture. Initially these adjustments were difficult and almost immobilizing; however, there was one key to survival—endurance. Through painstaking thought, which was the basis of my endurance, my mind and soul were stretched into larger proportions. Since the Navajo culture was primary in my life, my adjustment from the Anglo to the Navajo culture was less difficult than the other way around. In time, even this seemed to matter little as I began to better act the part of a cultural-chameleon, camouflaged upon a high branch of bicultural integration. In short, I had discovered how to navigate equally well, and better than ever before, within the confines of either culture. The pain of change lessened afterwards.

Many Indian students have traumatic difficulty in making

such transitions, whether on placement or in life itself. Some simply cannot deal with the stress. The inability to adapt has had a very bad effect on their self-esteem. But exposure to a new culture can be very rewarding. Even those whose resiliency is not sufficient for such an experience at least want to change. And those who are self-motivated appreciate the opportunity enough to learn to function in the new culture and even to help others.

The changes I had to make in Utah were easier because of the love, concern, and appropriate discipline given by my foster parents. While in their home I felt needed and wanted. From the beginning until my graduation from high school, I had an all-around positive experience.

It would be hard to believe that there has been an Indian placement student who has not undergone homesickness. I was no exception. But the homesickness was lessened by my considerate and genuine foster parents. I became loyal to my foster family. In turn, Glen, Joan, and Michael accepted me fully as a true member of their family. It was always Glen, Joan, George, and Michael. And in that last sentence, Michael himself would be the first to place my name in a position just before his own. You see, I really am his big Indian brother. What's more, in my heart, he verily is my little brother. There is nothing I would not do to help him if he were to need my assistance. In the Harker home, I was no stranger; I never went hungry or thirsty, and I always dressed like the best of my schoolmates.

Soon, my resistance to the Harkers' love and affection lowered. It became Mom and Dad, instead of Joan and Glen—and sometimes I even initiated the embrace upon one or both of them. (I could tell the first time I did so it greatly pleased them.) To be warm and affectionate, as well as to demonstrate these feelings, became part of my personality.

During my summer stays at home with my natural family, after I had learned to cope with reverse homesickness, I often thought about the little kindnesses the Harkers had shown me. As I did so, sometimes tears flowed down my face. I pondered how those small moments of attention sustained my self-confidence: how the corner of the bedspread was neatly done, the full garbage had disappeared, the tube of toothpaste had been rolled from the bottom, my haircut looked neat, and a hundred other compliments brought forth my deepest respect toward the Harkers. Every report-card day, especially after I had put forth my best effort that semester, I made a beeline right for the Harker home. My good grades were as much for them as for me. Joan would embrace me and give me a fond kiss. This would last only one or two seconds, but all the semester's academic struggle was worth it. Her next step was to show the card to Glen. His wide smile almost brought me off the floor. How I enjoyed bringing honor to the family I dearly cherished.

As March came each year, Joan made sure I had a birthday party. The first one she threw for me was a surprise. I had never dreamed of such a thing on the reservation. Because of the extreme poverty in my natural situation back home, birthday parties were foreign to us. I'd lie in bed at night, wondering when the dream would end. I even prayed to Heavenly Father for it not to end. I was not thinking solely about the material aspects of my new home. As I lay there, the detergent smell of the crisp sheets reminded me of the neatness and cleanliness of my current circumstances—clean sheets, clean-living foster parents, clean neighborhood, clean friends, and clean thoughts.

The Harkers constantly encouraged me to write to my natural family, and they always seemed interested in my family and in the Navajo people in general. In their love for me, they were firm but never domineering or overbearing. When I needed discipline, it was given. Their concern for my growth and development was genuine.

Of course, things were not rosy all the time. Our relationship had some trials, and stresses. Our one major disagreement came one time when I felt the Harkers were overly strict. Through my boyish eyes I saw the parents of my friends as more lenient.

It was one of those situations in which no one is really to blame, but which arises mostly from a lack of communication. Anyway, I became angry. For some time I did not say a word. As much as possible I avoided my foster parents. I didn't even eat with them. From what I understand, many patient foster parents and students have had a similar experience. This very thing, if faced by both the foster parents and student, is fertile ground for the sprouting of wisdom.

During this difficult time, one night I decided to hitchhike home. Although I knew I should face my problems and work things out, the easy way of running turned from mental plan to physical action. Many placement students believe this false creed: "There is never anything so threatening or great that you cannot run from it."

During the night, while the family was asleep, I quietly sneaked out the back door. For some time I walked toward State Street, and once there, I turned southward toward Provo, hoping to catch a ride from there. Soon I was in the vicinity of the high school.

Many things raced through my mind—foster family, life, God, church, the caseworker, and my natural family. Then, as I walked my hostility off, I mentally wound down. Finally, the right thing to do lodged in my thoughts—pray! I would ask Heavenly Father for help. Nearby was a grove of trees. Into this I entered. I fell to my knees and emptied my troubled heart.

Immediately after my prayer, the feeling came to return to the Harker home, that it was not wise to continue my night-time plan. I had no success in catching a return ride and ended up walking all the way. When I arrived home, I silently slipped into the garage, found a place to curl up, and remained there the whole night. At first light, I slipped back into my bedroom.

Things still did not work out between the Harkers and myself. Then the caseworker showed up on the scene, and I went to his home while things cooled down. I was there about two weeks before returning to the Harkers. I returned with a broken heart.

All of us felt miserable. We apologized and forgave one another and discussed the problem at length. For a short while, I was really hard on myself for my part in our differences, but with time that faded.

I'm very grateful to have turned away from the hitchhiking plan. So thankful am I to have listened to the Spirit in that grove of trees. I'm glad I faced my problems instead of running. What a lesson in maturity!

After this incident, we never again had a serious problem. Through the duration of my high-school experience, the Harkers and I had a most enjoyable time.

We had an abundance of trust and love between us; the fact, I think, that I was Indian seldom entered their minds. As for my own thoughts, I gradually forgot to think of the Harkers as white people. I was completely immersed in the Harker family, and I loved them as dearly as my own.

My adjustment in going back to the reservation was sometimes difficult. In contrast to the lovely home, with plenty to eat and a full wardrobe, was the one-room, dirt-floored hogan. It was like going from space age to stone age. Once back on the reservation, I was without most modern conveniences. Instead of well-balanced, nutritious meals, I now ate prairie dog or mutton stew. At first, changing back and forth in my eating habits was easy, but as I grew older and became more particular, I found it harder to enjoy the change. However the benefits of learning to change far outweighed the small inconveniences.

From year to year, however, the transition occurred almost without thought. When each school year closed, I prepared to return much as someone might pass from one room to another. The transitional sting was gone, but the scenery continued to change. The change became a season of peace, of flowing beauty. As much as I used to anticipate returning on placement to bask in modern luxury, now I also longed to return to my beautiful desert home, to herd sheep and goats. I wanted to hear the skinny dogs yap, to look for horses, to haul water and wood, and to run freely while jumping clumps of Navajo tea bush. I looked forward to the odor of sheep and horses, the desert rain, and the aroma of fry bread and mutton stew. I was developing into a new person, one with greater stamina for change, and one with deeper ability to see the constancy of movement within life.

With the maturing of intercultural thought, I did not mind the absence of electricity, running water, or toilet facilities. I

George as a sophomore in
high school

didn't get frustrated with not taking a bath all summer, for I understood our scarcity of water. I was more in contact with a cross-cultural reality, one that began to move me beyond the restrictional traits of either. After a restless night or two, I quickly adapted to the sheepskin bed spread on the dirt floor of the hogan. And when I returned to placement, it took only a few days to readjust to the soft, plush bed.

As I had to adjust to my natural home, so I had to adjust to the Harker home. Electric can opener, television, running water, top-of-the-line camping equipment, silverware, and blinking Christmas lights were part of a new reality that refined my view of the world. As I began to appreciate the simplicity of my own culture, the impact of Anglo culture, particularly its materialism, began to depreciate. I was not leaning with the gathering rebellion against materialism of the early sixties. By no means was I bohemian. But, rather, I began to fill with the buoyancy of understanding that came with innocent experience instead of perversion. I did not see materialism and immaterialism as opposites. Rather, my opinion was that both had a place in joy and happiness and the pursuit thereof.

It always seemed good to be out in the wide-open spaces, to get away from the congested city life where homes were built one right after the other. (I may even have felt this way living in a pueblo somewhere in the southwest.) The peaceful, serene beauty of the expansive desert appealed to the vastness of my Navajo innateness. I was born into a culture of living in harmony with nature. Because of this culture, the southwestern Indians fathom and fully appreciate the workings of Mother Earth. Their eyes have been taught attentiveness to even the smallest particle of the natural environment. The teachings passed to me were to respect and reverence the beauty of creation. Because of these teachings, my people love the land and are a land-based people. If offered a choice between money and land, a Navajo would always choose land, no matter the amount of money offered.

For the traditional Indian, religion is not a just-on-Sunday practice. The worldly view of religion seems to be formed around buildings, programs, and once-a-week devotion. Not that buildings are not important, for shelter is a must, but to emphasize them as the saving aspect of religion is incorrect. To the American Indian, religion is everything. This definition is simple yet complex to describe with mere words. To adequately define religion, as an Indian believes it to be, almost requires tossing out the word *religion* itself. Because the original meaning of the word has been obscured by time and misapplication, we must abandon its current usage to fully understand the Native American concept of religion.

As Native Americans, we understand spiritual fulfillment as our comprehension about land, animals, and people broadens. This is not to say Indians think pantheistically, or that they believe that God is in everything and everything is God, as some anthropologists seem to think. More proper is it to say that we feel the primary influence emanating from the Great Spirit into all things; it is the combining oneness of total nature. It is that background influence that pervades all life,

either animate or inanimate, with which an Indian com-
munes. My people, the Navajos, are this way. They strongly
believe that sickness indicates disharmony with nature, and
the traditional Navajo religion teaches that something must be
done to restore the harmony. Some have called this manner of
thinking amoral. But it is highly moral, deriving the sense of
right and wrong from without the individual.

To a Navajo, religion is life itself, with the major purpose
of being in tune with nature. This includes, of course, everything in the universe. It comprehends every living thing,
things that are in the earth and all things that are on the earth.
Personally, I understand this aspect of Navajo culture as proper
and good. Those who have not developed this already in their
hearts would progress spiritually by doing so.

I came to see that I could adopt the good things and reject
the bad things of both cultures, but at times it was necessary to
mentally switch to a set of values that applied only to one culture or the other. However, as the more transcendent understanding came, I developed a higher set of values that would
allow me to work in both cultures.

I was able to acquire high self-esteem in the Navajo culture
and also in the competitive Anglo world. Therefore I was able
to make the necessary and proper adjustments while crossing
between the two cultures, and I was comfortable and at ease in
both worlds.

If I had not had sufficient self-esteem in the Anglo culture,
I would not have been able to function in it. An Indian must
have adequate self-regard in his own native culture as well as in
the dominant culture in order to transcend both. Many Indians have high self-esteem within their own culture but feel
worthless and inadequate and lack positive self-image in the
non-Indian world. Do I dare say it? They have difficulty functioning in a dominant society. That is why the society is dominant, for it dominates the cultural self-esteem of the lesser
Indian society. The domination itself may be the lesser part of
the controlling society. So, the dominant society rules more by
majority than by actual right. I intend this not as criticism, but
as an insight that might be used to advantage for those lacking

proper self-esteem within the domain of the dominant. This even has application for personal relationships.

Those who lack confidence in both cultures might be classified as lost between two worlds. Some indians may completely reject their traditional upbringing in favor of living or mimicking the dominant culture. Often they encounter severe emotional difficulties when returning to the reservation. They are lost between two worlds.

My experiences on the placement program, living with a white foster family in a predominantly white society, helped me bridge the gap. The placement experience gave me the opportunity to develop my confidence and high self-worth. I now appreciate cultures other than my own, and I have come to respect, and even to love, the non-Indian and his culture.

Another positive effect of my placement experience was the realization that I was a United States citizen as well as a Native American. Knowledge of this combined heritage strengthened my self-image. This understanding has helped me to become a more balanced person.

Because I was able to function so well in the dominant culture did not mean I had lost touch with the Navajo culture. I do not espouse the idea that having benefitted from the best of both worlds makes me more like the Anglo. It does not mean that I have lost my Indianness or that I have devalued my own native customs. Many placement students have returned to the reservation only to be called "apples," the implication being that they are red on the outside, but inside are white. It is a cruel term applied by misdirected people. If the term "apple" is applied, let us think further about it than in an elementary-school sense. Yes, an apple may be white inside, but we sometimes cast it aside before realizing that the seeds in its core are very, very brown. Childish thinking seldom has the depth to understand the regions of the deep inner self; the hunger of a childish intellect goes no deeper than the skin itself.

I believe that Indians can take the best from both worlds and make a greater contribution to society. In the long run, they will become better people for it. It is possible for Indians to acquire the skills, knowledge, and even material possessions of the Anglo culture without sacrificing their native customs or innate feelings. More than anything else, the Indian Student Placement Program enabled me to acquire skills, knowledge, education, and even the material possessions of the dominant culture without sacrificing beneficial Navajo customs. I did not at any time feel a clash between my Indianness and my Anglo-ness. That an Indian life-style should replace my Anglo life-style was of no concern, and neither was I threatened that my Anglo life-style would overrule my Indian ways.

If Native Americans are unable to make the proper mental adjustments, they will have greater difficulty living in both worlds and will continue in low self-esteem. The counterparts to low self-esteem are personal problems, discouragement, and depression. Feelings of inadequacy lead to attitudes of racial inferiority. These attitudes manifest themselves in a militant spirit, or most of all, in turning to the bottle. People with these attitudes may have high self-esteem in their native culture, but their self-image will be low and challenged in the Anglo culture.

With the frequent changing back and forth from one culture to the other, I acquired attitudes and behaviors that allowed me to comfortably function in both worlds so that both cultures provided good health, physical well-being, love, and acceptance, along with emotional stability.

During my first two or three years on placement, the changes in my personality sometimes caused conflicts at home during the summer. My family thought placement was steering me away from our native customs. They thought I was too much a white man. They kept telling me to act according to the culture I was born into, to leave off the white man's world and religion.

My family and relatives found it strange to see me hitchhiking over twenty miles to attend church. It was less than amusing to them when I would no longer participate in native ceremonies, and they were concerned about my loss of interest in traditional activities, such as squaw dances, sings, and even rodeos.

The Native American Church was another big issue. My

family wanted me to join and participate in that church. My parents told me it was a church organized strictly for the Indian people. This church uses the narcotic cactus buds called peyote for their sacrament. Use of this bud induces hallucinations. During my growing years, our neighbors and my family entered this particular religious movement.

My older brothers and sisters ridiculed me because I would not partake of alcohol, coffee, tobacco, or peyote. From the training I'd received in Utah, I understood these things to be harmful to the body. Although I wanted to be part of my family, they held certain beliefs that I had to set aside.

I really did not have anything against the native Navajo customs. In fact, I still have love and respect for many of the beliefs of my people, which is difficult to convey to my family. Nothing serious ever developed between my family and me over cultural differences; nevertheless, these small differences were noticeable and occasionally came to the surface between us. This caused a little friction.

Unfortunately, after my initial years on placement, I was guilty of making light of Navajo beliefs and taboos. For instance, my people believe that anything struck by lightning should not be touched. On occasion, I made light of this belief by deliberately touching things that had been struck by lightning. Also, the Navajos are careful to not leave pieces of clothing or nail clippings where evil-thinking people or witches can grab them to bewitch someone. I made fun of this. At other times, I made light of a coyote running in front of us, the nighttime hoot of an owl, or whistling in the dark.

During one summer home, after my second year on placement, my brother Bob and I did something to really test some of the things we'd been taught. My mother had always told us that monsters foraged and lurked on the highest point of Sleeping Ute Mountain. The mountain, when viewed from the highway between Blanding and Bluff, Utah, resembles an Indian in full headdress lying on his back. We were told never to go up there. I talked Bob into going up to this mountain with me. We even took a .22 caliber rifle in case monsters were there. Bob was scared to death. I was, too, but I was determined to see if the monsters were there or not. Halfway up the mountain, Bob informed me that that was as far as he was going. Nothing I could say would convince him to continue, so I continued on my own. I made it to the top but could find no monsters there.

When my mother found out what we had done, she gave us a real scolding. It did not even help for me to tell her there were no monsters up there. She would not listen. Out of respect for Mother, I did not go up there again.

Of course, my family made light of some of the things I'd learned as a Latter-day Saint, especially my abstinence from alcoholic beverages, cola drinks, and profanity.

The use of alcohol may be widespread among my people, but not everyone uses it. If more than 50 percent of national automobile fatalities are caused by drunken drivers, that indicates widespread abuse of alcohol even within the Anglo society. But, admittedly, there is a problem with alcohol on the reservation, as elsewhere.

Most Indians do not drink for the taste of liquor or for social benefits. They generally want to escape from a slow-paced life and to ease cultural conflicts.

Among my people, drinking alcohol is not a slow, relaxing affair. The liquor is gulped down immediately. For two reasons this is done: (1) they want to inebriate their culturally pained minds as soon as possible, and (2) the drinking habit stems from the days when it was illegal for an Indian to drink, either off or on the reservation. For that reason, not to get jailed for alcohol possession, the drink was hastily swallowed. Even today, though drinking is lawful off the reservation and prevalent on the reservation, my people still have ingrained in their subconscious minds to drink fast before the booze is taken by the law.

When I refused to drink with my brothers and sisters, they were offended and said I was not trying to be part of the group. The Navajo cultural expectation is for the group to stay together. If one group member differs, he is ridiculed until he capitulates to what the group desires. One must not rise above or strive beyond what the group is willing to permit.

In many ways this expectation is good, particularly when the group has good goals in mind. In past years, clans united to work field after field until a corn harvest was finished. They did this as a group instead of demanding that each family harvest its own crop.

Being a member of my family, I was expected to drink like everyone else. I was expected to frequent the Gallup slum row, and to involve myself in other unwholesome activities. When I did not do these things, my family, friends, and neighbors increased the pressure, thinking I might give in. When I still refused, they became angry. Sometimes they actually ganged up to fight me.

As time passed, they realized I was serious about not drinking. Eventually I was left alone, and in time my former persecutors began to respect me for the things I believed. Yet, I know I could not expect my brothers and sisters to understand my position fully. There is no hatred, but only love, in my heart for them. I just wanted them to respect my right not to drink, as I respected their right to do so.

I was witness to the day my three younger brothers began drinking. They were very young then. Not long after this, one of them had too much to drink one cold day. During the night, he wandered away from the hogan and was found the next morning frozen to death upon the lonely desert.

Alcohol has brought tragedy upon tragedy to my family. In addition, the bottle has destroyed the ambition and initiative my family members might have had. Total chaos and frustration were the contents of the liquor bottle. And my family drank it right down.

Alcohol robbed my family of education, vocational skills, and employment. In marriages, alcohol continued to devastate, causing marital clashes and poor examples for friendless children. Alcohol snuffed out the lives of my older sister and her husband. Eight children at that time were left without father or mother. As these eight grew older, instead of the milk bottle, there was the alcoholic beverage. Finally, it took the life of a beautiful fourteen-year-old niece and a handsome nineteen-year-old nephew. Whatever mortal potential they had is now gone. Another older brother left his family, and nine more nephews and nieces grew up without parents. Instead of nutritious meals, they were raised on paint-sniffing and alcohol. There were days when they didn't eat. Their lives were a total wreck. What a tragedy! There was nothing I could do for them but cry and pray.

Alcohol led to other habits, such as glue- or paint-sniffing. These and similar bad habits soon occupied most of the days for these beautiful young people, the hope of the Navajo nation.

Many summers ago, upon returning home, I sensed something wrong as I approached our hogan. Things just did not seem right. The usual barking of dogs running out to greet me was absent. From where I was, the summer shadehouse appeared deserted. No one was walking about the place. It was as still as death.

As I cautiously turned the corner into full view of the hogan and the surrounding area, my suspicions were justified. What I saw was worse than death. There in the shade of the hogan sat many of my nieces and nephews, helpless, with little to eat. Old rags soaked in paint covered half their faces; their minds were somewhere else. Some of them had also been drinking. I stood there in deep grief and cried. All I could do was encourage them to do better. I knelt down and poured out my heart to God for them.

What did I have? I was just an Indian like the rest of them, poor and penniless. Yes, I was wearing fine clothes brought from Utah, but that is all I had. Would no one else feel the despair for my family and people? With tears flooding my eyes, I just stood in a state of shock. "O Great God and Creator, hear our cries and grief. Hast thou forsaken thy Indian children? How long must Indian Israel suffer?" If I had any money, at least I would have given them temporary relief. Their awful plight and wretched condition has given me the motivation to move on to greater heights. With God's help, I hope to help them someday.

I resolved never to use liquor or drugs or to slip down to that level. I prayed to someday have the means and knowledge to reach out and lift them from the treachery of their circumstances. I prayed "O Great Spirit, how long must my people suffer! How long must America's Indian children struggle and cry in vain?"

I could still hear the voice of my father: "George, help me! I don't like what I am doing. I don't like to drink. I am helpless and have become a slave to it!" These same pleas, my family gnashed into my hurting ears. All I had was prayer; my entire heart was full to bursting in their behalf, like that of Enos of old in the Book of Mormon. I tried to get help from government agencies and from local missionaries, but the existing resources were not much help. In those days, alcoholism was not even understood as a disease, but as evidence of weak wills and minds.

I always remembered the expression on my father's face, the painful times when he pleaded with me to somehow help him overcome alcoholism. I had always been helpless. I was too young and immature. In my heart, though, was the remembrance of my father's desperate imploring. Even when I thought about the good times, they were always counterbalanced with the sorrowful image of a pleading alcoholic.

After I had filled my first mission and had later received both a bachelor's and master's degree, I had occasion to give my father the help he had requested long ago. Then, after I had seen his constant battle with the bottle, a solution appeared very complex, but now it occurred to me that my father should simply make up his mind to quit. On one of my trips to New Mexico to visit my family, I decided to tell him just that.

The thought of assuming responsibility to tell my father collided with my Navajo cultural upbringing. As a youth, I had been taught to honor my parents by always being their son, believing that their wisdom would be in excess of mine. As with most tribal customs, I had been taught to profoundly respect my elders, always receiving counsel at their hands. Even among the elders of our clan, my father was respected for his wisdom and for his ability to heal and counsel others. By Indian standards, even though I may have had high white man's degrees, I was considered young and still learning. I knew in certain respects that I would be approaching a very traditional father with counsel I had come to understand as effective.

Because I loved my father more than I did traditional family roles and expectations, I decided to tell him my feelings about how he could help himself. Besides, he had asked me on several occasions earlier. I did not have the answer then, but now, by the Spirit, I did. My father, despite his strict Navajo upbringing, always had an ability to step outside cultural bounds in order to consider what might be truth.

"Father, I want to talk to you about alcohol," I began.

"Yes, my son. What is it you want to say?" And in asking this, he gave me his attention while his attitude was one of listening with respect. His dark eyes were filled with love as they focused upon my face. I knew I could talk to him about anything. I also understood that I had to use Indian directness, because beating around the bush was not good Native American policy.

"This drinking problem. Why don't you admit that you are an alcoholic, then commit yourself to overcome it immediately. Just keep telling yourself you can do it. I know you have the will power to stop. I know with God's help you can conquer alcohol now. Decide now that you will never take another drink. Father, I know you can do it. I will pray for you. If you will help yourself, with God's help, you can do it."

My father was looking deep into my soul now, feeling to discern if I was sincere in my counsel. After he had determined I was, he responded, "I know that what you are telling me is true. I promise you and the Great Spirit that I will not touch another bottle. I give you my word on this. It is the only answer."

From that day on, my father never touched alcohol again. He kept his promise. However, the many previous years of binge drinking had taken their toll. He was never to recover sufficiently to live in good health. Alcohol had destroyed his liver and severely damaged other vital organs in his body, and he had terminal cancer. The last few months of his life, he was in excruciating pain. No amount of medication seemed to help. He couldn't eat or sleep.

When I was mission president at Holbrook, I received news that my father was dying. He had begged me several times previously to quit being mission president so I could live with them. That he needed me by his side was more important to him than my mission. Because of my commitment to spread the gospel among my people, I could not honor his wish, and somehow I knew he understood.

I did leave the pressing duty of the mission to visit my family for one day. Father's condition had worsened. In the back of my mind was a notion to stay as long as my father needed me. When I arrived home, I found my father in critical condition. He was pleased that I had come. When I looked upon him in his emaciated condition, my heart wrenched inside. The love I had for my father was very deep and uncommon. I knew he did not have long. Even in his intense suffering, he spoke of others, his family and friends. We talked and shared our love that day. Finally he asked for a priesthood blessing.

With tearful eyes, I laid my hands upon his head, and when I did so the Spirit of the Lord came over me. I was impressed to ask the Lord to take him so that he would no longer suffer and endure the crosses of this world. The next day he passed on to the next life. I was saddened to see him leave, but the family's worry for his suffering was eased. We had a beautiful funeral and burial service for him.

It would be easy to condemn my father for his drinking, but I don't. A medicine man is an extra-sensitive person who gives up a comfortable life-style in order to heal and help others. They are always on call, and most never say no to those who ask for help. When they heal someone, they give of their own energy and spirit to do so. After a healing has taken place, the medicine man needs time to recuperate, to recharge through prayer. These men are possessed of great charity for those around themselves. They are truthful, meek, and humble. Time after time of healing others can leave the medicine man vulnerable to considerable pain because he has given so much of himself. It is a conscious decision to give up part of oneself for another. My father was filled with this Christ-like compassion.

I have learned to tolerate what alcohol has done on the reservation. That I approve of it, no, absolutely no! But what can I do alone? I hate the sin of alcohol, but I have great compassion for the user. Throughout the years, I have observed how my people, the first Americans, have become the last Americans in terms of employment, education, health, sanitation, income, and every other standard. They are far behind the general population of our country. When a person's emotional, social, mental, and physical needs are not being met, he will do anything for survival in those areas. In the case of the Navajo, some of them tried to literally fight back, ill equipped and ill educated. They failed. Yet again and again they strove for the best interests of the tribe. Not only were they ill educated and ill equipped, but prejudice, hate, and discrimination had taken their toll, too great a toll at that. Such feelings within the dominant society ought not to exist. Ultimately, these valiant souls, after meeting defeat time and time again, met it one more time as they turned to the bottle.

I have seen my fellow Indians try to succeed, but because they did not have a good command of English, or because they didn't know how to fill out the forms, because they didn't have the qualifying credentials, because of lack of skill or education, they were repeatedly turned away. Worst of all was to be rejected because of having a different skin color. Small wonder they turned to drink to get away from it all.

It is a long, hard road for an Indian to succeed in a world dominated by non-Indians. It is not that my people are lazy or unambitious. It is who they are that brings such ridicule. This is a fact. When our communities and our local, state, and federal governments are controlled and dominated by non-Indians, it is particularly difficult for an Indian, or any other minority, to survive easily in modern society. These people need much support, encouragement, understanding, and compassion from others to succeed.

Alcohol, though it loomed large, was not the only challenge I faced when returning from placement for the summers. I felt that I was being pulled in all directions. There was pressure to attend ceremonies; pressure to conform to the Navajo life-style; pressure from the elders of my people, who encouraged less involvement in the white man's ways and religion. In addition, there were the many Navajo cultural taboos that presented extra burdens.

Not having enough to eat, not having money for basic needs, searching for firewood in over-gathered areas, hauling water long distances, and catching horses over miles of rangeland all presented formidable obstacles to bare subsistence. One of the factors protecting a reservation Indian from undue stress and related emotional problems is that he does not seem to be pressured by rigid time schedules, appointments, and long-range plans. The reservation life seems to revolve around the sun—morning, noon, and night.

My first exposure to schedules was at the government boarding school, but I really understood the clock when I had lived a few weeks on the placement program. The clock, it seems, has more power than Tito, Mussolini, or Hitler. The weight of the modern-day world is carried by the small hands of the clock. In my white foster home and in Utah, the clock was the master. At home on the reservation, the sun and other natural elements ruled my life. As I grew older, I was able to quickly adjust to each situation and function as the need demanded.

A strong cultural factor facing the Indian who enters the dominant society is the idea of material accumulation. In the Navajo way, riches do not belong to the individual. The whole clan, or extended family, has claim on what each member may possess. Wealth is measured not in dollars, but in the accumulation of horses, cattle, or sheep.

Even though a clan may accumulate material wealth, they keep a close eye on the individual clan members. If one collects too much wealth, he is a prime candidate to be considered a witch. So a Navajo will cease accumulating material possessions after he has reached his personal comfort zone, or even sooner if others hint that he may be nearing witchhood.

For this reason, and partly for lack of education and work experience, a Navajo will work only as long as it takes to make enough money to satisfy his cultural expectations. Then he quits. This work ethic has long been a source of frustration to employers who wonder why Navajos quit right when performance is high and progress excellent. Also, long-range financial planning is not done by Navajos.

The needs of the Navajo are simple and basic. They have not been taught to desire the things the world can offer.

Work is a most positive value in the dominant society. For this reason, the value of striving and succeeding is stressed. "Idleness is the devil's workshop" is a common phrase used to sum up this value. Mormon people adhere to the value of work, to be self-reliant and to be independent. All of this may be good, but we must understand that the Indian people are not oriented in this direction. Their attitude toward work and enthusiastic activity is much more relaxed. To an Indian, success, progress, and accumulation of property is interpreted as being selfish. Navajo parents teach their children that the aggressive values of the dominant society can be achieved only by destroying good relationships with family and friends. Also, they teach that the accumulation of wealth causes many anxieties. Because of these ideas, many Navajos are not prepared for success in the dominant society. They just do not feel it is worth striving for.

I can still vividly remember the teachings of my father about these things: "My son, with the Navajo way and clan system, you will never need to stand alone. Someone will always have something you can use in time of need. We hold all things in common as a clan. Never be embarrassed to ask one of your clan brothers or sisters for help. It is their duty, and yours, if called upon.

"Why should you desire to outdo the other person? Where does it take you? What will you gain in this life to take to the next? Very little, my son, very little. An Indian should share what he has with others. This is the way the Great Spirit intended. Consider the bees. Look how they work together. Do you see any of them fighting to try to become the queen? Do you see any one of them wanting to do the most in the hive? No, they all work according to the good of the colony. This is the way an Indian should act.

"Remember the Navajo footrace. Did you hear any of the elders say, 'I wonder who will win?' No, you did not. Just to finish the race is enough to prove manhood. This is our way of life—we cooperate. Each person is willing to give his last bread to the next if necessary."

We had no thoughts of saving for future needs. There was nothing to save. The needs always existed now. My people considered the lily of the field, how it was clothed of nature, and, as people of the earth, they operated upon this principle. The Great Creator would take care of them if they exerted faith. Talk of checking and savings accounts would have been incomprehensible.

Museums, zoos, picnics, operas, birthday parties, vacation trips, credit cards, art galleries, anniversaries, and movies were something of another world. Rides on trains, planes, and ships never entered our minds. Any kind of books, magazines, or daily newspapers never passed through our hogan doors. That is the way it was when I grew up. Today things are different on the reservation, but back then these luxuries were nonexistent to us. The rush of crowded city streets seldom caught a Navajo in its current—for sure it never swept any of my family along.

All of what middle-class America enjoyed was completely foreign to my family during my childhood days. The only fraternity we belonged to was poverty. The only business organization was when we children listened to the order of hitch-hiking to the bean fields. Our only insurance was rain, which helped us capture prairie dogs for dinner, and we hunted only to survive. No sport was really involved. Reservation life was a world unto itself.

Life with my family was simple. There was no need to hurry. Life was considered good when there was food to share, friends to enjoy, and ceremonials to attend. Wisdom was associated with age, the older persons being greatly respected.

These are just some of the cultural differences that may cause stress if one is not careful when trying to transcend both cultures.

While in Utah on placement, I changed year after year from the Indian orientation to that of the Anglo culture, which revolved around competition, saving time, conquest over nature, aggressiveness, and so on. The people totally immersed in the dominant society will compete with peers, relatives, and even family members. They are threatened by being outdone as status urges them to move upward. Schedules govern their lives; they often seem unsatisfied with the present, almost as though it does not exist, and they are preoccupied with the future. They live in a state of anticipation. When I returned to placement, I had to get used to this life-style.

Glen Harker was the breadwinner in my foster family. To fill this role, he had to have regular and gainful employment. We lived in a neighborhood where all the neighbors knew each other. Church activity promoted that closeness. As a family, we participated in the activities the Church offered, and we took part in school and community events, too. Some of the values I learned while living in the dominant society were right and good, such as thrift, punctuality, inquisitiveness, and competitiveness. Those I kept. They were beneficial then and have continued to bless my life since.

As the values from both of my cultures blended, I developed strength of character, integrity, and iron determination to accomplish good and to hold myself above temporary pleasures and self-seeking interests. Confidence came, not cockiness.

As I grew into the teenage years, I developed a beautiful, peaceful feeling in my soul, and with it came courage and strength. I was becoming less afraid of the traditional things I had been taught, less fearful of taboos about owls, coyotes, and witches. I realized that some of the teachings I'd received really did not make connected sense. My life had changed, and these cultural restrictions had lost application for me. By that time, I understood why I was upon the earth, and many of the childhood teachings I'd always taken for granted did not fit into the greater understanding. I began to move into my own world of understanding rather than claim citizenship in either Navajo or Anglo cultures.

From The Church of Jesus Christ of Latter-day Saints, I internalized the great truths taught about God, his creations, our purpose in life, and life after death. I began to see the traditional Navajo teachings as incomplete, and, in many cases, too negative about life.

Even though I began to question the Navajo religious beliefs, I still have respect for that way of belief. Many Navajo teachings are valuable—for example, respecting Mother Earth and her creations. This is ignored in the dominant society. Some people confuse wildlife range management as respecting the earth. This only begins to scratch the surface of the more respectful belief. Although there were moments when I joked about certain taboos that did not seem logical to me, I generally didn't outwardly devalue the beliefs of my family.

As I studied the Latter-day Saint religion in my foster family setting, it became clear, making a lot of sense. My mind began to comprehend the mysteries I'd never understood before. God became more real to me. I began to relate to Him personally. I visualized Him with a body of flesh and bones, and I knew that we were made in His image and that He is the Father of our spirits. I knew that his body was perfected and glorified, and I learned that God had blessed me with some of His attributes and qualities.

I compared this concept of God with that of the Navajo religion. I thought about the holy people, the Navajos coming from beneath the earth, the story of Changing Woman. These things became more abstract and didn't make sense. The holy people my father told me about were both good and evil. This, too, seemed wrong. Why should I follow many when I could follow the one Supreme Being, God, the Eternal Father of all?

Soon I was praying more and more to the eternal God taught to me in my foster home. More and more I received answers to my prayers, more than before. At home on the reservation, I often knelt in prayer while in the hogan or out with the sheep. There, in those sacred places, I yearned to have my words reach into the ears of the great God.

Several times, as I prayed in the hogan, my brothers would see me through the cracks in the wall and make fun of me. My God did not make sense to them, so they laughed at their own lack of understanding.

"Hey, George, what are you doing in there?" one of them would ask. "What are you begging for out of the air?"

"Hey, come over here, look in that crack at George. I never saw anything like it!" another would say.

Then another brother would ask, "Where's the corn pollen, George? You can't pray without that. Everybody knows that you have gone crazy on that white man's religion." Then they would all laugh. I realized that they were just teasing, but sometimes their teasing turned into anger.

During the summer, the desert was very hot. Not only was this hard on my family, but it was hard on the livestock. Sometimes we lost sheep for lack of water. When our reservoir, which was about seven miles away, dried up, we had to carry salt water from a spring on Ute land just across the border. This was an inconvenience for my family. We took our livestock there, but the Utes asked us to leave their property. During the drought years, we received no winter moisture. The land was then more desolate, brown, and dry.

During those times, while out herding sheep, I fell to my knees asking God to send rain. My prayers were not always answered immediately. Yet I knew an answer would come. I knew that eventually we would be blessed with moisture so the little lambs could quench their thirst. Often rain came immediately. Sometimes it took a long time. But rain always came.

Once we had not received moisture for some time. The reservoir had completely dried up. My aunt and uncle spoke of driving the livestock to Shiprock, twenty miles away, so they could be near water. We were in dire circumstances. Seeing this and firmly believing in the power of prayer, I decided to go before the Lord with our problem.

Going out onto the barren desert, away from all, I knelt

and fervently poured my heart unto the Lord. We were so grateful to see a quick answer to this humble prayer as the rains came. Again, water, life, had come to thirsty people and animals.

My summers at home each year helped me to grow and develop, especially during my teenage years. I first saw the ways of my people from the viewpoint of a child. Before I finished high school, I had acquired an adult's appreciation of the Navajo culture. By the time I was twenty, I had matured enough physically, spiritually, socially, and culturally to take the best of the two worlds.

16

THE MISSION
AMONG THE NAVAJOS

S tay home. You have finished school. We are happy
that twelve years of school are over. Now no more
schooling. It is time for you to stay here. Get married.
Your father and I will find you a good Navajo wife. Family is
the most important. It hurts us because you want to leave. Get
married and live with us. We need you. Help us!"

The suffering must have shown in my eyes more than I
wanted. So discerning was Mother that it was impossible to
hide feelings from her. A warm smile spread over her aged face,
a face worn through many seasons of trial.

"My son, it is up to you," she said. "Whatever you want to
do, this is what we want as well. Your father and I want the best
for you. Out of our family, you are the only one who finished
high school. I don't know much about schools and education.
But they must be important. We will trust and believe in you.
We have confidence in you.

"You will be back one day to help us and your people. This
we know. The Great Creator is watching over you. He has put
these desires inside you. He also wants you to improve your
life. These feelings are not your own but belong to the Great
Creator. It is the holy people. We will support you in whatever
you do."

Mother had always been understanding. She restrained her tears. It was not easy for her to say what she did.

Two weeks had passed since I returned home from my work at the Grand Canyon. I had just told Mother about my wish to attend college. Father was away in Nebraska working seasonal employment for the railroad. His desire would have been for me to stay home, to marry a Navajo and settle down. However, I knew he would not stand in the way of my desire to improve my life. It was a comfort to have the support of my family.

The two weeks at home had been one of the most enjoyable and peaceful times of my life. To go cut firewood, haul water, laugh with my family, herd sheep, and go to squaw dances, rodeos, and Ute bear dances brought me into the tradition of my family. I seemed to have sweet peace within. I had begun to understand what the old ones meant when they said we should have quiet inside ourselves.

All during those two weeks, Mother had been satisfied in thinking I was home for good. To her, as with most Navajo adults then, a contented life meant having the family near. Though she sensed the encroachment of the dominant Anglo society, she had little understanding of how education would help me to later help our family and our tribe.

Yet, toward the end of those two weeks, a forceful urge enveloped my being. It was impossible to ignore. This type of feeling had been with me frequently. It was like the feeling I had had at the Grand Canyon to return to my natural family. Now it was with me again, and I explained my desires to my mother. She was so kind and understanding. Her embrace had been warm.

The next day found me out by the highway. Hitchhiking, I think, is a Navajo institution. I needed a ride to Cortez, Colorado. From there I planned to catch another ride to Mesa Verde National Park to seek employment as a cook. I needed to feed my family; they had nothing to eat. A ride came soon, after only a little waiting; and not much later, I was hiking up the paved road leading into Mesa Verde National Park. Mesa Verde was nestled in the mountains just east of Cortez. As I walked up the last incline toward the administration building, the scent of pine lifted my soul. It was not long before I found myself sitting with the man in charge of hiring.

Because of my previous kitchen experience at the Grand Canyon, I was hired on the spot. Again, I would start as a dishwasher. After doing this for a while, that driving urge came over me again. I knew it was the Spirit telling me to move on. I knew I would have to do better than dishwashing in order to help my family and also save money for college. After a few weeks, I terminated my employment. I had decided to seek a better job and more significant opportunity.

Again the roadside became my companion. From town to town I hitchhiked. The nights were lonely, and food was scarce. Each town had a dump, and there I scavenged for food. If someone had opened the door of an old rusted-out truck at night in the wrecking yard, they would have found me asleep on the seat. For almost a week, I lived like this. There was little else that I could have done. I was broke and without a friend.

I found work at last with a mining company in the Dove Creek, Colorado, area. The pay was better. When I sat down for the job interview, I mentioned to my prospective employer that I had thought of going back to school in the fall. I would be working for him only a little over two months. He was looking for someone who would become more permanent. At least I had been honest with him. Then he did a surprising thing: he hired me.

I went to a nearby grove of trees and there offered a prayer of gratitude to my Heavenly Father.

The next day, outfitted with boots and mining headlamp, I descended over one thousand feet into the deep recesses of the earth. With another Navajo as a working companion, I drilled and blasted, mining for both ore and coal. At lunchtime, we ate underground.

After eating, usually I turned out my headlamp. Then, in the darkness, I would think about my family and my people. My heart burned, and I ached to accomplish something pleasing unto God in their behalf. My face waxed pale, and often tears dropped in the silent darkness to spot the sleeves over my folded arms. I likened my situation to that of the Indian people

and other true Israelites sitting in the dark pit of adversity, crying out for help. I yearned to help the God of Israel heal the
heartaches of Lehi's children.

Soon I decided to dismiss these thoughts that brought too
much despair. It was far better to content myself with the
work. To do my very best as a miner became my objective. I decided that unless I did well as a miner, there was no way I could
do well in any other facet of life. Life, being one large whole
like a pie, insists upon being cut into uniform pieces. Those
pieces are determined by our daily actions. I was determined to
make pie à la mode out of my mining experience.

Sometimes my work companion and I would lean against a
shoring beam, whispering back and forth about the plight of
the Indian people. We spoke proudly of our forefathers, of
their greatness, and of the spiritual prowess of the renowned,
wise, and learned medicine men of the tribes. Though we
sometimes seemed to be in the grave, especially when we lay
back to rest after eating, yet through the darkness there was a
lively hope in our dreamings. Echoing through the silent
shafts, our familiar hopes whispered from wall to wall. I wondered if those standing around the dusty entrance above were
ever quiet and still enough to hear our conversation.

A pay raise was not long in coming—ten dollars a week
more. This was good pay in those days. Again the grove of
trees arbored my heartfelt prayer of thanks.

Thinking to help my family, I bought an old, beat-up Nash
car. It was in fair condition, and it cost just seventy-five dollars. Some work had to be done on it, but it ran. My family
would be proud of this "chiddy." I could just see Mom's smile.
Her heart would burst in pride that her son had bought something to help the family. Dad would be happy, too. The hauling of firewood and water over long distances would be easier
now. To please my family caused my soul to smile.

On weekends, I took my family for scenic cruises. With a
car, we could go to new places. My family saw more of the non-
Indian world and began to realize the existence of a world other
than their own.

Because of the things I was able to do for my family, the

temptation to permanently work in the mine intruded rudely into my future goals. Again came the restless feeling, which soon mushroomed into an urge, that I should leave the security of my mining employ. I kept telling myself to have the courage to do what the Spirit was telling me to do.

I quit my job and began hitchhiking home. I had terminated my job with the mine without really knowing why or what to do next. I left everything up to the Lord. As I was between Cortez and Towaoc, Colorado, the LDS missionaries picked me up. They had been trying to find me all day, asking in every small town that dotted the highway. They did not know I had just left Dove Creek, some miles to the north. The restless feeling began to be explained. My Mormon foster parents in Utah had contacted the elders, hoping I would enroll at Brigham Young University. School had already started four weeks past. I would have to make haste.

I spent a few more days with my family. (This is how an Indian makes haste.) My brothers and sisters urged me to stay just one more year. On the other hand, the Spirit kept urging me to go.

"I'll be back," I told them. "One day I will help you build a house with running water, electricity, a toilet, and nice furniture. When I get out of college, I will do this. You won't have to chop wood anymore or haul water. You won't have to live in rags anymore. As my family, you deserve at least these things."

I embraced my mother one last time and started to leave. Just at the door, I looked back to see tears in her eyes. That caused me some pain. But I took my journey. Soon I was in Shiprock, New Mexico, waiting for the first bus to Provo. My foster parents had sent some money for my bus fare. I was thankful for that.

In Provo, my foster parents met me at the bus stop. The next day, I stood at the student services window in the administration building on the Brigham Young University campus. I was all alone. No one there was assigned to assist Indian students. In later years that changed, but for now everything depended upon my own initiative.

Since I was over four weeks late getting registered, most of the general courses were already full. I ended up with some stern classes, like zoology and microbiology. They were the only ones left. Also, in my naïveté, I signed up for twenty-one credit hours.

I tried to secure a scholarship or some financial help from the Navajo Tribe. However, the tribe did not look favorably upon BYU because it was a church-related school. Tribal scholarship officials encouraged me to attend some other college or university. The situation looked bleak.

Then my wonderful foster parents stepped in, offering to help with tuition and fees. I had saved some money from the mine; this went to purchase books. Soon, although it was difficult, I rented an apartment within walking distance of the campus. I needed more money, though.

I got a job on the BYU grounds crew and also worked as an early morning janitor on campus, getting up by 3:00 A.M. and to work by 4:00. My first classes started at seven-thirty in the morning. In addition to the twenty-one credit hours, the demands upon my time this first year were tremendous. In spite of these demands, I was still able to socialize with friends. I even helped organize a small club for Indian students. All in all, it was a fun and challenging year. And I did well academically.

Then I was confronted by another decision: whether or not to go on a mission. It meant postponing my education and the help I might give to my family. But in the end, I held to the goal I'd set in high school—it was as though I were submitting to an earlier will. Then my determination to serve a mission became as hard as flint.

It was not long until my mission papers were filled out and submitted. A couple of weeks later, I received a letter from the First Presidency informing me of my call to the Rapid City South Dakota mission.

Somehow President J. Edwin Baird of the Southwest Indian Mission heard of my being assigned to the Rapid City South Dakota Mission. It prompted him to action. He wanted any Navajo elder down in his neck of the woods, right on the Navajo reservation.

Shortly, I had another letter in my hands reassigning me to

George just before his mission

the Southwest Indian Mission. This was a direct answer to all my previous prayers, since I had wanted to teach the gospel among the Navajos in the Southwest. Since I knew the language, it would be less difficult to teach the gospel there.

Elder Spencer W. Kimball of the Council of the Twelve set me apart for this special mission. He blessed me to have utterance to teach the gospel through the power of the Holy Ghost: "I bless you, George P. Lee, that you will astound many wise and learned men among your tribe, the medicine men whom you will teach and convert and bring into the Church. You shall be most fluent in the Navajo language. Your tongue will be loosed many times."

This blessing I needed, as the many years of speaking English while on the Placement Program had almost replaced my native tongue. I felt slow of speech and stammered in Navajo.

Because of the confidence this blessing gave me, I was most desirous to go among my people and preach of the Lord Jesus

Christ. I wanted to baptize people by the thousands. I was a typical missionary, full of zest for the Lord. I had set my goal high. And I tried to keep it there.

Another Navajo elder and myself were flown by small aircraft down to Winslow, Arizona. The ride was so choppy I got airsick. If there had been a parachute, I probably would have bailed out! I was ever so glad when we finally landed.

President Baird met us at the Winslow airstrip. He seemed very pleased to see us. He drove us right to the mission home, fed us, and then began our mission training. This man didn't waste time; right after dinner, he directed my companion and me to the town of Holbrook to street proselyte. This excited me. I felt like Samuel the Lamanite preaching from the wall to those who would not listen. I did manage to give away some copies of the Book of Mormon, though. It seemed that I had to shout the gospel at the top of my lungs in order to be heard over all the cars and street noise.

After two or three days at the mission home and more Holbrook street proselyting, President Baird assigned me to the Piñon area. My new companion was to be a Navajo elder. Not long thereafter, he came to pick me up. We arrived in Piñon after midnight.

The next morning I was up early and ready to baptize. The mission field seemed to me to be the celestial kingdom. Little did I realize that I was still on the telestial level.

My companion and I studied scriptures that morning and then reviewed missionary lessons. A special feeling came over me to go out and begin preaching the gospel. My senior companion, the Navajo elder, was not so inclined. And wanting to be obedient to mission rules, I followed his counsel. All the while, though, I kept waiting for him to say that the time to preach the gospel had come.

After lunch, we finally went out. We traveled from hogan to hogan, gathering the little children inside and teaching them Primary songs. I was biting the bit by then. It was hard for me to contain myself. I wanted my people to know that Jesus Christ Himself had walked the Americas! I wanted them to know that Jesus Christ had visited their ancestors. I yearned to teach by the Holy Ghost. We continued from hogan to hogan. I was the junior companion. I tried to subdue my own desires, but the impatience still came. Little did I realize that we were laying a foundation for further work in the future. The glorious preaching would come.

After a week, my companion approached me. "Elder Lee," he said, "I notice you are a little impatient with the way things are going. I have an idea that I've prayed and pondered about. We will begin to take turns being senior companions. This coming week you are to be the senior companion. You will make the decisions."

I could hardly believe what I was hearing. This man was more in tune than I had given him credit for. Of course, I was elated. At the same time, I was humbled for having been so apparent in my anxiety.

"Thank you," I said. "I would like that. But what if you do not agree with my decisions?"

"I will abide them just as if you really were the senior companion."

This choice elder's idea of shared leadership appealed to me. I resolved inside not to let him or the Lord down. My prayers had been answered. I had the highest respect for my companion.

"Elder," I asked, "would it be possible to sit down and go over the names of families you've contacted in the past? I think we should put them all on a map."

"Elder Lee, that sounds like an excellent idea. It fires me up!"

I quickly noted that he was just as able to follow as to lead. His leadership and support were subtle.

I added, "We should start teaching the adults. We can have cottage-hogan meetings. We need to get two or three adults into one hogan together. Then I think we can teach."

Piñon was a very large area spread with sagebrush and sprinklings of piñon pine. The hogans were scattered widely apart throughout the area. To go from one to the other took an immense amount of time. Each visit to a hogan had to be timely and productive.

George with Navajo missionary companions Elliot Murphy (left) and
Jim Dandy (right)

Piñon proper consisted of a small trading post, one gas station, and a chapter house. A chapter house is for community
gatherings of any kind. Also, a small Bureau of Indian Affairs
school was located there. We held church services in the chapter house.

We were not too successful with the adults of the area because of their strong beliefs in their own religion. Our success
came with the children (because of the LDS Indian Placement
Program) and with the inactive members. We also did a lot of
public-relations work with local tribal officials. Parents and
tribal leaders on the reservation recognized the value of the
placement program in helping their children receive a better
education. It would help them learn skills and trades and even
further themselves in college. Also, the contrast of living in an
Anglo society would further help them understand who they
were—the *Dineh,* or the people. It would help them appreciate
a culture other than their own.

Before the children could participate on the program, they
first had to become members of the Church. Yet most of their
parents never did join. We taught the children with flip-charts
illustrated with pictures of other Indians. Still our success with

the adults was limited, although we did baptize a couple of families and activated a number of families. Somehow they lacked the power of the Spirit. With my attention on the visual flip-chart, I found it difficult to concentrate on the person to be taught. But the Lord continued to assist us in our greatest times of need, although I lamented the fact that we were not baptizing a lot of people.

After one month in this area, I received a letter from the mission president transferring me to the Steamboat, Arizona, area. My spirit became restless. Something whispered, "You are not to go to Steamboat." I was deeply torn. What could I do? The mission president had thus directed me. But the thought kept going through my mind that the Lord needed help elsewhere.

After I had questioningly packed my clothes, and just as I was getting ready to step out the door to go to Steamboat, I received an emergency message from President Baird that I was not to go to Steamboat. The elders there had hepatitis; therefore, the area was closed down. I was to go to Chinle, Arizona. This was to be a temporary assignment until further notice.

In Chinle, I received a new companion from Spanish Fork, Utah. We began teaching early morning seminary with some success. I then mentioned to this companion that we should start centering our teaching around the Book of Mormon and Jesus Christ. But we continued with the seminary program and the routine Sunday School classes. Many people came out to Church, but few entered the waters of baptism. We worked hard on activation to build up the branch. We did not have a church building, so we met in the chapter house.

It was not until we began teaching primarily from the Book of Mormon that we had baptisms. When we taught Jesus Christ as contained in the book of my forefathers, then came the power of convincing necessary to convert the Lamanite. Jesus Christ cannot be taught with program or flip-chart, but only by the piercing power of the Holy Ghost. Two months in Chinle brought a letter from President Baird asking my companion and me to come to the mission home for a special orientation.

"Elder Lee," President Baird began as he looked me in the eye, "I have been watching your successes for some time. Your diligence to your mission call is apparent. We have an area in our mission that has been barren for some time. We have had no elders there for quite a while. I would like to assign you to this area with a new companion. I feel this is what the Lord would have."

"President, I will do whatever the Lord wants. What area is it? What is it like?"

"The area is a difficult one. The last missionaries to serve there were driven out at gunpoint. There is one church in particular that dominates this area. The ministers of it have been responsible for spreading false rumors about our doctrine. They have quite a hold on the people. I want you to go in, assess the situation, and correct the problem. Then preach the gospel to those good people there. Can you do it? Can you build the Church and organize a branch?"

I now understood why the Lord did not want me in Steamboat.

"Wherever the Lord wants me, President, is where I will have the most success. If the Lord wills it, it will be done."

A big elder then lumbered into the office. I sensed something special about him. Though he was quite large, over six feet, an air of humility attended him. Though his body was rugged, his spirit was quiet and meek.

"This is your companion, Elder Lee. He is from back east." Without waiting for so much as a nod, President Baird continued: "You should work closely together, placing any feelings of difference aside. Stay close to the Lord and you will stay close together."

As we walked out of the president's office, my Anglo companion conversed with me in Navajo. I liked him right away. We headed toward our assigned area. On the way, we determined to make fasting and prayer part of our routine.

Once in our area, we rented a hogan from an Indian family. The president was certainly correct about the feelings of the people. Doors were slammed in our faces. Hostility toward us abounded. People reviled and cursed our religion. Many

Navajo woman weaving traditional rug

Navajo children on reservation

taunted and told us we should join with their native way of
thinking. No one would talk with us about spiritual matters.
We were accused of being polygamists who had come to get

wives. Others said we were communist spies sent to undermine the Navajo way of life.

Even though we became discouraged and frightened at times, yet we continued our work. The other church in the area held meetings in the local chapter house to condemn the Mormon Church. The more we labored, the more the opposition increased. Then the thought came to us that we should attend one of these meetings. We invited ourselves.

During the meeting, we asked for the opportunity to speak. Many Navajos, devout in their native religion, were gathered here. Both the antagonistic ministers were in attendance. They greatly tried to persuade the chapter president not to let us talk. However, we greatly pressed the chapter president until he relented. I was asked to do the talking because I was Navajo. The chapter president asked me to speak in Navajo to the people.

As I approached the microphone, a most captivating feeling embraced me. It was as though a strong wind rushed upon me from all directions. When I reached the microphone, all fear had left, and in its place a great confidence had settled upon me. The Lord had poured his Spirit upon me.

As soon as I opened my mouth to speak, the Spirit took over, and I said things of which I had no former notion. The people looked at me with amazement and marveled. As the blessing of Elder Kimball began to come to pass, I looked out over an astounded congregation. I give no credit to myself, but know it was of the Lord. Many had considered me to be a white man's Indian, a cavalry scout. But as they heard me speak, the Lord gave them a different opinion. The audience was completely silent, and the Spirit of the Lord filled the room. There was standing room only at this meeting—the Spirit had been working on the people all that day. The Lord brought them there because he wanted them to hear the gospel.

One particular man who mocked the things being said approached the podium and strove to yank the microphone from my hand. He actually got a firm grip on it once. But so strong was the Spirit upon me that his strength could not match that which the Lord had given to me. In resignation, he finally walked out of the building.

After the talk, I asked my companion what I had said, for I could not remember. He said I had spoken about the Savior, about his having come to this land in times past—of how the Book of Mormon testifies of the things he said and did. And that it was to these people, to their ancestors, the true blood of Israel, that he appeared. I spoke of their great destiny and that it was imperative that they be restored once again to the true gospel of Christ as contained in the holy record of their forefathers. I had also spoken of the inspiration behind the Indian Placement Program, of how it strengthened the Navajo youth and prepared them for greater service to God and man. It was a day never to be forgotten.

Afterward whenever we went out tracting, homes were more eagerly opened to our visits. The man whose hogan we had earlier rented opened his home to us. Then his relatives opened their homes. And then their relatives. We were profoundly thankful to the Lord.

We could not help but remember the charge given us by the mission president to open a branch there with local Lamanite leadership and to do it in less than one year. This also meant baptizing a considerable number of Navajos. We began to catch the vision President Baird had in assigning us this area.

Soon his vision began to become reality. Although the ministers tried to hold more community meetings to propagandize against our church, the numbers of people who would attend and listen dwindled.

As we went out among the people, we felt an entirely different spirit in their hogans. Before, we had felt hostility, but now there was kindness and open hearts. Medicine men began to listen. Instead of elementary Navajo, I used a more elevated form, like that I had heard my father speak when he taught me of the Navajo ways. My father began to become wiser in my eyes.

The medicine men were surprised that I knew so much

about my native culture. Of course, there were times when the Spirit helped me understand things I had never before considered. Humbly I thanked the Lord whenever this happened.

To approach these medicine men would be like Anglo elders approaching men of MIT, Harvard, Yale, or Columbia. But there is one difference. In the area of spirituality, the medicine man focused his learning and ability. Many of them are ready for gospel meat and not doctrinal milk. And the difference between meat and milk is not so much in verbiage as it is the power of the Spirit. As we taught the medicine men, they desired to teach us as well. We listened for as long as two hours at times. Their beliefs we respected. Many times I may have considered something one of them said as being out of gospel context. But then, some time later, I would finally realize the truth of what the man had spoken. I found it best to remember what they had said, to tuck it back in my mind. Then, if it were a good seed, it would sprout into something good. This happened many times, and it helped me understand how to more effectively preach the gospel and to bring spiritual blessings among my people.

When it became our turn to talk, we spoke of the Book of Mormon, but we did not minimize blessings derived from reading the Bible. We taught about the great accomplishments of prior Indian civilizations. Of the glory of Christ's ancient visit to this continent, we bore unimpeachable witness. And after having talked about these things for a while, the Spirit would descend, and testimonies flowed from heart to heart, bosom to bosom, soul to soul. The words of life again found their home in Israel.

Contrastingly, there were some who told us we were wasting our time because our church had no mission center to give out food, clothing, and medicine. We then tried to teach the idea of self-reliance. The more we taught this, the more interested the people became. Soon we were telling them of the blood of Israel that flowed in their veins, of the great ancestors they could claim, and of how in the last day they would rise again despite any opposition peoples, governments, or other churches could give. That they were destined to become a great civilization again was of no question. That this land had been given specifically to them by Christ was a truth that sank into the depths of their Abrahamic souls. And as they are a people who live at one with the land, this had great meaning. They began to understand that they were the descendants of great Nephite and Lamanite prophets. They began to comprehend their vast spiritual heritage.

Frequently these same people would stop drinking coffee. Several families handed us coffee cans still full of granules. They put aside peyote. Baptisms came. The people began to return to a knowledge of their fathers and of Jesus Christ. As missionaries, we were invigorated and encouraged by the turn of events. Many prominent medicine men stepped into the waters of baptism. Soon a branch presidency was called. We were well ahead of the timetable given to us by the mission president.

Then the storm began again. The ministers of the other churches began threatening to withhold the much-needed medical supplies and clothing from the people if they continued to attend the Mormon Church. Members from our church began to attend the other one again in order to receive the needed help. Though our members had a sound testimony of the gospel and of the Book of Mormon, when it came to seeing their families suffer, they could not forbear. Their temporal condition was so miserable that it gave them very little choice. Even the local cemetery was controlled by the other church, which refused to let the Mormon dead be buried there. The opposition and persecution had become so great that my companion and I decided to fast and pray about the matter.

After we had fasted a few days, the Lord revealed to us that we were to write the ministers a letter. It was to be kind but firm. So we wrote it. In this letter we thanked the ministers for the many good things they had done for the people of the area. Toward the last of the letter, we told them that we were there under direction of the Lord and that if the persecution did not end, something would happen to cause both of them to leave the area. We gave them two weeks to consider the matter. We heard nothing from them. We tried to call a meeting with them, but they would not see us. Two weeks went by.

Then, one of the ministers became so sick he had to leave the area. He was carried out on a stretcher. Another week passed, and the other minister was overcome with sickness. He left also, and did not return.

They were replaced by two new ministers, and we knew that this was an answer to our prayer and fasting. The new men were cordial, kind, and willing to work with us. They believed in freedom of religion. We felt good about that. Especially, though, we felt good about our members receiving the medical supplies and other things they needed. All opposition ceased. No more doors were slammed in our faces. Not all joined the Church, however, but always thereafter the people were kind to us.

It was not long until a letter arrived from the mission president reassigning my companion and me to different areas. I was given another companion, a new one. Then, as the supervising elder, I was charged to cement the opening that my former companion and I, through the Lord's help, had opened. This we did.

Many people had been converted and baptized in our area. Miracles had taken place to demonstrate the hand of the Lord. Less than a year earlier, most of the area had been anti-Mormon. Now every door opened to show a kind face to the missionaries. A branch was organized. Children attended seminary. It was a beautiful and exciting feeling to see all of that take place. Three Indians were called and formed a branch presidency.

Elder Spencer W. Kimball of the Council of the Twelve Apostles was coming to tour the mission—we had received notification from President Baird. Of course, we were excited. The letter instructed us to call a special meeting in which Elder Kimball would talk with the new members of our area. There was only one problem—we had no chapel. There had been talk of building one, but nothing had officially ever been started.

After prayerful consideration, we approached the local

trader, asking him for permission to use his trading post as a meeting place. Fortunately the trader was LDS and readily consented. We were greatly relieved to have found a place.

The appointed day came. Strangely, a few local people became upset because the Mormons would be using the trading post for a religious meeting. They even went so far as to file complaints with leading tribal officials. The trader became anxious, as his business was at stake. We assured him that the hand of the Lord was in this and that everything would work out. So we continued as planned. President J. Edwin Baird and Elder Spencer W. Kimball arrived. It lifted our spirits greatly to see these two men.

That evening President Baird spoke first, delivering an uplifting and outstanding message. I interpreted for him. Then Elder Kimball gave an inspiring talk. The Spirit was present in great abundance. All listening were attentive and bent forward on their seats. I again interpreted Elder Kimball's message.

When Elder Kimball finished his talk, he asked if any had questions. The questions covered a wide range of topics, and many were about the history of the Church. Some asked about the anti-Mormon rumors that had been circulated in the area. Infused with the Spirit of the Lord, Elder Kimball answered the questions forthrightly and in satisfying detail.

Then a hand was raised somewhere in the back. Elder Kimball nodded, and the man asked: "Elder Kimball, we would like a building to meet in." His head hung in humility as he asked: "Can the Church build us one?"

Elder Kimball was evidently quite moved by the petition. He explained that there were certain criteria the Church required before a chapel could be built with Church funds. He had spent much time among the other leading Brethren trying to convince them of the Church's responsibility to the Lamanite, and he had managed to get the Placement Program recognized as an official Church program despite some opposition. It might have been asking too much in too short a time to push for a chapel in some remote area of Navajoland. However, Elder Kimball understood well the Book of Mormon prophecies regarding the Church's responsibility to the Lamanite. One could tell he was grieved not to be able to give consent right then.

Sensing his hesitance, the man continued, "We need a place. We do not want to wait until tomorrow. Jesus wants it too. We are not willing to wait."

The man's testimony penetrated Elder Kimball's heart, and this great apostle tearfully lowered his eyes. "I am sorry," he said. "I can only check for you when I go back to Salt Lake."

"We do not need Church money," the Navajo man softly said. "We will build our own church. We love Jesus and his Church. Your permission is what we wait for."

Mute tears began stretching themselves down the lone apostle's cheeks. He was humbled by the situation. His love for the Lord and the Lamanite was evident.

With quavering voice, the Navajo continued. "There are trees in the mountains for logs. We have our wagons and good horses. We can cut the logs and build our own place. Will this be all right with you?"

Sobbing steady tears, the Lord's representative could barely choke out an answer: "Yes, yes. Build. May God bless you."

The Spirit of the Lord filled that little trading post. That evening the inspired gentle apostle and humble Israelite Indian

Branch meetinghouse under construction

melted their mutual care and concern for the Lord into one
heart and mind. There in that post, the realities of the world
were traded for the visions of Zion.

The trader no longer worried about what the people in the
community might have to say about his trading business, for
the higher transactions of the Lord had passed beneath his roof
that evening.

After the meeting, Elder Kimball and President Baird continued their tour of the mission. True to their intent, the local
members began cutting timber from the nearby mountains to
build a chapel. It was a beautiful sight to behold. Old trucks
and horse-drawn wagons brought the logs to the chapel site.
The chapel was built in less than a month. Then, the members
built another building for Relief Society, Primary, and youth
programs.

Many members began coming to meet regularly in the
buildings they had constructed. It was a marvelous thing.
Many times I found a secluded spot to kneel and offer thanks to
the Lord for his blessing. We continued to baptize new members. More children were signed up on the placement program.
We counted our blessings daily. The blessing Elder Kimball
had given me earlier really began to come to pass.

It was not long before I was able to read and write in my native Navajo tongue. Ways to more effectively teach Navajos in
their own language began to come into mind. Elder Witherspoon, our supervising elder, would come to visit from his area,
and during his visits we investigated the idea of starting a mission school to teach the Navajo language to all of the Anglo
missionaries. Elder Witherspoon, though an Anglo missionary, spoke almost fluent Navajo. When the idea was presented
to him, President Baird accepted the idea wholeheartedly.
Elder Witherspoon and several other seasoned missionaries
were called into the mission home to develop the school.
Though I had been involved in much of the planning, I elected
to stay in my area to proselyte. With so much happening—the
new chapel, more new converts—it did not seem wise to leave
my area. Elder Witherspoon was quite capable and sufficiently
fluent in the Navajo language to organize the school. Mean-

while, I continued to receive and train new junior companions, and I helped Elder Witherspoon develop training materials for the mission's Navajo language school.

One night there was a knock on our hogan door. It was Elder Witherspoon and his companion. He said, "Elder Lee, can you take my companion and me into town? Our Scout is stuck back in the sand. We've got to get to town as soon as possible."

It was nearly 1:00 A.M., but understanding the remoteness of the area and our dependence on one another, I consented. "Sure," I said. "It will only take my companion and me a minute to get dressed. Come on in."

After having driven in our car to where their vehicle was stuck and having freed it from the sand, we began our journey. My companion and I led the way, pulling Elder Witherspoon's Scout behind. About three-thirty in the morning, I fell asleep at the wheel. Our car veered and then tumbled over several times before finally coming to an abrupt stop in a ditch. Luckily, the towing chain had broken. The Scout had been catapulted on past our rolling car by its forward inertia. Stopping as hastily as possible, Elder Toledo, my companion, jumped out and came running back to where we were.

Elder Witherspoon and his companion were in the Scout I was driving. They had been thrown out but were all right. I received a concussion. When I came to, I was in a hospital bed. For a day or two, I had partial amnesia and could not even remember my companion. President Baird called me at the hospital. All things will improve, was his comforting counsel. By the third day, I was out and on my way back to our assignment area. At the request of President Baird, we met with him briefly in a nearby town before returning. After being reassured that I was all right, he sent us on our way. It felt good to be working again. The newly baptized members were delighted to see me again.

Some time passed. A letter came from the mission president directing us to a regional missionary conference in Tuba City. While there, I was interviewed by President Baird and called to serve as one of his assistants. What an assistant to the

mission president was, I really had no idea. To me it was just
another assignment. When I arrived at the missionary conference and learned about my new responsibilities, I was unsure as
to whether I could handle the assignment or not. It was much
more than I had expected. An assistant would travel the whole
mission teaching, leading, and directing zone and district leaders. My first priority was to be obedient, even though things did
not always follow my way of thinking. I would rather have had
an area and proselyted.

My new calling gave me opportunity to supervise and tour
the Shiprock area. If I were to be in the area, it would give me a
chance to visit with my own family and relatives to teach them
the gospel. It was an answer to my prayers.

In this particular assignment, one of my responsibilities included overseeing the Navajo language school that Elder
Witherspoon and I had planned earlier. Not long after this
school had begun, great results were seen throughout the mission. More baptisms came. More families attended Church.
Lives were blessed both temporally and spiritually. Diligent
members began to rise above their impoverished state. Many
began to become involved with literacy programs; others overcame alcoholism. Yet others, particularly those returning from
the Indian Placement Program, went on to college or specialized occupations. The mission Navajo language school was so
successful in training Anglo missionaries to speak Navajo that
it was later incorporated into the BYU Language Training Mission. I could not have been more delighted to see one of my
dreams realized.

It was my privilege to help organize youth conferences and
scouting programs, to develop filmstrips, flannelboards, and
other visual aids. We even put together a Lamanite show using
the talents within our missionary force. With this show, we
went from town to town both entertaining and teaching. From
activities such as these, we found people to teach, and many
baptisms came.

Toward the end of my mission, I asked to be transferred to
the Shiprock area. It was my desire to begin teaching my family
and many relatives there. Also, it was my dream to secure a

chapel site, to have a Church building to serve the people of that area. For the last two months of my mission, this is where I served.

From hogan to hogan, my companion and I traveled, talking with the people. We were laying the groundwork to obtain local permission to build a chapel. We even spoke on the local radio program. And we talked with the tribal leaders. By the end of my mission, we had received a tentative commitment from tribal leaders for a chapel site. However, I was released from my mission before the site was secured. Not long after my release, the site was approved by local tribal officials.

I did have a chance to teach my family the gospel and to sign up some of my brothers and sisters on the Indian Placement Program. Elder Witherspoon had been in this area earlier and had come into contact with my family. I am thankful he did so, for they must have been touched by his tender and sincere spirit. To my great joy, my mother and father consented to baptism. This was a wonderful day. I soon realized, however, that they might have joined the Church only to please their son, for later they became inactive, something that hurts very deeply even now. My parents soon went back to their own Navajo ways. It was hard for them to break with their own native religion.

After being released, I stayed in Shiprock with my family. After a couple of weeks, I began to feel restless. Once more the driving urge of the Spirit permeated my being. Although my mother wanted me to stay home now, she did not appear shocked when I announced that I would be leaving to go to college again. It hurt me to disappoint my parents again. They wanted me to settle down, marry a Navajo, and live with them. But the yearning to achieve and the dogged determination to succeed in life prompted me to move on.

Before leaving, I asked my father to give me a father's blessing. Although his manner was awkward, he gave me the blessing, which in the Navajo way did not consist of placing hands upon heads. Nevertheless, it was from my father, my patriarch, that I received the blessing. He gave me many wise words of counsel in this blessing. Afterward, I reluctantly made preparations to leave. Our separation was tearful. Since my family had no money for bus fare, I hitchhiked to Provo.

The next day, after having arrived in Provo, I went to BYU to register. Unlike the first time I enrolled, there was someone there to help me. While I was on my mission, BYU had assigned certain faculty members to look after the Lamanite students on campus. And there was an Indian club, the Tribe of Many Feathers. It did not take long to find some of my former friends.

It was great to be back in college, to enter higher learning.

17

COLLEGE
—A HAPPY
HUNTING GROUND

The rustling of leaves as I walked was in contrast to what the media had portrayed about the silent, stalking Indian. I had not slept all through the night. Now I had entered the orchard, not knowing yet what to do. It was a beautiful autumn morning, an Indian summer. My mind was heavy and my heart was troubled.

I dropped to my knees. I had walked far enough into the orchard that only the faint drone of an occasional passing vehicle could be heard. I felt forsaken and alone. I began pouring out my soul to the Lord. It was not the first time I had knelt there.

Not long before, I had sat in the office of the bishop of the Brigham Young University Indian Ward. I held him in good esteem, and I respected the office he held. Several hours passed before I left his office. We talked of many things, but mainly about interracial dating and marriage. It was his feeling that such should not occur. I had been counseling my Indian friends that it was all right, but that whoever they dated should have a strong testimony of the gospel. It was my feeling that as long as two people really cared about one another and that there was genuine love between them, then race didn't matter. Also, I thought that along with love and caring, as long as the two people were strong in the gospel, then the marriage would be a success. This philosophy unfortunately ran counter to the feelings of the administration and the bishop.

There was no desire on my part to go against priesthood counsel. I loved my bishop and felt that he loved me. I sincerely felt that nothing was wrong with interracial dating and marriage. In fact, I had been dating a young lady who had been on a mission among the Indian people. She understood Indian ways. Almost in every way she was Indian, except for the color of her skin. In her heart, she was numbered as an Indian. Of course, I dated many other non-Indians, and Indians as well. All through junior high and high school, I had dated non-Indians, since I was the only Indian around. I had conditioned myself to be color blind. I met a girl in Geneva Elementary School, my first year on placement, whom I really admired and respected. She was beautiful, intelligent, sweet, kind, understanding, and caring. I dated her more than anyone else through my teenage years. I never for a minute thought about her as white.

It had taken a lot of courage to ask the bishop for an interview. Because of his feelings (and not only his, for that was the prevalent view at BYU), I felt out of sorts. This was something that really needed to be talked out, not only for me but for the other Indian students as well. Many had been interracially dating and received the same counseling from campus advisers and priesthood leaders. They came to me for comfort and direction. Because I was president of the Tribe of Many Feathers, Indian students came to me for advice. I sat with many who had the same trial to face as I did. So there sat the bishop and I, eye to eye, but not yet single in our opinions. We did not quarrel, but we earnestly sought the Spirit to increase our understanding.

At the conclusion of this extended, private interview, I decided to follow the counsel of the bishop. I desired so much to be one with my priesthood leaders. I felt it my duty and responsibility to be an example and to lead the right way. I had always been obedient. This time would be no exception. To say I left his office without sadness would not be true, for I then had to face the girl I had been dating. Her thoughts had been as mine; we thought ourselves to be rising above the prejudices of the day. Though I had given her temporary custodianship of my feelings, now it was not to be, and it was up to us to accept it. It was not the day for racial and cultural strangers to be joined together. It was my intention to accept the matter and put my heart to rest somehow.

In a very emotional setting, she and I discussed the matter. I told her of my feelings about the importance of being obedient and the blessings that would bring. Though there were tears, we both agreed to part ways. We understood that we would always have wholesome memories of one another. Now I knelt in the orchard. The hurt I felt was for my friends and Indian students in general. Also, the pain centered around why such an attitude existed among us.

Once I began to pray, the tears would not stop flowing. I cried to the Lord for faith, strength, and His divine care. I cried for the Indian students and the Indian people in general. Arising from my knees, a powerful, sweet influence pervaded my whole being. I cannot tell how long I basked in that blissful and divine enlightenment. I learned that pain is part of life. I had prayed for understanding and received it. I now understood the reality of life a little clearer. The understanding I had gained was not what I had expected it to be. Part of the understanding included coming to know that the counsel of the priesthood leader was not an appeasing cover-up for prejudicial attitudes. That night, I enjoyed the most peaceful and sweet sleep I had had for a long time. I departed the situation much wiser, and life went on.

More Indian students attended BYU in 1965 than when I first went in 1962, even though the BYU Indian student government did not exist as it does today. The Indian campus government existed mainly with the Tribe of Many Feathers. Assigned to work with this organization was a kind adviser. He had a great heart toward the Lamanites and always did his best to give us good direction. Another great person who worked with us was an Anglo in the capacity of Indian education director. Like the first brother, he tried to be sensitive to our needs. As Lamanites, we were thankful to have their direction and assistance.

Elections of student officers had been held in the fall, including officers of the Tribe of Many Feathers. I was elected as club president. Though it was not one of the larger clubs on campus, I shouldered my responsibilities seriously. I spent many days fasting, praying, and asking the Lord for help. I wanted nothing but the best for the Indian students. I wanted them to succeed in college. I wanted them to succeed in the white dominant society. I desired so much for them to become tribal leaders among their own people. Clearly, educated, trained, experienced, and qualified Indian leaders were needed on all Indian reservations. I spent much time laboriously thinking of ways their participation in the Tribe of Many Feathers would prove fruitful. The Lamanite adviser and I met often to discuss what we could do to improve the Indian Educational Program. Many different tribes were represented among the Indian students. We wanted the best Indian program in the whole country.

I searched for ways to make the Indian students feel a part of the campus life. One idea that came after much pondering was to have a Miss Indian BYU contest. I had never organized a beauty contest before, but why not? I decided to fashion it after the homecoming queen idea. I knew that Indian queens could be just as charming, talented, intelligent, and beautiful as Anglo queens. There were times when I thought about not doing it, but then thinking back on how impressive the idea originally had been, I forged ahead with it. So many ideas kept coming that I could not sleep some nights.

After I had thought it out well, I proposed the idea to fellow student leaders. Everyone caught hold of the idea. As president, I asked a young Indian woman to direct the Miss Indian BYU contest. As chairman, she did an outstanding job. Millie Chestnut became the first Miss Indian BYU. In more ways than appearance, she was a most beautiful person. She was a beautiful Indian princess. She was full of grace and charm. BYU was represented well by Millie.

Also that year, we initiated an all-Indian basketball tournament. This gave many Lamanite students an opportunity to participate competitively in sports. More than the competition, though, we just enjoyed getting together in some organized games. It helped us let off steam. We found that our studies were easier to bear after a good physical workout. We invited outside Indian teams to compete and had an outstanding tournament. We also wanted to sponsor a national Indian leadership conference. We were thinking big-time. To begin with, we organized an all-Lamanite conference in conjunction with Indian placement students. Our keynote speaker was a tribal chairman.

In student leadership workshops held in the mountains, usually at Aspen Grove, we found time to plan for upcoming events. This time was used to train new student leaders. It also was a time to socialize and drop the burdens of campus life from our tired shoulders.

The Lamanite adviser and I were tossing ideas back and forth one day when the idea hit us to seriously consider bylaws for an Indian student government that would be patterned after the Associated Student Body laws of BYU. After deciding that this was a good idea, we selected and asked a committee to come up with bylaws and to draw up a constitution. This was accomplished with great success. When put before the Indian students, it was sustained. The same organization still exists today at BYU, a system of presidents and vice-presidents.

After the bylaws were approved, the designated positions were filled by election. Then those who were elected met to discuss upcoming activities. The activities were not to interfere with studies or to distract in any other way. The primary goal, after all, was to help the Indian student succeed in college and in life. Social activities and events such as leadership workshops, seminars, and conferences were planned, as well as American Indian Week.

While trying to organize the Lamanites, I felt many other pressures. My own family on the reservation was having problems, and they had wanted me to stay home. It was stressful not to have complied with their wishes. That my parents wanted me to marry a Navajo and stay home to begin my own sheep flock was a constant pressure to me. And the last time I had spoken with my father, it was his desire for me to succeed him as a hand trembler or part-time medicine man. He said, "My son, it is time for someone to learn of the ways of medicine. As I have watched you, I can see that the Holy People have given you wisdom. I will teach you of these medicine ways. You must learn these ways to help your people."

I was in a difficult situation. I felt that I could be of the most help to our people by finishing college. "Father," I said, "I respect your wisdom. I am honored. But there are other things I feel I must do. It is not my desire to hurt your feelings. But I am not prepared to take the medicine learning way." I wanted to prepare myself to be useful to all Indian tribes, not just the Navajos. Eventually I wanted to make a significant contribution to our whole nation! I was just as proud of being an American citizen as I was of being an Indian.

I sensed his hurt.

Continuing, I tried to explain my decision: "The Navajo people and other Indians need someone who can learn the white man's college and ways. The day is with us when we must know of his ways in order to best help our people. This is my desire. To learn the ways of medicine and to graduate from college will not come easily to one mind. Our ways are powerful, but there are other ways in which I must help our family, tribe, and nation. I appreciate and love you with all my heart. I do not turn you down because I think medicine learning is not important. But an Indian must learn to compete in the white man's world in order to survive."

"That you have chosen another path, I see," Father said understandingly. "Ashkii Hoyani, I have trust in you. You have never let your family down. The Great Creator has plans for you. This I know. I respect your beliefs as a Mormon. You can go to any church. It does not matter to me. I, too, love you. If you tell me that the Book of Mormon and the Bible are true, I will believe you. If you say you must be educated like a white man to survive and to help our people, I will believe you."

To have my father respond in such a way was a warm experience that bordered upon being deeply spiritual. To have the love, trust, and confidence of my father was most rewarding. I vowed never to let him down.

Pressure also came because some of my brothers and sisters had quit school. This hurt deeply. Schooling, as I saw it, was one of the essential remedies to remove them from impoverished circumstances. Idleness and boredom wedged into their lives after they quit school. My anxiety for their welfare was deep; I spent many sleepless nights in mental struggle trying to think of ways to lift them from such poor circumstances. My family was never lazy, but the simple truth is that there were no jobs available on the reservation. They were young at that time—too young to have quit school. After quitting school, they began to drink. The more they drank, the more their hopes for the future dimmed.

How deeply this pierced my soul is beyond what words can describe. During that year, my brother, Clifford, died. After having become intoxicated, he wandered away from our hogan and never returned. Lonely and helpless, he stumbled around and lost his way in the bitter cold night. The next day he was found frozen. He was just sixteen. How I loved him. I had taken care of him when he was but an infant. I had changed his diapers, fed him, wiped away his tears, and held him to my bosom. A part of me passed away too.

Studies were a constant pressure. I carried between eighteen and twenty credit hours. Being president of the Tribe of Many Feathers was a pressure. Because some members did not follow through on assignments, many times I had to do what others would not do. I also had two or three Church jobs at the same time.

Another pressure I had to deal with was that some people felt I was a rebel, for I felt obligated to represent the other Indian students' views. Often the Indian students were hurt by insensitivity from the dominant society, particularly over the issue of interracial dating and marriage. Students threatened to leave because a few well-meaning campus advisers had called Indian dances satanic. And here I was in the middle of all this.

Because my father was a medicine man, I knew that these dances were not evil. My father had explained that the Creator gave these things as spiritual gifts to Indian people to help them survive in a harsh environment. I believed my father, for I saw him do only good for people. He was a good man, and his spiritual knowledge had helped many Navajos.

As president of the Tribe of Many Feathers, I felt it my responsibility to help the untutored to understand the sacredness of these dances and other Indian ways that were good. I believed strongly in combining the good from both cultures. There are both the good and evil in American society as well as in Indian cultures. Consequently some people branded me as a disbelieving Mormon. Some thought just because I believed in Indian ways, I was not a good Mormon. It was difficult in those days for people to understand that Indian cultures could blend into the gospel just as well as the European cultures, and possibly better. Why? Because many of our traditions held close ties to Israelite thought and expression.

Also, some of my roommates were not members of the Church, and some advisers thought I was being misled or influenced by them. But this was not true. I knew that the Lord had brought us together so I could help bring them to the gospel. So intense was the mandate to forsake Indian ways that I was even told to tell one of my nonmember roommates to leave BYU. I was told to break all ties with him and that he was an agitator and militant Indian. Never could I have done this, for I had seen the man's awesome spiritual potential and ability. I stood up for him and defended him. I promised the advisers that one day my friend would become a well-loved and respected leader in the Church and outside the Church. Today he has risen into leadership positions at BYU, and as a good member of the Church he holds responsible positions therein. He is also well respected throughout the nation and Indian nations as a great youth leader. He is one of our outstanding Indian leaders.

My roommates and I became known as the "basement boys," as we lived in a basement apartment. Most of the Indian students came to our apartment to receive counsel about personal problems, studies, dating problems, and other matters. We always counseled them toward success and toward patience with those who did not understand Indian ways. In a sense, our apartment became a refuge for lost souls who had been disembodied from campus life. Always it was our intent to give them uplifting and positive counseling.

Also, I held several positions in the Lamanite ward on campus. That was tough. I grew from it, but it was still very hard at times. Church callings or positions I held at the same time were elder's quorum president, Sunday School superintendent, Sunday School teacher, and Young Men's president. This was all in the same year I had attended Clifford's funeral. Man Who Halts, my beloved uncle, had also passed away that year. Indians tend to mourn deaths longer than those within the dominant society, and I grieved deeply over their passing.

Somehow I persuaded one of my younger brothers to stay in school. I arranged for him to stay with the Harkers in Orem. Then I helped him get into BYU. Not making wise use of his time there, he did not last too long. At least he had tried. But it still hurt to see him drop out and head back to the reservation and to the wrong crowds.

I tried my best to help Mike, Joe, and Bob, and my brothers and sisters in their struggles, along with trying to take care of the needs of the Indian students at BYU. My own studies had to be considered as well. The year presented a grueling challenge, to say the least.

I learned to treasure, as did my father, afflictions and adversity. Problems and trials can be turned into blessings. From them greater faith and strength come. From this standpoint it was a wonderful year, for the spiritual and emotional growth I experienced was phenomenal.

I had planned to go to school right through the summers, to get my bachelor's degree as quickly as possible. But because of the pressures on campus, I decided to take a break. I wanted to find a job on the reservation in order to be closer to my family. On the reservation, there would certainly be less stress, and that is what I needed then.

I was fortunate enough to land a job as park ranger in the

Canyon DeChelly National Park in Chinle, Arizona. I spent two summers working there, both in 1966 and 1967. My responsibility was to patrol the park and to enforce park regulations and policies. I was furnished a trailer in the mountains nearby. Rather than stay at park headquarters, I stayed in the trailer and then drove to the rim of the canyon each day. Driving the rim took most of the day. The rest of my time I spent walking into the canyon and greeting tourists. Also, I spent time talking with the Navajo families who lived in their hogans on the floor of the canyon. I met a lot of people that way. Tourists came from all over the world to visit the historic site. It was there that Kit Carson had starved the Navajos into submission before taking them to Fort Sumner on the Long Walk. Also, right on the canyon floor, the Navajos had for years raised beautiful stands of Arizona peach trees.

After work hours, I was usually involved in LDS district or branch activities. My assignment in the Church at that time was to work with the young people. As Scoutmaster and youth leader, I was busy all the time.

Whenever I was not occupied in Church work, I usually traveled home to be with my family. My paychecks came in handy to help them buy needed commodities, especially food. Also, I helped them bring in firewood and haul water. In that way those two summers on the reservation were completely filled. I also spent a lot of time in meditation and prayer. It was handy to do since my trailer was located away from anyone else's. Meditation in solitude, in the high mountain tops, though not to be overdone, is a good way to commune with God. My father taught me that the best place to worship was up in the mountains.

As college continued, things did not seem as hectic as before. I either got used to my problems or they lessened. Campus advisers began to respect the good in Indian ways. Time and experience brought this understanding on both sides. The administration and the Indian students began to become of one mind and heart. Soon BYU developed the best Indian education program in the whole country.

Then I met Katherine Hettich, a Commanche from Okla-

homa. It was the spring of 1966. We had worked together as
Indian student officers. It was during this time I noted her firm
testimony and delightful personality. The more I was around
her, the more my feelings turned to love. But I didn't know
that was what was happening, never having experienced such
poignant, subtle feelings before. She was outgoing without
being offensive, and relating to other people seemed to be one
of her greatest strengths. I was attracted by all these fine
qualities.

On one occasion, I was in charge of setting up a Book of
Mormon pageant. The part of the Savior was being cast. A
very effective Polynesian actor was playing the part of the
Savior, so the scene itself was reverent. The lighting had to be
just right to give the special glow that represented the light
that radiated from the Savior as he came to visit the Lamanites. The scene reminded me of the time when I read of the
Savior's coming in Third Nephi when I was shepherding one
summer day years past. I reflected back then to that time when
I had gained a profound testimony of the Book of Mormon, a
record of the forefathers of Indian people.

Dimming and lowering the overhead lights began to make
the scene seem even more real. Then I looked to the front row.
One of the stage lights, a soft, lovely one, had fallen upon one
of the most beautiful, angelic young women I'd ever seen. How
my heart was lifted with her beauty, mingled with the thoughts
I was experiencing of the Savior. It was Katherine Hettich,
and I knew then that I wanted to ask her out for a date. The
young man sitting next to her was her date for the evening. It
was my plan to end that type of coed life-style. The Spirit directed me to get better acquainted with her.

A little before that, I helped start an Indian student news-
letter. Not coincidentally, I think, one of the students assigned to work with me was Katherine, vice-president of publi-
cations and publicity. She eventually became editor of the
newspaper. She edited and set some print in my heart. Our relationship went from elite to pica to boldface, blossoming into
a wholesome and genuine friendship. We dated a lot. One
night after she returned from a date with me, she asked her

roommate if there was anything wrong with her because George had not even held her hand after several months of dating.

She and I worked closely together to organize other functions and activities for the Tribe of Many Feathers. We planned and initiated many activities during BYU Indian Week. Also, we planned numerous youth conferences. By the fall of 1967, we both realized our commitment to one another.

There was one more step I had to take—I had to talk with her father. When I asked his permission to marry her, our chat turned into a lecture. He told me that under no circumstances was I to marry his daughter and particularly since I was going into the LDS seminary work. Though he was a member of the Church, his understanding of all its programs and precepts was not broad. He associated my entering into the seminary program with some of the monastic orders of other churches. He was very upset. I was to leave Katherine alone.

I tried to talk with her mother (I forgot there were two steps!) and got the same reaction. She did not want her daughter married to a reservation Indian. She had seen unhappiness in Oklahoma. If her daughter had a chance to marry an Anglo, so much the better—it would save her from a life of misery. Being a full-blooded Navajo was one strike against me in their eyes. Both Katherine and I received her strict admonition not to marry. It was extremely painful for us because of our deep love for each other.

Her parents got in touch with the Indian ward bishop on campus and tried to persuade him to discourage us from getting married. He called us into his office one day, mentioning the fact that her parents had contacted him. But he had told them that George Lee was not just another Indian. He had told them about some of my accomplishments and Church positions, and about the way I carried them through. He said that I had a great future ahead of me. Furthermore, he had told them that priesthood interference in the matter was not appropriate because we were both worthy individuals. If it was the mind of the Lord, then who was he to counsel us to part? This made her parents even more upset. We did not want them to be upset.

We wanted their blessing to start marriage. Time is a great healer. So is personal appearance! Once I met them in person, I completely won them over in seconds. Ever since then, they have been thrilled and happy about our marriage.

Elder Spencer W. Kimball agreed to officiate at our marriage in the Salt Lake Temple in December of 1967. Our bishop from BYU, advisers, and other close friends came to our wedding, making it a special experience. Both Kitty and I feel it was a very sacred and spiritual event. Elder Kimball gave us some wise and encouraging counsel never to be forgotten. Though small physically, Elder Kimball became a giant in our eyes because of his compassion, faith, and awesome spirituality.

After our marriage, because we were always together, we found it easier to concentrate on our studies, because being apart was no longer a worry. With she and I working as a team, it was easier to accomplish the many duties that were placed upon my shoulders in the various campus leadership positions. That year I was a senior in college, due to graduate in the spring of 1968.

As graduation time approached, one of my first concerns was to find employment. My wife was pregnant with our first child. Marriage had brought unavoidable responsibilities. I began to send out résumés. After some time, we had not received any replies. As a husband and prospective father, I began to have some concern. Both my wife and I prayed that something would come forth to help us sustain our family financially. It was not long until our prayers were answered.

A letter arrived inviting me to come to Rough Rock, Arizona, to teach school. The administration of this school, the first of its kind in the nation, wanted me to help initiate a new bilingual, bicultural approach in teaching Navajo children. School officials had heard about me from someone; I still do not know exactly from whom. So they wrote a letter asking me to come. I had not sent a résumé to this school district. Of course, we accepted the offer. I would rather have taught in the LDS seminary system, but there were just no openings there at the time.

With thankful hearts, we prepared to leave. Kitty began packing suitcases while I tried to take care of my graduation requirements. Both of us were satisfied with the direction the Lord had opened. It was hard to leave campus life and all of our friends, but the outside world was begging to be challenged and tested. With a little apprehension and anxiety, but with much faith, it was not long until we were chatting in the car, with tearful eyes, on our way to Rough Rock, Arizona, on the Navajo reservation.

18

ROUGH ROCK

The trip to Rough Rock was pleasant. To have such a nice job was the dream of a lifetime. During the days when I was young, just a boy chasing prairie dogs for dinner, I had never even imagined that I would be in a position like this. I thought back over my time at BYU. I had graduated with a bachelor's degree. Presently it was my desire to one day receive a master's degree as well. My plan was to work for a year or two and then pursue a graduate degree. I just knew that opportunities would be opened up for me to pursue my master's and doctor's degrees. But for now, I was looking forward to getting fully involved in Rough Rock. I desired deeply to help others, particularly the Indian people. I had seen so much despair among my own people. My desire was to give others a key to happiness.

"Kitty," I said, "why do you think there were no openings in the seminary program? I sure wanted to teach the youth in the Church. Why is it that out of the clear blue this job turned up in Rough Rock?"

She was quiet momentarily and then responded, "There is something to it, all right. It must be where we are meant to be for now. Somehow I feel this will not be our permanent home, though." I had thought the same thing. It was just a feeling, a small one, but there nonetheless.

"I wonder what kind of housing they'll have there," she asked rhetorically. Then she lapsed into silence.

I returned to thoughts of how I had wanted to help others gain a better appreciation for life. My first desire had been to teach seminary, but that did not come to pass. The Lord had other plans for me.

Rough Rock was to be a pilot project for a completely different approach in teaching Indian children. It was to feature bicultural and bilingual education and Indian community control and involvement, including adult education. Emphasizing free interaction between community adults and the school, this program was indeed a departure from the traditional Bureau of Indian Affairs standard of education within Indian communities.

The decade of the 1960s was especially important in the education of Native Americans. Innovative things were being done throughout Indian reservations across America. Democratic administration in Washington seemed to be more sensitive to the needs of America's poor, especially the Indian poor. I was thrilled to join the team of committed and dedicated Indian educators who were making a valiant and gallant effort to raise the educational status of Native Americans. The awakening of America to its native children was almost to full height by 1968, the year of my graduation.

Even though there was a governmental trend favoring Indian education, still the Indians in general lagged behind the white population of the country in educational attainment. Educational achievements of Native Americans were low as measured by standardized tests, number of years of schooling, number of graduates, college enrollment, and college graduation. It seemed that Indian students were two or three years behind white students, and that Indian children fell progressively behind the longer they stayed in school. Many studies indicated that Indian dropout rates were twice the national average in both public and federal schools. Startling research reported that the average length of education for all Indians under federal supervision was five school years, and more than one out of every five Indian men had fewer than five years of schooling. Thousands of Native Americans were functional illiterates.

Fortunately, during this time there were many sensitive citizens across the nation who felt the need to improve the standard of living for the Indian American. A national survey and study of American Indian education was implemented. The National Indian Education Advisory Committee was organized. A Senate subcommittee on Indian Education was created to look into problems of Indian education and recommend ways to solve them. Ted Kennedy and other concerned and sympathetic United States senators served on this subcommittee.

President Lyndon B. Johnson sent to Congress a special message on goals and programs for the Indian Opportunity Committee and appointed Vice-President Spiro T. Agnew as chairman with six cabinet officers as members.

I viewed this era, the 1960s and early 1970s, as a period in which America's Indian children were truly discovered. I thought that their contemporary educational deficits and other related problems were being exposed for the first time to the general public.

Turning its sometimes lazy eye toward the first children of America, national attention began to see the brown cataract mirrored before itself. The eye of America had neglectfully allowed its visionary element the blindness of poverty. The pulsing heart that had given the early colonists much native richness had been finally given due attention. The aerobics of the American political machine began to exercise in favor of the Native American. This was an exciting and thrilling time.

We pulled over to fill the car with gasoline at the Bluff, Utah, trading post. It was hot there, but the stately red bluffs that lined the south side of the San Juan River helped divert attention from the dry heat. Cottonwood trees abounded in this small village. Dust lay quietly at the base of all the trees, darkened only by the leafy shade. Now and again a dog barked. I wiped my brow and looked over at my wife.

She was uncomfortable with the heat. The pregnancy. When she didn't respond, I smiled. All my friends who were already married told me it might be this way, moods and all associated with pregnancy. I was new to the idea, but I had enough respect and love for my wife that it did not matter—to experience what some say is much different than just hearing it.

When the car was filled, we climbed back in and were on our way. Once the wind began to whisk into the windows, the heat was more bearable. Kitty shifted in the seat a little and looked more comfortable. I read that as a sign—it was all right to talk now.

"How are you feeling?" I gently asked her. I watched intently for her facial reaction even before she spoke.

"Oh, I'm feeling much better now. How many more miles is it? In a way, this desert country is beautiful. Is that Monument Valley over there in the distance?"

"Yes. I've hitchhiked through that area before." With that, both she and I began to enter our own thoughts once again. My own thoughts picked up where they had left off before. I had been thinking about the general awakening in this country to the needs of the Indian population.

Study after study about Indian education seemed to be popping up all over the country. These various studies demanded a bicultural and bilingual approach to Indian education with understanding of and respect for Indian cultures and suggested the use of Indian cultural materials in the instructional program. They demanded bilingual instruction in teaching English as a second language. A special kind of teacher, sensitized to Indian culture, was needed. Also, the studies included the pinpointed need for control of community schools by Native Americans.

Rough Rock School was receiving a tremendous amount of favorable publicity nationally as well as locally, ranging from magazine articles to television documentaries and to statements by prominent educators as well as by United States senators.

Rough Rock School started in 1966 as an elementary boarding school on the Navajo reservation. It was built by the Bureau of Indian Affairs and was contracted out to a small corporation of Navajo tribal members called Dine Incorporated, who were to administer the school. The purpose of this arrangement was to provide a setting for an innovative educational experience that would include bicultural and bilingual education and community control of the school. It was agreed that the school would be free of control by the Bureau of Indian Affairs.

The Dine Incorporated hired as director a Navajo educator long interested in the objectives of the project, and he recruited a fine staff, of whom I was a part. An all-Navajo board of education was elected with the understanding that it would have effective decision-making powers over the school. Most of these board members were traditional Navajos who had never had an opportunity to attend school themselves. Now, here they were as school-board members deciding key issues affecting Rough Rock School. Amazingly, they demonstrated a high ability to make wise and effective decisions about the school.

When we arrived at Rough Rock, we immediately took a liking to the area. The drive had been long, but we were now at a place we would call home, at least temporarily. The ride had been pleasant. My wife, in her motherly way, was tired from the long ride but pleased to arrive at last. We were assigned a medium-sized trailer to live in. Kitty began housekeeping duties immediately while I began work at school in preparation for the upcoming year.

I spent many hours in the Navajo curriculum center producing materials for my classroom, materials based on Navajo legends, history, biographies, and language. My goal was to present the Navajo students with a clear history of their race, to give them pride in their heritage. Traditional history courses often gave a negative image of Indians. My goal was to give the Navajo children an understanding of cultural values and how they arise historically, often for economic reason. I wanted them to hear the truth. So the materials I developed included a comparative study of Indian and Anglo values. I was also involved in creating instructional material for teaching English as a second language.

In faculty meetings, seminars, and workshops, I advocated that Indian parents and tribal leaders should assume increasing interest in and responsibility for the education of Indian children. I strongly believed that local Indian adults should be on school boards elected by the community and that there should be some form of specialized training for these native school-board members. I felt that they should have full authority to administer their own schools and not just advisory powers. There were Indian community members on school boards before at the Bureau of Indian Affairs schools, but they were there in name only. Their function was merely advisory. Indian voice, I urged, meant power and action, not just words.

Rough Rock became a model for Indian communities. Later during the year, I was given more responsibilities, including counseling, in which I made sincere efforts to contact the children's families and parents to encourage them to come into the classroom. I wanted them to see the wonderful things that were happening for their children. Always the suggestions of parents were given serious consideration, and most of the time they were put into operation. The Indian parents, though lacking an education themselves, were very wise about life. They knew how to teach, for they had been passing on traditional values that their parents had taught to them.

A traditional Navajo word for white man is *anaa'i*, which means "enemy." For too long, schools were, in a sense, enemies to Indian families and communities. Schools were the white man's institutions. Government boarding schools had teachers and administrators whose credentials would not be accepted in good public-school systems. Turnover was high, standards were low, and working conditions and personnel policies were poor.

Unfortunately so, teachers and administrators in BIA systems were often given employment as political rewards without consideration of their qualifications. The bleak reservation environment matched the depleted salary scale. This turned qualified personnel away. The isolation of the schools on bare reservations, devoid of restaurants, shops, and malls, seemed only to breed more isolation.

An invisible wall of separation existed between Indian community adults and the school systems. A desert cold war existed. Indians knew their own values and what they must have for harmony, and BIA schools insisted on following policies from Washington that denied Indian community individualism.

Many teachers were insensitive to cultural differences, which separated them from their Indian students. Sets of values and habits completely foreign to local Native American customs were inculcated within the cinder-block walls of boarding schools. Way beyond this, the differences were magnified when school personnel were utterly oblivious to these cultural contrasts. That there were some sensitivities to dress and language differences did not preclude the fact that almost total ignorance existed about subtle values and feelings. Indians had, for the most part, always been depicted as stoics. Many Anglos bought this dime-novel idea wholeheartedly. The fact is that most reservation-born Indians had been reared in a surrounding of simplicity and serenity, which only created more poignant feelings.

Indian dwellings were seldom visited by BIA school personnel. They had no knowledge of the living conditions and family backgrounds of the children they had been teaching for years. They had little contact with the Indian community life and no understanding—and wanted it not—of Indian attitudes, values, and standards.

With this kind of negative relationship between teachers and communities, which had long existed, I had difficulty persuading parents to come into the classroom. It was not easy for them, and understandably so. A great reluctance existed that projected an image that they were not interested in their children's well-being. How far from the truth this was.

Who could blame them?

When teachers of their children had labeled Indian children as lazy, stupid, mean, and hostile, who would want to expose parental sensitivity to that kind of comment?

The philosophy of Rough Rock School was that a child's success depends largely upon the help and encouragement from home, so I visited many parents and invited them to assist me in the classroom. They were afraid at first. Many were surprised, and more were shocked at such an invitation. It was unheard of. And to be visited by a teacher genuinely interested in their child? Impossible! Suspicion of white man's schools still loomed in their minds. They were afraid that the school might rob their children of their Indianness and identity. Some parents were simply afraid to turn their children over to strangers, particularly non-Navajo strangers.

I shall never forget an experience I had with John Todachinnie's family. When John first stepped into the classroom, he was very shy and extremely reluctant to participate. One day I asked him to be class president and gave him an achievable assignment to hand out pencils and paper to the other students. He was fearful at first, but after a week or so, he began to look forward to this responsibility. Slowly he began to emerge from his shell. The other students began to look up to him as their president. When they needed something, he was the man to ask. Two others were subsequently asked to serve with him. Each had assignments designed to build their self-confidence. How they changed was a miracle. After a term, three other class officers were selected by vote of the class. Many had turns in being class officers.

It was not long until I found myself on a rough and bumpy road headed to the top of nearby Black Mesa. John Todachinnie's parents lived there. It seemed to take forever to get there. Anyone unfamiliar with reservation survival would have thought nothing could have lived out there. The pickup truck I drove up the mesa bounced me up and down in its steel spring seat like tumbling clothes in a dryer. I was nonetheless determined to get there.

As I drove up to the humble hogan, I could see immediately that John and his family were living under extreme poverty. My heart sank. I had lived in similar circumstances when I was about John's age. What kind of a chance would he have in school? Despair fell over me as I walked slowly up to the hogan door, not really knowing what I would say. I knocked on the door.

"Hoshdeé," a faint voice from inside responded. I caught the aroma of frybread and mutton ribs.

I pushed open the latchless door and entered. Inside I found Sally Todachinnie, John's mother, preparing dinner for her husband, who was still out herding sheep. Five children were with her. (They had four boys and two girls, I later learned.) I kept thinking about how important the atmosphere and condition of the home were in the early years of a child's education and life. It hurt.

"Ya'at'eeh. My name is George Lee. I am of the Bitterwater Clan. I am a teacher at the school. One of your sons, John, is in my class. I like John very much. He is doing very well in school. In fact, he is one of my class leaders. He was made a leader just recently."

I surveyed the family inside the dirt-floored hogan. I thought about how familiar this life seemed. I was reared in a hogan like this. How had I ever made it myself?

I remember thinking that I wished more white teachers would do what I was doing. Perhaps they would be more tender in the classroom. Perhaps they would be more sensitive, patient, understanding, and compassionate with the Indian people. Maybe they could learn something from this culture that would benefit their own lives. They would begin to see that day-to-day survival in such economic misery makes even

George P. Lee teaching a student to write in Navajo at the Rough Rock School

the smallest of tasks, such as getting a child off to school, a great hurdle. How can Indian children, I thought, be compared to white children in academic achievement? It is unfair. Satisfactory academic achievement could hardly be expected from Indian children who come from such a poor and wretched home environment as the one I then saw in the Todachinnie hogan.

I reflected back on some of my college educational lessons. The number of books in the home, the number of people in the home, the educational level of parents, the number of square feet in the home, the English-speaking ability of the parents, the age and condition of the home, the parents' attitude toward schooling—all are related to a child's academic success. A home without the proper combination of these things has little chance to produce academically successful children.

I began to understand why John had come to school inadequately clothed and malnourished. Sally Todachinnie and her family were totally unexposed to the dominant societal values and ways. Her family was unfamiliar with piped water, sanitary toilets, oil lamps, electric lights, fuel oil, plastered walls, wallpaper, ocean liners, two-story houses, elevators, mail carriers, fire engines, credit cards, supermarkets, department stores, movies, and all other modern conveniences. Yet these things around which the modern school system developed were commonplace to the Anglo child.

More significantly, I noticed the absence of newspapers, magazines, and posters and the many other examples of the printed word that introduce white children to a variety of vicarious experiences that enrich their lives. The Indian child is therefore deprived of the supplementary teachings that have become an unconscious part of life for almost every white child from birth. I told myself again that it was unfair. Why?

I said to Sally, "Ha'at'iish Dine'e nili?" (What clan are you?)

"Naakai Dine' [Mexican People clan]," she meekly answered.

I asked, "Where is your husband?"

"He is out herding sheep. One of our boys is with him. They should be home soon. I am making this frybread and ribs for them. I am sure they are hungry. They have been herding all day."

I thought as I looked at Sally how many of my people, the Indian people, despite all the strong external pressures, have not yet become assimilated into Anglo society. While making continual superficial adjustment to economic and political exactions of the dominant society, families such as Sally's continue to preserve basic Navajo values.

I said, "I would like to invite you and your husband to visit my classroom to help me teach your son and others. I need your help. I want to help John, as well as help you, in any way I can. This school is different. It is interested in you. We want you to know what is going on." And as I paused between thoughts, Sally began to look at me in a different way.

I continued, "The school here is good. It is doing some wonderful things for the community children. We are a demonstration school. This is a new approach in education. The other teachers and I are trying to teach the children right. We teach them the Navajo language and culture as well as the white man's culture and language. As a parent you can help us because you know our ways. We need to blend good Indian ways with the good ways of the white man."

Her furrowed brow began to uncrinkle as she understood my words. The newness of the idea at first held her spellbound. I informed her that Rough Rock School had made national headlines, not to impress her, but to show her the importance of what the teachers were trying to accomplish. I spoke to her about the United States president's address given in favor of Native Americans. Then I implored her to help in my classroom.

Before I was finished talking, her husband and other son walked in the door, greeted me with a wide smile, shook my hand, and sat down on the bare earth. The husband was still suspicious about who I was and what I wanted. I quickly identified myself and tried to put him at ease. I gave a similar speech to him also. I stressed the importance of education for the progress of our people.

As I looked at him, a thought went through my mind that he, like many others, had resisted the efforts of the white people to destroy his culture in order to supplant it with that of their own. Schools were looked at only as devices to hasten the assimilation of Indian culture into that of the dominant society. Indians resist this through withdrawal, indifference, and noncooperation. Tom Todachinnie was this way. Sally was more responsive. Tom and I still continued to talk, but not about schools necessarily. But eventually I asked Tom and Sally again to help in my classroom. The atmosphere in the obscure hogan was momentarily hushed. Again I asked. It was apparent that Tom was resistant. I hoped he would tell me why. When he did not respond, I repeated the same message as I had given before, about John's leadership ability and need for education, and about what our school was doing to improve Indian education through parental involvement.

After a long pause, Tom finally asked, "Is your school trying to make white men out of my children?"

With this simple question he taught me much. Many years of schooling could not have taught me what that one utterance did. He was so deliberate in its delivery. I knew that he wanted his children to retain their identity, their Indianness, their culture and language. He wanted to perpetuate valuable tradition and saw the white man's school as a threat.

Tom had the more traditional Indian's perception of education and schools. But in spite of their apathy, hostility, and suspicion, Indian people in general were beginning to place a high value on schooling. In time, both Tom and Sally entered my classroom. They assisted me and made valuable suggestions and comments on what I taught and the way I taught. My teaching greatly improved because of their help. They were beginning to understand more and more that in order for an Indian child to succeed in the white man's world, he has to compete and become more aggressive academically.

Many traditional Indian parents began helping at the school. Whenever they became involved, their enjoyment was obvious—they were there day after day. Even parental self-esteem was lifted, and they too grew from the experience.

Tears often came to my eyes as I saw Navajo women in bright velveteen blouses and silk skirts come into the classroom to help. And men came adorned with traditional Navajo jewelry reserved for special occasions. More than the jewelry, they wore smiles. It was hard to hold back the tears as I saw bright-faced children eagerly responding to teachings of Navajo language and stories, along with English and American history. Rough Rock's philosophy was that teaching Indian children their own language and history facilitates their learning of the English language and history. This philosophy seemed to be working. It was gratifying beyond compare.

The wall between parents and the school soon crumbled. They understood it to be their school, not the typical Bureau of Indian Affairs school. To have observed Indian people directing the affairs of their own local school was a memorable experience. No longer did the school represent an alien or terrifying environment. Both parents and children were proud of their involvement. In the past, government schools often sat in a fenced compound completely apart from the communities they served. In the past, the schools had not served as community resources, nor did they serve community needs or desires. Rough Rock made great strides in achieving community control. School board members were exceptionally well known in the community and were indeed in control of school direction. Contacts between classroom and home were frequent.

Though for the most part things were positive, some things were not. The many studies done about Rough Rock provided no substantial evidence that bilingual and bicultural education and other innovative programs resulted in a better command of English and other basic skills as measured by standardized tests. But the most important thing was that parents became involved in the school and were exposed to the educational process.

Perhaps we went overboard in the bicultural and bilingual areas. The students would be forced to deal with the dominant society more and more as they grew up. A better command of

English and a better understanding of mathematics would have served them well. Still, good had come from the bilingual and bicultural study.

During the course of the year, I was assigned to coach the school's basketball team. I had to start from scratch. Some of the students had never been exposed to the game. These were the ones who came from the more remote and isolated part of the reservation. I began by teaching the basic fundamentals of basketball. The boys responded very well and became very team oriented. Their hard work and teachableness paid off. The discipline didn't come easy. I had to work with them day and night to shake off the undisciplined run-and-shoot reservation-type basketball. As a result, we went undefeated, with eighteen team wins and no losses. We won the league championship and all of the tournaments in the area. It was a miraculous season. We won the respect of all the teams in our league and brought honor and a good reputation to the school. John Todachinnie became a valuable member of the team.

The *Navajo Times* headlined our team and included a team picture. All the boys cut out their picture, of course, to show their parents back in the hogan. What they accomplished that year was amazing. I tried to teach them to be leaders off the court as well as on. Hard work paid off. The unity of the team was beyond description. The self-respect and confidence of each team member were greatly enlarged and strengthened. This success alone seemed to offset the many negative experiences they might have had. Pessimism was replaced by optimism and hope in their lives, as well as in the future.

Other assignments I was given during the course of the year were guidance counselor, curriculum materials developer, and summer-school supervisor. In addition, I provided leadership for the educational programs at the school by disseminating information to the community while promoting coordination between the school and community.

On the spiritual and religious side of things, my choice wife was Relief Society president in the local branch. I was a counselor in the branch presidency and held other positions at the same time, particularly one of trying to activate members. Later, I was asked to serve in the district presidency. Our church meetings were held in another community almost twenty miles away. All during the year we went to church. In the hard winter, through sloshy mud and slippery snow, we traveled the same rutted dirt road, getting stuck many times. Yet, this did not prevent us from going to church. Sometimes I had to attend with mud on my pants, but what was I going to church for anyway? To be a fashion model? The Spirit always seemed to be the same as long as I kept my conscience unsullied. My wife never missed a meeting as called for in her assignment. Never did we miss a Sunday meeting together.

We did much long-distance home teaching and missionary work with good success. In order to visit the families we were assigned, I put many miles on our car in an evening. That year we were assessed a substantial amount of money for the building fund. We came up with it all right, but we had to tighten our financial belt. We have never regretted making these sacrifices.

Our branch president, Alton Johnson, an Anglo, was often viewed as a modern-day Jacob Hamblin. He was well loved and respected by our Indian branch members. His love and patience for them were unsurpassed. My family and I became dear friends with this gentle and spiritual man. He spent much of his life among the Indians. He was a great example and leader among them. Clifford Young, like Alton, was another Anglo leader who dearly loved the Navajos. He was district president for years on the Navajo Reservation.

I was also involved in the Navajo Youth Organization as one of the youth officers. This was a Navajo tribal organization. We planned, organized, and set up youth conferences for Navajo youth on and off the Navajo reservation. One conference we planned lasted three days, and we invited more than five hundred youth. Local tribal leaders and personnel, Rough Rock School personnel, and Bureau of Indian Affairs school personnel were invited to come. It was a wonderful event in which Navajo youth were inspired and motivated to do better.

I was president of this organization for all Navajo youth throughout the nation while I was still an undergraduate at Brigham Young University.

On our way to a district conference one time, Kitty began to have labor pains. Elder LeGrand Richards, one of our favorite speakers, was scheduled to speak at this conference. What a time for her to go into labor! I had really wanted, as she did, to meet Elder Richards. But, Duane, our firstborn, had different notions about where we were to go. We ended up at the Gallup PHS Hospital. It was all right, I guess, to have missed Elder Richards's talk, for I found out early enough that Duane could get just as wound up vocally!

After a few days, I brought my wife and newborn son back home. Then, two weeks later, we were on our way home from a trip. After I pulled up to the house, I got out of the car with two-week-old Duane in one arm and a sack full of groceries in the other. The rain was pelting down so hard that the droplets hurt when they hit my body. The sidewalk had become dangerously slippery. I had made a rush for the front door. In the process, I dropped Duane. He landed hard, head-first on the edge of the cement sidewalk and rolled off into a puddle of muddy water. My heart sank. Dropping the groceries, I tearfully and frightfully picked him up. My soul shrank.

With my wife right on my heels, I rushed into the house. Duane had turned blue all over and had a faint heartbeat. In panic, we did everything possible to revive him. Nothing worked. He did not cry at all. In fact, he was not even moving. This alarmed us greatly. Instantly, it seemed we were both impressed to kneel down and ask the Lord to help us. I then gave Duane a priesthood blessing, and as soon as I had finished, he opened his eyes and began to cry. Oh, how many nights before had I wished his cries would not have awakened me! Now tears came to our eyes, and we knelt to thank the Lord for this great blessing. From that day forth, Duane has been healthy.

The year before I had started work in Rough Rock, both Kitty and I knew we were going to be there only a short time. So at the beginning of the summer after my first teaching year, we began to look for some type of signal that would indicate a different direction for us to take. We discussed the idea of enrolling in a graduate program, or applying elsewhere for employment. With all the discussion, we never came to a resolution. In June I was assigned as the summer program director for Rough Rock—I had not applied for work anywhere else. What we were to do was uncertain, but at the same time, we both knew and had faith that the Lord would bless us with an opportunity to further my education.

Then, one day in June, a letter came from Utah State University. The dean of the department of education was inviting us to come to their campus to help organize and implement an effective Indian education program. This program was to have a special Indian-related curriculum and was to recruit Indian students with the use of federal funds.

The university was willing to compensate me for my service by offering a full scholarship with living expenses in an educational administration graduate program. After my wife and I read the letter, we rushed to each other in a happy embrace. This was it. This was the message we were waiting for. Our prayers were answered.

I immediately went to Rough Rock School to make an appointment with the school director to tell him of our changed plans. I was the summer school program coordinator. It was hard to tell him, for I had grown to love and respect him as a friend. I didn't want to hurt his feelings. Reluctantly he let us go when he heard the good news. Though he was hesitant, he was also pleased for us.

In less than two days, we were packed and on our way to Logan, Utah, to Utah State University. We found it extremely difficult to leave our friends, especially Lewis and Donna Singer. They were our close, dear friends. Lewis is also Navajo. We had served in the same mission and even went to BYU together. At Rough Rock, we had played on the same community basketball team as well. It was hard to leave him and his family. But the Lord had different destinies in mind for Lewis and me. He and his wife had our highest respect and love. Paul Platero was another good friend whose love and friendship were hard to leave.

Asdzaa Lichii, mother of George P. Lee

We drove to Utah by way of Shiprock in order to see my family, to give them the exhilarating news. This time my father was home. Both he and Mother were glad to see us. As usual, they did not want us to go but wanted us to stay home near them. I explained again what I had to do. They seemed to understand. I'm sure they always thought it was the same old story. And it was. But the leaving was always the same—painful.

All during the drive to Utah, after having left my beloved parents and family, I thought of the previous year. I thought in particular about Ted Kennedy, who had spoken to our first graduating class. He had impressed me as a benevolent man, sincerely interested in the cause of the poor and downtrodden. He was unique. Despite his very busy schedule, he took the time to visit Rough Rock School, which was located in a remote and isolated part of the Navajo reservation.

Ted Kennedy was at that time the chairman of the Senate Subcommittee on Indian education. I often wondered why he went all the way out to Rough Rock School. What political motive could he have had? I could sense it thrilled him deeply to see the successes. He had a great heart for the first Americans and had done much to promote their well-being in this land. His brother, John Kennedy, had first looked into the Indian situation and attempted some dramatic things favoring Native American welfare. Ted was only following his brother's great example in lifting the burdens from America's poor. God bless him. I thought it would be a tremendous experience to someday work in Washington, D.C., alongside such a great humanitarian.

I had arrived in Rough Rock wrapped in collegiate linen, with no experience in the real world. I had to learn to apply to real life the knowledge I had acquired in college. Though not impossible, it had not been the easiest challenge either.

For so long, the Black Mesa area had been a dark cavern of suspicious thought regarding school. My role had been to break the bands of debilitating doubt and mistrust. Doing so required the forsaking of traditional educational approaches in order to touch the more individualistic Indian. And now, somewhere back in Rough Rock, was the collegiate robe I'd left behind. A more significant experience awaited; all it would entail was not yet apparent.

19

IN THE
NATION'S CAPITAL

As we drove to Utah, many of my fulfilling experiences at Rough Rock came to mind. While on political runs, Ted Kennedy and other political leaders came to look into our educational program, which had been heralded earlier in Washington, D.C. Their own testimonies showed their enlightenment.

Though Robert Kennedy was scheduled to visit, unfortunately he was assassinated before his trip came to be. Truly he was one of the great forerunners in Indian education, along with his brothers John and Ted.

The senators who had come to the Rough Rock project had left in astonishment. It was as though public opinion had shrouded the idea that Indians could assume responsibility for self-education. They had seen that the Indians of this obscure community had risen above the deathly grip of traditional fear toward educational involvement. These same men witnessed firsthand what had only been told them back in the nation's capital.

Heretofore throughout the nation, the belief had been made sure which more than intimated that Indians could not direct their own educational process. Rough Rock School, though initially owned by the Bureau of Indian Affairs, was given over to seemingly unchangeable traditional Navajos. Begun as a government pilot project, the Rough Rock educational trial had seen the BIA stand clear and wash its bureaucratic hands of responsibility. The innovation would either diminish into theoretical pauperism or increase as educational regality.

Though deficient in dominant society understanding, the all-Navajo school board became the redeeming body that successfully steered the school aright. Among the hierarchy of our nation, an educational earthquake had jolted the slumbering sentinels of traditional teaching approach. Rough Rock had proven the crucial point of Native American self-determination and had become an educational shrine that attracted the attention of future innovators.

As we reviewed the year back at Rough Rock, intermittently we stopped for gasoline and food. But it did not seem long before we pulled onto the Utah State University campus. We spent the rest of the day going to the various departments to get acquainted with professors and department heads. Our housing and my class schedule were arranged. We then introduced ourselves to the dean of the education department, who had written me the letter of invitation. He was warm and congenial. For some time, he and I chatted. I began to feel more and more comfortable.

He later introduced me to a prominent and renowned Jesuit priest, Dr. Leary, on leave from Gonzaga University, where he was president. Dr. Leary had been asked by Utah State University officials to work on several projects for the school, one of which was to work with me in order to obtain federal funding for the Indian Program I had been asked to organize. We spent much time discussing Indian people in general. The problems and issues affecting Native Americans were the main focus of our conversation. So sincere was the visiting professor and administrator to learn of Indian ways in order to understand Indian needs that we took several trips to various Indian reservations.

From this informal research, we developed and promised a coordinated educational approach to serve the interests and needs of Indian communities and organizations. We took several trips to Washington, D.C., to obtain federal funds to help us set up an effective educational program. We worked with local and state departments of education, and the university staff helped us develop a federally funded special-services program for recruiting Indian students. Our desire was to eventually recruit a Native American coordinator to supervise the programs we had initiated. This was done.

It was also my fortune to learn from Dr. Leary some of the educational theory and administrative tactics he used as president of Gonzaga. I came to respect his integrity, as he was a man of great character and commitment. His interest in Indian people was genuine. I absorbed a great deal of mature, professional counsel from this intelligent man.

The year at Utah State was very successful. Through diligent efforts, a proposal for funding was taken to Washington, D.C., and there approved. Before, there had been only a small quiverful of Indians at Utah State, but by the end of that year there were over sixty. The endeavor was complete. The campus educational department was pleased. The department also sent me a personal letter of commendation and praise for my academic achievements in the graduate program.

It was during this same year that our second son, Chad, was born at the Logan hospital. The birth of our children has always been by far the greatest blessing in our lives. It was a great day for Duane, for now he had a baby brother to play with.

At some point during our stay at Utah State, the dean of the education department encouraged me to apply with the U.S. Office of Education for a fellowship. Before, many Utah State graduate students had applied, but none had received the award. The fellowship offered top educators throughout the nation a rare opportunity to work a full year as an intern in the United States Office of Education in Washington, D.C. Though the dean encouraged me to submit an application, he did not pump up my hopes about receiving this special and unique fellowship. No one in the Intermountain West had ever received it. Most applicants had many years of educational experience, having been principals, superintendents, professors, and even college presidents. The program was very prestigious and was not an Indian program.

Being the very first Indian to apply for this fellowship, I was not even given a speck of a chance. However, to the surprise and astonishment of the school, community, and others in the Utah State Educational Department, I was awarded the fellowship. I was ecstatic, elated, and, at the same time, numb and speechless. The following letter was sent to me from the U.S. Department of Health, Education, and Welfare in Washington, D.C.:

> Dear Mr. Lee:
> The Regional Office of Education has again been successful in their endeavors to identify potential leaders in American education and recommended to this office a list of fifty-four finalists for the US Office of Education Fellowship program. I am happy that you have been selected from these candidates as one of twenty US Office of Education fellows for the 1970-71 academic year.
> Dr. Russel Ruffino
> Director, USOE
> Fellows Program

My appointment had stunned everyone except me. There had been something deep down inside that told me I had a chance. That this was a blessing from the Lord I do not deny, for with the little experience and education I had, my chances had not been very great—only minimal at best.

The next day there was an article in the newspaper about my appointment. Kitty and I were very disappointed in what the article said. I felt it to be a personal affront. More, it was an affront to all Indian people. The following is a part of what the article said:

> George Lee, a Navajo Indian from Shiprock, New Mexico, will complete a master's degree program in educational administration from Utah State University this spring. Then he will represent the Rocky Mountain area as a US Office Education fellow in Washington, D.C., during the 1970-71

academic year. Lee is one of *twenty Indians* [italics my own]
in the United States to receive the fellowship.

To me, my appointment as the first person from the Intermountain West and as the first Indian to receive this fellowship
was downplayed. The oversight was that the other nineteen
USOE fellows indeed were *not* Indians.

I hurt for my fellow Indian people. It was not the first time
things like this had happened. It seemed to be the lot of an Indian to be the low man on the totem pole. Corn, tobacco, and
medicinal herbs were not the only contribution that Indians
had made to the wealth of this great nation, as history books
generally depict. Indians have historically, though silently,
given much to the spiritual stamina of this land. Also, their social ideals have long been sought after by great men of utopian
dreams, such as Ralph Waldo Emerson, Henry David Thoreau,
Thomas Jefferson, and countless others. The camouflaged dis-
play of my appointment was par for the course.

After having received the letter, I took the time to offer the
gratitude of my heart to a kind Heavenly Father. Again, I knew
the Lord had had a hand in my selection, just as He had done
in times previous. I was so thrilled and proud of my appointment. I was not so proud of myself as I was for my Indian
people. As I accepted the award, my thoughts reflected on
Billy Mills, a Native American who had won the 10,000-meter
race in the 1964 Olympics in Tokyo, Japan. No one had given
Billy Mills a chance to win the race. Yet he had shocked the
whole world by coming from behind to win over the world's
best runners. Everyone was stunned but Billy.

The USOE internship provided full salary. The work
would entail organizing, evaluating, research, administration,
proposal inspection, and witnessing congressional sessions as
they pertained to education and other related programs. This
opportunity to exercise leadership would be valuable. Before
leaving for Washington, I set my mind to be of worth to my
country and to those with whom I would serve. I was proud to
be an American as well as a Native American.

It was difficult to believe that this was happening to me, a

Navajo who had been reared in dire poverty on a barren reservation, going to the nation's capital to rub shoulders with the nation's powerful and influential leaders. I could not believe that I was going to make decisions about our nation's problems and concerns. Though I had a hard time believing it, I certainly was not going to reject it. It was a happy occasion for my family that day when the mail came. It was a happy moment for the first Americans. It was indeed a proud moment for a native son of our mother country.

After graduation exercises, and after I had completed my thesis, my wife and I packed our suitcases and left for Washington, D.C., thrilled and excited. Our travel expenses had been defrayed by the U.S. Office of Education. It was our plan to stop over in Shiprock, New Mexico, to tell my family the good news. Their reaction to my appointment was nonplussed. Mom and Dad had no idea as to the significance of my award, though I tried my best to explain. After a short time of visiting with my family, we were off to Washington, D.C.

Once we arrived in the nation's capital, the first item of business was to find an apartment. It was difficult to find one suitable to our needs. Finally we found one in Alexandria, Virginia, which was not too far away from where my office would be. I rode the bus to work every morning. It proved to be far better than driving. The traffic was a mad morning sprint into the mayhem of the political day. Our apartment did not prove to be the best. Both above and beneath us were families whose every movement could be heard. With our young and active sons, living was uncomfortable, for we could not let them frolic and play as little boys are wont to do. If we did, someone would either bang on the floor from beneath us or stomp on the floor above. I think the year was much more inconvenient for my young family than for me.

When I reported for work, I was told I had a choice of working in any department I wished. Those available were the department of education, the department of justice, the departments of elementary and secondary education, the department of colleges and universities, and many others. I chose to work some in each department.

The first meeting I attended was with the nineteen other USOE fellows. I really felt insignificant as I sat among these high-powered educators from all across the land. I felt a little insecure and bewildered, and I lacked confidence at first. As I looked around, there sat gray-haired men and women with years and years of experience in the American educational setting. Most of them already had a doctorate. Silently I asked myself, "What am I doing here? I don't belong here." Then I quietly excused myself, found a small empty room nearby, and offered thanks to my Maker and asked him for blessings of courage and faith.

Several times while sitting there, I wished I could be somewhere else. This certainly was a very ambitious and prestigious group. The other fellows, dressed in their business suits, made me feel uncomfortable. After all, I had just come from the reservation where fine clothing is not considered as very important.

I marveled at these men and women who were leaders in educational institutions across the country. They held such positions as school district superintendent; state department of education superintendent; and elementary and secondary school principals, teachers, and administrators. These were educators with a wealth of well-balanced experience and training.

During the break times, I mainly stood back from the group and observed how I was supposed to act by what I saw them doing. I was reluctant to mix in right away. Being the only Native American, I felt a little bit out of place. Most of the fellows were Anglos, with a couple of black educators.

I was going to be making decisions for America's school children. The nation already had a hard time believing that Indians could guide education for their own people, much less for any other group. Yet here I was, a lone Indian, chosen to affect the national educational system. My first desire was to set aside feelings of inadequacy in order to become effective. Soon my mind was made up to do all I could to help with all of America's children, as well as Indian children.

As my headquarters, I selected an Indian desk in the department of education. "Indian desk" did not mean just one lone desk. It referred to a staffed office within a department. The first person I really got acquainted with was an intelligent and hard-working Native American woman who at that time was the director of the Indian desk. Right off, she informed me that the Indian desk was more or less a token desk with no funds for assisting Native American projects or programs. My first task was to see that funding was made available to this desk.

It was not long before I began to see the various ways in which the Native American cause could be better served throughout the land. Vast storehouses of programs and prominent people had been long waiting for someone to use proper diplomatic keys to open them up to assist Indian people. Prior to this period, a dearth and famine had long existed in terms of meeting Indian needs.

The NCAI (National Congress of American Indians) had been struggling and was then operating in the red. The leaders of the NCAI were concerned and approached me to ask for financial help for their programs. Before this, I had succeeded in opening several outlets for federal and private monies to Indian tribes and organizations bent toward the Indian cause. As a medicine man, my father had never refused help to anyone. From him I had learned this trait and understood the growth it could bring in kindness. Even though it was difficult to assume one more task, I consented to help.

After dropping important seeds for Indian sympathy in the ears of certain influential Washington people, I then passed their names on to the leaders of NCAI. Some I directly asked to help NCAI. Generally, they consented. It was not long until NCAI began to prosper and become dramatically effective in assisting with Native American needs.

It was fulfilling to see the financial storehouses in Washington open up in favor of the Indian people. I had great satisfaction in knowing that lives somewhere, somehow, had been blessed. NCAI leaders worked so wonderfully with me as a team, and I thought how truly marvelous it was that Indians of different tribes could work so well together.

Before this time, Indian tribes were working more in competition with one another. What federal funds they knew about came mainly by chance, and the sources for funding were indeed bleak. It was no coincidence that at the same time Indian leaders began to communicate and cooperate, funding began to open in Washington. The leaders began to behave as the Creator would have had them do. The Native Americans who initiated and continued NCAI were excellent examples of how tribes all over North America should cooperate. Today, because of NCAI efforts, we see more intertribal affiliation and cooperation.

Financial help continued to come for Indian Americans. Success was ours. I was sought after when key issues involving Native American policy were to be formulated. I was always honest with those seeking my advice. Sometimes they did not like what I had to say, but I always stated what I believed to be the facts. Since I really had no personal desire to permanently locate in Washington, I had nothing to lose in being as direct and as honest as I wanted.

Soon I had a reputation for being honest, and not one for seeking personal or political aggrandizement. It is not easy to be honest in Washington. Besides having to accomplish my assignment there, I felt I had a heavier and more significant responsibility to Indian people. And for all this, I was awed and overwhelmed by my appointment, which began in low key. But once I decided and committed myself to swim in Indian and Washington politics, I began to enjoy it very much. In fact, I loved my work. I suddenly found myself in one of my life's dreams, and that was to make decisions about Native American issues, whether in educational circles or otherwise.

I could not believe what was happening. Of myself I cannot really claim any glory, for every step I took seemed to be already paved by a higher power. President Richard Nixon casually committed to a policy of Indian self-determination, and Congress also committed to providing maximum Indian participation in the government and education of the Indian people.

Federal and state governments were miraculously saying

that they would not only listen to Indian views and honor Indian agendas, but that they would also give Indians a central role in the implementation of policy.

For the first time, America seemed to be listening to the soft and humble voice of its Native American children all across the land. Everywhere I went, the Indian people pled only for survival. Among other things, they wanted jobs, health care, functioning economies, and good schools, and, especially, they wanted the federal government to keep its promises. All of the first depended upon the last.

I was in the midst of President Johnson's "Great Society" programs, which opened up new links between Indian leaders and the federal government. It was so refreshing and so heartwarming to see the Indian tribes given opportunities, for the first time, to bypass the Bureau of Indian Affairs and to pursue their own political agendas in new ways and means. A glad voice of hope had permeated Indian reservations throughout America.

Working in conjunction with other departments, our Indian desk made dramatic political decisions and dispensed federal funds to Indian tribes and organizations for economic development, establishing legal services, and helping tribes sustain tribal and other Indian organizations. The more I saw Indian people benefit, the more willing I was to give even more of my own time and energy. There were times when I went home to my family so fatigued I could hardly sit. But dreams were sweet as tiredness took me into sleep.

Indian legal organizations were springing up all over, staffed by Indian lawyers and supported by both federal and private funds. Indeed, Indian awareness all across America was at its peak. Indian people began to exercise their political muscles all across the country. They began to understand that it did not violate Indian traditional beliefs to fend for themselves in the political arena.

In the eyes of state and local officials, urban Indians, just like reservation Indians, were the sole responsibility of the Bureau of Indian Affairs. Most state bureaucrats looked upon state tribal issues with blind eyes. BIA believed that its responsibility stopped at the reservation's edge. So between the two, the states and BIA, the Indian was the only one who lost out. Indian activists rightly protested the policies and failures of the bureau to meet urban Indian problems. The eyes of the nation began to look upon the issue. Indian issues were publicized as they never before had been. Native Americans all across America seemed to be taking a cue from the tactics used by the American blacks.

I cannot describe the joy I felt as I observed the new assertiveness shown, the emergence of a new generation of Indian leaders all across the country. It was a delight to be in meetings with powerful senators and congressmen as they discussed and dealt with Indian protest movements in favor of restoration of federal jurisdiction and services and the return of terminated tribes to tribal status. My heart and mind were in constant prayer for my people, all Indian people, during those meetings. Many times the room was filled with the Spirit as a positive decision would be made in favor of Indians.

I had an opportunity to discuss the issues about the Menominee Restoration Act, which would reinstate federal services to the Menominee Tribe in Wisconsin, and to recognize that tribe as a sovereign Indian tribe. Indian tribes saw termination of Indian reservations as the greatest threat to tribal survival, and termination did not officially die until about 1970, when President Nixon repudiated it. Indian culture was paramount. Without the survival of Indian culture, America would lose its main means of understanding unity, a resource they yet have not tapped.

I was asked many times to represent the United States department of education on official trips to various parts of the country. One time I was asked by the department to make an official trip to New York City to the state department of education. The New York department of education had requested assistance about educational matters. When I received this assignment, I became quite anxious because many knowledgeable and high-powered educators worked at the New York educational headquarters. I felt as though I knew nothing. I was completely overwhelmed, yet I had the faith that I would get the job done.

After I got off the plane in New York, I took a taxi to downtown New York City. Even catching the taxi was an overwhelming experience for a skinny Indian just barely twenty-eight years old. All the street noise was disconcerting and confusing. I had never been to New York City before. I had read about it and I had seen pictures of it, but never in my life had I actually visited this city until then. I was anxiously looking forward to this particular trip. Though somewhat frightful, the challenge, I knew, would have its rewards.

In New York City, I felt like I was in a concrete mausoleum. All of the buildings were concrete and gray. People were walking so fast, and I wondered if they truly knew what they were doing and where they were headed. No one looked at another person, it seemed. It was cold, almost devoid of feeling. I wondered what the people I was to meet with would think of me. I began to doubt my ability to communicate, especially with them.

As I continued on, the smell of fish markets assaulted my nostrils. Generally, Navajos have not taken any kind of fish as part of their diet. The fishy smell, along with the diesel vapors of passing buses, added to my dismal feeling. Somehow I found myself near a park. It felt so good to see live trees. It was like an oasis. I stopped to regain my senses and confidence. My spirit was lifted to see pigeons, green grass, and infants in strollers.

When I arrived at the New York City education offices, people were already there waiting. Heads all turned as I walked in. There was complete silence as all eyes looked toward me. Though they tried to hide it, their looks of surprise at seeing an Indian walk in gave away their thoughts. It was as though they were saying, "We ask for professional help, and what does Washington send us? An Indian!" It didn't do much for my self-confidence either. I would rather have been somewhere else. The setting was austere and formal. Again I thought, "What am I doing here? I don't belong." I began to silently pray to my Maker to assist me in this hour of need.

When the preliminaries of the meeting were over, I was introduced. They did not know what to expect from me. Frankly, I didn't know either, but as soon as I began speaking, the spirit of God came over me, and things I didn't even know began to come into my mind. Soon their questioning looks began to turn into studies of contemplation. I spoke from both my mind and my heart. My prayer was being answered.

After the meeting was over, many of the group spent extra time asking me questions. Afterward, in the solitude of my motel room, I offered a prayer of thanks to the Almighty God, knowing that He had been with me and that He was the One that had strengthened me and increased my confidence. My worries had come because I had thought to rely only upon myself, but, as it was, the workshop, or the meeting, was an outstanding experience for all. Later the state education department people who were in attendance wrote a letter to the commissioner of education in the U.S. Office of Education and commended me. They had nothing but high praise for my recommendations. They were thrilled at the help I had given them.

My experience in Washington, D.C., was one of great growth. Though I learned more about education, political ropes, and red tape, the greatest thing I gained was confidence. I learned the importance of being confident in new experiences. That faith I applied in New York City and Washington, D.C., worked as well on the Navajo reservation as anywhere else.

In the course of my work, I met with Sidney Marland, commissioner of education, to discuss Indian needs, problems, and priorities. As well, I met with key senators who could be influential in helping to develop funds and other aids for Indian people.

One day it was my privilege to meet with Senator Ted Kennedy, a member of the Indian subcommittee. When I mentioned Rough Rock, he, of course, remembered having addressed the first graduating class there. In a warm and friendly way, we spoke of Native American needs. I spoke with him about the need for funding the Indian desk. He then commit-

ted his help to introduce bills for legislation in that direction.
After I left his office, I thought back to the time he had come to
Rough Rock and how I then had hoped one day to be able to
work with him, so great had been his influence upon me.

On numerous occasions, in a consultant and advisory capacity, I represented the commissioner of education to major
Indian and non-Indian conferences and workshops throughout
the country. In addition, this responsibility entailed conducting workshops and seminars for various state departments of
education and giving educational speeches at local, state, and
federal levels. Another sideline function was to assist the commissioner of education in monitoring major federal programs
conducted by colleges, universities, state agencies, and nonprofit organizations.

In giving assistance to the commissioner of education, I
stood in many Senate hearings on Indian education and on
education in general. I took frequent trips throughout the nation to receive feedback and communication from Indian
tribes. One objective was to increase the understanding of Native American communities about what federal funds were
available and how to obtain them.

My attention was drawn to projects that involved Indians.
I did extensive lobbying for Rough Rock and other Indian
community-operated schools. Success also came in being able
to procure more federal funding for Navajo Community College, which, by the way, was the first Indian college organized
on an Indian reservation in the United States.

I spent week after week going through proposals coming in
from universities, colleges, state agencies, and nonprofit organizations that requested federal funding. It was my job to
select the proposals most likely to succeed. During this process,
I became acquainted with the different departments of education as they related to bilingual education, student special services, talent search, teachers core, searching institutions, and
adult basic education, just to mention a few.

This was an exciting time in my life, full of promise and
hope. The great people I was able to meet influenced my life
and helped me gain a better understanding about our govern-

ment. I tried to give those with whom I worked a better understanding about the needs of the long-neglected Native American. By channeling funds toward Indian reservations, I sought to place straw in the clay mire in which the first children of America were struggling.

Of all the senators I met and talked with, Senator Ted Kennedy was the most helpful and outstanding. He took time to listen, and he listened with his heart. Because of him, many Indian projects were funded and many bills passed to aid the American Indian.

Also, because of President Richard Nixon's concern for Native Americans, many land-claim bills were passed giving land back to Indian tribes, such as Blue Lake, which was given back to the Taos in Taos, New Mexico. I felt fortunate to be in the midst of all these events. What joy filled my being to have a small role to play in declaring the war on poverty. I envisioned my people on an equal basis with others. I saw the chance for self-respect, cultural preservation, and greater contribution by the poor of America.

Many week-long conferences were held that year on Indian self-determination. At one of these conferences held in Kansas City, Missouri, Vice-President Spiro T. Agnew was the keynote speaker. Accompanying him was Lewis K. Bruce, who then was commissioner of Indian affairs. Both men spoke powerful, encouraging words to the more than five hundred Native Americans assembled there. This conference studied such issues as native land claims and discrimination against urban and reservation Indians. The meeting was important because the National Congress of American Indians was virtually bankrupt at the time. After this conference, I spent considerable time trying to secure funding for this congress. During the conference, I had my first dose of Indian activism. There was a small group of anti-everything Indians in attendance who could have angered the vice-president and commissioner. However, because the government leaders were well-seasoned and understanding, they continued their support of Indian programs.

To my dismay, I was not well received on some reservations. In the Plains area, I was conducting a seminar on proposal writing when a militant Indian group approached me and told me to leave the reservation.

"Go back to the Navajos," they jeered. "We do not need a Navajo helping a Sioux here." How this statement hurt, because I had heard it several times before on other reservations. Why, I asked, cannot Indian tribes learn from their past errors to become unified and to assist one another? What would it take? Contention and restlessness seemed to pervade the Indian reservation systems throughout America.

One of the Indians in the militant group kept raising his hand to speak, but he only jeered at my words. I thereafter avoided calling on him. Finally he came up front and began to verbally abuse the audience. He told everyone there that he was anti-white, anti-government, and that he hated the white man for what was done to his people in this country. Then he turned to me. "You talk just like a white man," he said. "You wear a tie and suit just like them, too. You are just an apple, red on the outside and white on the inside. You are a white man's Indian."

I was upset, but I determined in my mind to be kind, loving, and patient—to respond with the respect I was not receiving. When he was finished with his tirade, I asked him a few questions: "You said that we should go back to the old Indian ways? Will you please tell me what you mean by the old ways? Do you mean we should go back to the tepee? Go back to buffalo hunting?

"You said I looked like a white man. If that is the case I suggest you take your clothes off right now, because your clothes came from the white man and were made by him. Take off your eyeglasses while you are at it; they came from the Anglo factory. Take your shoes off—made by white men. Throw your car away. I assume you live in a house with electricity. Get rid of it. No more television either—made by white men. Stop eating the food in stores and restaurants. Eat fish and berries. Everything you have has come from the white man. The white man built America. America is for everybody. Mother Earth is for everybody. Let us live in peace with our white brothers."

At the end, he did not say very much but turned away embarrassed and left the room. I tried to say these things in the kindest way possible, but sometimes the truth can be difficult to handle. I had always been taught to get along with our white brothers and sisters, that there would come a day when some of them would understand how an Indian felt and thought. For Indians to succeed in an aggressive society, they must learn how to be aggressive in the right way. It is possible to know when to be appropriately aggressive without losing one's self-identity and integrity. The Great Creator enabled us to come to this earth to partake of its fullness—each race of people has the same claim. It is up to us to respect this idea.

I went on to give this gathering of Indians a good, positive speech. My tongue was loosened and my mind was clear. What I then said came from a higher source.

I remember a few times when I found that federal funds were being misused. One school used federal funds (given to them in the name of Indian needs) to outfit an entire football team. Not only that, but they constructed bleachers to watch the games, using these funds. School districts, colleges, and universities, in the name of Indians, were receiving millions of dollars and then misusing the funds. Their dishonesty appalled me. Where would our great nation stand in the eyes of the world if such dishonesty prevailed?

Though I saw some negative along with the good, the year in Washington, D.C., was very exhilarating and rewarding. I always looked forward to going to work in the mornings. Even though I liked my job and had been offered several different positions within various departments, a restless spirit came upon me, and I knew my time was coming to a close at the nation's capital.

Unexpectedly, I received a letter from the Ford Foundation in New York City with a tremendous offer. I could select the university of my choice for postgraduate work and they would take care of all expenses. I could not turn down this offer. Both Kitty and I knew this was the message I had become restless about.

I also received wonderful offers from Harvard and Princeton with similar proposals. Despite the attractiveness of such prestigious universities, my wife and I desired to return to the West, our home.

During that year, a member of our ward was mugged and almost killed while walking home from work. It seemed a constant fear, day by day, to live where we did. My wife especially feared for the welfare of our children, as I did. She also worried about me, since I commuted by bus to and from work. So, going back to Utah was appealing. My sister, Lucy, had been living in Washington also. I was able to help her find employment in the Bureau of Indian Affairs office. She, too, gained much valuable experience. Like ours, her heart was really in the West. She made plans to accompany us to Utah.

To be headed toward the setting sun caused many thoughts to sift through my mind. I thought of the prior year's experience. Where would life find me tomorrow? The influence of the many senators, legislators, congressmen, commissioners, educators, foreign diplomats, and wonderful citizens of this great nation was inside me somewhere. Where would this influence move me?

Again, I thought of my patriarchal blessing, which said that friends would be raised up in times of need to help and assist me. This blessing was being fulfilled before my very eyes. Without a doubt, I had made many friends all across the nation.

When I first arrived in Washington, the towering image the media had given of our nation's political leaders gave me a feeling of awe. Now, in retrospect, I could see that all people are human, no matter what their station. Yes, we owe them respect because of their achievements, but every person has an inner integrity. Some become blinded by their own success and thus endanger themselves and others.

I was able to gain a unique, comprehensive view of what was happening with Indian people all over the nation. Because of my inexperience, and in order to function in an environment generally foreign to Native American thought, I had to fasten my mental talons firmly upon the crags of unfamiliar territory.

The sensitivity to Indian needs was right at its peak during this time. From the height the Washington view afforded, I watched this long overdue sensitivity develop into crescendo, and then, unfortunately, begin to wane. America, for however briefly, had sincerely and truly recognized its many racial colors. And while in Washington, D.C., I gained a broad understanding of racial awareness.

The times I had met with Senator Ted Kennedy and with senators from states with large Indian populations gave me a chance to speak in behalf of all Indian people in the United States. Many times I sat in the presence of dignitaries, and always on the forefront of my mind was "What can I say to influence these people in favor of Indians?" What a great blessing and responsibility that was.

As I traveled with some powerful national leaders, I saw that many of them were evidently caught up in the ways of the world. In city after city, they became engaged in questionable activities, such as going down to various parts of the city that would normally be avoided by family-oriented people. I declined to accompany them to these places and to inappropriate movies or other questionable activities.

Because of the position I held, it was necessary to make appearances at various social gatherings. Though I was able to maintain my standards, I did not go untempted. Fortunately, I was able to fall back on the teachings I had received from my father, my foster family, and the Church. I did not submit, though the forces against me were great at times. There were times I used my position to let people know of my moral values. I did not lose friends or face over my stance. They ended up respecting me, but, more important, I respected myself.

It was difficult to understand how men of powerful political position, in control of millions and millions of tax dollars, could degrade their own character by succumbing to the vices that existed so prevalently and seemed to array themselves at the fingertips of these political giants.

I traveled with one such man. He told me he and his wife had an agreement whereby each consented that the other could have physical encounters with others. This appalled me.

He talked unashamedly and openly about this nuptial arrangement. To reciprocate, I talked about the gospel and the values the Church taught. I also talked with other men whom I traveled with about the same subject. Some listened, and their lives changed.

On our way back west, we stopped in Shiprock to visit my family. Both Mom and Dad were there. When they saw us, they were elated. They embraced my family for some time. Again they wanted me to find a job in the Shiprock area and live with them. Again I had to say no. I told them I was going back to get my doctorate in educational administration. They had no comprehension or concept of postgraduate degrees. They did not understand what that meant. I had to explain in quite some detail. We spent a couple of days with them before going to Provo.

Once in Provo, we moved in with Kitty's family until we could find our own apartment. It was sure good to be back in Provo among family and friends. Once we were a little more settled, I immediately had BYU and the Ford Foundation in New York City come together to work out the financial assistance for my doctoral program. This fellowship included our living expenses. This financial arrangement was indeed a great blessing. I could hardly wait to get started.

$$\underline{20}$$

THE CALL

I enrolled in the BYU doctorate program and carried a heavy academic load. The time I spent with other doctorate students was enjoyable; we spent considerable time discussing life, religion, politics, and what we wanted from life. After one year, I finished most of my classes, while the second year marked the beginning of the dissertation required of doctoral students. Fortunately, I had a very helpful committee assigned to help with my dissertation. Also, my doctoral committee chairman proved to be of inestimable help. I did very well academically and even received a letter of commendation from the BYU department of education. I had spent hours and hours in the library studying for my classes. Kitty was working on her bachelor's degree on scholarship at this time. Grandma Hettich gave us a tremendous lift by looking after our kids while we studied hard. Tony, Richard, and Adam (Kitty's brothers) gave me a break from my studies by playing ball with me. They loved sports and were good young men.

A letter arrived one day from the president of a college in Arizona. It was a church-related college, but not of our faith. He said that the board of regents and the search committee from the college strongly encouraged me to consider a position there. They were looking for a president to replace the incumbent. To find a Native American with the proper qualifications was their desire. The one then holding the position was Anglo. I don't know how they found out about me, but I was pleased they had. Other applicants had applied, but the regents were not satisfied with those. So I was sought out.

I also received two other excellent job offers during this time. One was to head the educational department for the Navajo tribe, and the other was to be superintendent of a school district in Arizona. Kitty and I fasted and prayed to find out what our Heavenly Father wanted us to do. The BYU education department did not want us to go. I, too, had some mixed feelings about going, and Kitty would have to give up her scholarship. I had finished all my class work for my doctorate but still had my dissertation to complete. We both wanted to complete our degrees, but all three were such tremendous job offers.

After much fasting and prayer, we both received a strong impression that the Lord wanted us to accept the offer from the church college in Arizona. We felt that if the Lord wanted us to go there, that was the thing to do. I would be going in as a vice-president in order to effect a smooth transition when I became president six months later. We felt good about going. We both turned in our scholarships and accepted the position. There was no doubt in our minds that this was what the Lord wanted us to do.

When I went for the interview, and after having seen the campus, I was hired on the spot as vice-president and dean of students, with the understanding that I would assume the presidential role after six months. During this interview, I was not questioned about my membership in the LDS Church.

My wife went through the packing routine again, and in a short time we were on our way to Arizona. I had already contacted the Ford Foundation in New York City, informing them of the opportunity we had accepted. I thanked them for their financial assistance. Their response was to tell me that if I ever wanted to finish my dissertation, the money would be there. And so, we were on our way to Arizona, but we really did not know why. The restless feeling had come over me again—I suppose that was part of the reason I had accepted.

Once I started work, the Anglo board of regents, who were all ministers, began to ask me about my religion. Was I strong in the Mormon Church? Did I believe it? Had I gone through the Indian Placement Program? Did I hold any leadership positions in the Church? I answered yes to all these questions, even to the point of letting them know I was serving as a counselor in the Arizona Holbrook Mission presidency.

After having found I was a staunch Mormon, they began to do things to find fault with my work. I sensed a strong anti-Mormon sentiment among the minister-regents. The battle was on. I have heard of religious discrimination before, but all of a sudden, I was right in the middle of it. They threw hurdles in my path to thwart my assumption of the presidential chair, which would soon be left vacant. They tried to change the initial agreement that had brought me to the college—that I would be president after six months. Everything was done to try to discourage and upset me, yet I did my best as the vice-president and dean of students.

This particular college, before it had become such, had been a parochial high school that had been directed by some of the same people who were still present at the time of my appointment. In all fairness, I must say that some of the best students on the reservation came from that church high school. It was worthy of praise. And even though some negative things may have happened to me there, I still say that this college and its board of regents had done much good for the students who had attended there. The community college had an open-door admissions policy, as it accepted students of all races from different parts of the country.

I traveled frequently to recruit students and to do public relations work. Many students came to me to talk about their problems—spiritual, academic, or personal. The president had also asked me to write proposals to seek federal funding. This was not too difficult, since I had worked in this area in Washington, D.C. In finishing the proposals, I knew exactly where to send them. I knew people in the various offices, and so I wrote them personal letters asking for their support. The funding came.

Before I knew it, six months were up. The president who was leaving strongly recommended to the board of regents that I be installed as president. But they had other ideas. Because it was a church-related school, they had second thoughts about an Indian with a different church affiliation taking over the presidential seat. In spite of the opposition, I felt very good about my accomplishments up to that time. I wanted to demonstrate to these concerned people that I could do a good job.

In many of the board meetings, instead of discussing problems and programs in the college, the members criticized my beliefs and my association with the Church and the Indian Placement Program. These men indicated their own displeasure with the LDS Church. I had to stand and defend my beliefs. It was not always an easy thing to do. I had never had a job in which I had worked so hard and accomplished so much but yet received no compliment or praise.

I could not believe this persecution was happening, especially in the United States of America. The opposition grew stronger and stronger. Several ministers who usually did not attend the board meetings suddenly came to all the meetings, and the board of regents released all their hidden hostilities against my beliefs and the Church. I prayed many times in their behalf that they would judge me as an individual, and not just as someone representing the Church.

Never at any time was I upset or depressed. I was more than happy to answer their questions and their criticisms. The Spirit rested on me greatly during all their questioning. I was thankful for this, because I needed it. It was my desire to turn the other cheek in these meetings.

The former president was not affiliated with the ruling regents' religion, and, although he took a neutral position, and understandably so, he did support me by telling the board of my qualifications and of my track record during the previous six months.

Since the board did not want me, they tried to organize

another search committee to hire someone else as president. Eighteen applicants sent résumés. All the while, the incumbent president and I tried to reason with the board, emphasizing the agreement under which I was hired. To not honor this commitment would be dishonorable. The incumbent college president could not believe what was happening.

I could have left at any time. That would have been exactly what the board of regents wanted. My wife and I prayed and fasted a great deal. We asked Father in Heaven what to do. In each instance, we were told to stay there. Kitty wanted to leave. My own desire was to leave. I had had it. But I had learned to obey the voice of the Spirit. I could not leave. We did not know the reason we were to stay. Deep in my heart, I wanted to win the approval of the regents without compromising my integrity and beliefs. The adversity became so great for my sweet companion that she had three miscarriages.

Finally, the incumbent president, several faculty members, students, community members, and I met to discuss the issue. We went together to one of the board meetings to remind them of the agreement under which I was hired. Community members placed pressure on the regents as well. Under this lobbying, the board gave the contract as it was initially offered. I was to be president. I respected them for this, as it showed that they were, after all, men of reason. From then on there began to be more respect between the regents and me. I had finally been accepted, but my religion had not.

I was now in the hot seat, and I mean it was hot. I chose to ignore the stiff criticisms. Work went smoother that way. In every way, I tried to improve the college by bringing in excellent instructors and curriculum.

The student body wanted to have a basketball team to compete with other colleges in the area. After many meetings, we approved the hiring of a basketball coach. This person would also set up an athletic program for the college. Many applied for this position. Finally, we narrowed the twenty applications down to two men, both with outstanding qualifications. One of the two was LDS, but he had the highest qualifications. His record indicated that he could turn a losing program into a winning program in one year . That was his specialty. He was highly recommended by some of the outstanding basketball coaches throughout the nation.

So, finally, we hired this excellent basketball coach from West Virginia. He was a short man, stocky, and looked nothing like a coach. But he was a superb coach and an outstanding individual, husband, and father as well. As soon as we hired him, the board of regents caught wind of what we had done, and they were extremely upset because the coach was LDS.

Before he came on board, I told him about the problems with the board of regents. I could not believe the strength and faith he had. He even looked forward to the challenge. He was a great competitor.

He and his family moved in. Within one year, he had recruited a mixture of ball players—whites, blacks, Mexicans, and Indians. Some of these athletes had been overlooked by other colleges. He molded this unlikely mixture into a winning team. I have never seen such enthusiasm and teamwork as were brought about by this selfless coach.

The boys became leaders on the floor and off as well. What a determined man! He was magnificent. He had developed our program of nothing into something respectable. Our team won game after game and then went on to the national tournament for junior colleges. It was phenomenal.

The publicity we received over our sports program was tremendous. Many fine students then became attracted to our school because of our sports program. Many had seen the basketball team play freshmen from other Arizona colleges and universities and beat them! That was the type of team we had. The board of regents came around even more! They were perceptive men when it came to success in sports. In time, they did not fund the basketball program because it brought too much success and because the coach was a Mormon.

As our programs in the college began to expand, there was need for more space. We built new dormitories and a student union center. The student union center was furnished with game rooms, pool tables, and movies. There were seminars and workshops to strengthen our faculty in their ability to instruct the students.

Suddenly our college was receiving recognition both locally and nationally. More federal grants came our way. We received three hundred thousand dollars from the National Science Foundation for our science program, and we developed the best science program on the whole reservation. This brought recognition. We introduced courses on Indian history and culture, along with English and American history. Adult classes for traditional Navajos were offered in the evening. Arts and crafts were going. GED classes were offered. Things were moving in favor of this community college. We developed the best and only computer center for the whole area.

At first, the college was financially unstable. One of the first directions I received from the board of regents was to scare up some funds. Because of my Washington, D.C., experience, they knew before my hiring that if anyone could come up with money, I probably could.

I met with many well-to-do people who were willing to donate funds to our college. I took many time-consuming trips throughout the nation nurturing and cultivating these wealthy donors. I even visited the church that ran the college in New York City. All the while, our student body was expanding. We formed satellite branches outside of the area. Students who transferred from our college did not have a hard time having most of their courses recognized by other receiving colleges.

The dean of financial affairs was also LDS. He had served a mission among the Indians in the Southwest. For them, he had an abiding respect and love. He worked miracles for us in the area of finances. Of course, he also received opposition because he was LDS. I tried to convince the board that I had hired him for his qualifications. But no matter how successful we were, we continued to receive opposition. As more success came, more opposition arose.

The college continued to progress and grow. Students had to be turned away. We engaged in a building program so we could handle students who might have been turned away.

Temporary trailers were set up for student housing on the football field. And since we did not have a football team, this posed no problem.

We had the support of the community, faculty, and student body. But there was the ever-present thorn—the board of regents. Always came the criticism. My vice-president, an Anglo, also of the same church as the board of regents, was in constant communication with them, always giving them information to make himself look good. He tried to record everything that I did, even to the point to record my phone conversations. We had a little Watergate going on. I tried to deal with the man as kindly as I could. He would have been the most likely candidate to be president if I were out of the picture. And frankly, he probably would have done a good job. His only problem was his fear of not succeeding.

Also, the dean of academic affairs was trying to bring about my downfall. Some of the faculty were also in cahoots with the dean of academic affairs and the vice-president. The board of regents even tried to get some of the student-body officers to act as informants. Some students did. The pressure and opposition became great. But nothing gave them justifiable reason to fire me.

Eventually some lies were listed on paper and presented to the board. Among other things, I was accused of showing X-rated movies on campus, flirting with girls on campus, using my church for self-promotion, using the Indian Placement Program for my own self-interest, and forcing teachers to give A's to some of the students. By then, though, some of the regents had been able to feel my sterling determination to stick by what was right and moral. Slowly, some of these men began to question some of the slander. Many said to let the thing pursue its course; if it were ill-planned, it would come to naught. If well-planned, then who were they to stand in the way?

Some of these things came out from the board meetings. I knew their source, for I had watched the behind-the-scene activities of those who were aiming for my downfall.

Our third child, Tricia, was born in the midst of all this turmoil. She was our miracle baby. She brought joy and blessings into our home.

One day I went into the vice-president's office and said, "If you had a friend who was close to you, a friend you trusted, a friend in whom you had confidence; and this friend stabbed you in the back, criticized you, talked behind your back, and did everything he could to make you look bad, what would you do with him?"

He said, "I would fire him—let him go."

As soon as he said that, he knew he had incriminated himself. The next day, he quietly left without my asking him to leave, without having to be fired. He had known what he was doing. His ambition was to be the next president, so that is why he did what he had done. Naturally, the board of regents learned about this and accused me of firing him. They tried to rehire him. But he would not come back. Inside, he must have known it would not have been right—he must have started becoming an honest person. I gained respect for him in his declining that position.

The next person in line was the dean of academic affairs. He was promoted as the next vice-president by the board of regents. I knew that he would continue to supply false information to the board. He met with students and faculty to clandestinely plan my overthrow. This secret combination was against me and all I stood for. I did not fire or expose them. I knew that, one by one, all would leave of their own accord, just as the first vice-president had done.

Through all this, Kitty and I did not leave but decided to tough it out. We were not wrong and were therefore not willing to capitulate. She and I continued to fast and pray. Though we wanted to go, we could not, for the Lord wanted us to stay. Why, I did not know. My sweet wife began to actually feel in her heart the physical pain brought about by the intense opposition.

One by one, I called those who were combined against me into my office and had some earnest discussions with them, trying to point out their better qualities. I told them of their constitutional rights as citizens, and of the rights of all citizens. I reminded them of how some of these rights were being denied to some citizens in our great land of promise, that many citizens were being denied freedom of speech, religion, and the pursuit of happiness. They began to realize that what they were doing was wrong. Soon they left campus.

I then did the same thing with the faculty members involved. I discussed the greatness of America and the freedoms we should enjoy. After they understood what they were doing, one by one they left campus also.

One day while meditating, I received a strong spiritual impression that we needed to leave. I knew, without a doubt, that it was time to go. The Lord had made known His will. I planned to make a farewell speech in the next board meeting. All of the board members were geared up for another fight with the Mormon president. How surprised they were as I told them of the secret meetings and the information that had been passed on to them. I told them all that they had done. I told them of the greatness of America, the freedom of religion, speech, and press. I turned the other cheek and fought back with compassion. All of them, especially the ministers, knew that what they had done was wrong.

I could have exposed to the media all that was happening. But I did not want to cause the fall of the college. Instead, I told them of my love and appreciation for the opportunity of working as president of their college. I fought back with kindness and righteousness. I felt a tremendous compassion for them and let them know that I loved each one of them. I let them know that I did not harbor any animosity or hard feelings for them. Then I resigned my position.

My wife and I packed and were on our way back to Utah. The only thing I knew to do was to recontact the Ford Foundation to continue my doctorate program. So, BYU and Provo once again became our home. We had just been through a refiner's fire. The reason was not apparent.

However, during that past year I had received many wonderful blessings. In the Doctrine and Covenants we are taught that after much tribulation come the blessings. This particular scripture took on a new meaning for me as I reflected on the trials and tribulations I had experienced as head of the college in Arizona and also the blessings I had received. I had received the following honors:

1. Presented with an Outstanding Young Man of America Award from the U.S. Jaycees.

2. Received the Spencer W. Kimball Lamanite Leadership Award.

3. Received the Outstanding Indian Education Award.

4. Was selected to be a Utah State Board of Education advisory board member.

5. Was selected as president of the Indian Alumni Association.

6. Received the Ford Foundation Fellowship Award.

7. Was selected as consultant to the Bureau of Indian Affairs schools, Rough Rock School, Ramah High School, Navajo Community College, and the Navajo Education Offices.

8. Was selected by the president of The Church of Jesus Christ of Latter-day Saints to testify before a Senate committee in Washington, D.C., to acquaint the committee members with the Indian Placement Program.

In addition to these blessings, I later had the great blessing of completing my dissertation for my doctor's degree before a deadline imposed by President Spencer W. Kimball. Also, I was later recognized as the first Indian to receive a doctorate from Brigham Young University.

I began going to the library from early in the morning until late at night to work on my dissertation. A few weeks later, I awoke one morning feeling very strange, almost as if I were coming down with an illness. I was weak, so I decided to remain in bed and rest. My wife was up when a telephone call came. She had to shake me three times to wake me. I thought I was dreaming. It was President Spencer W. Kimball, the president and prophet of the Church.

He began to interview me over the phone. I wondered what was going on. I was still half asleep, but I did not take long to revive.

The interview was long and in depth. Finally he said, "The Lord has called you to preside over the Arizona Holbrook Mission."

There was a long silence. I could not believe what I had just heard. After the utter shock wore off, I responded feebly, "How could that be, President? There is already a mission president presiding over that mission. What will you do with him?"

"You just leave that up to the Lord."

I then realized what a foolish question I had asked. I asked myself how I could even be questioning the president of the Church. Unknown to me, that mission had just been divided. The current president had been called to preside over one half of the split mission, and I was to preside over the western half, the Arizona Holbrook Mission.

President Kimball was very cordial, kind, and loving. His questions were very difficult and penetrating. He then said he would like to visit with us in person. I spoke with him at length on many matters. I told him that I had planned to develop my dissertation through the rest of that April and throughout the summer into the fall. I wanted to finish it by the coming December. Very plainly he told me to finish my dissertation by July 1, before we left on our mission. There was another long silence. I was thinking, "How can that be possible? I can't finish the dissertation by July 1." I did not question him at all. If he thought I could do it in less than three months, I knew it could be done. After I hung up the phone, Kitty and I sat down. She spoke with me, but I could not hear her.

"How can it be?" I asked myself. We were not prepared, I thought. We had no money. Certainly I was not a man of prominence, influence, or affluence. Fortunately, we had no debts except for a new truck we had just bought. We quickly sold it and earnestly began making preparations to leave on our mission. Three months was not a long time.

Two weeks before, I had been in Oklahoma at a Lamanite leadership conference with other stake officials. The stake president there invited Sister Lee and me to come and speak with his people. While there, and on a Friday night, I had a dream in which I received a call from President Kimball, and we had a long and pleasant conversation. The dream had been beautiful. As soon as I awoke, I felt uplifted. I then told Kitty that we might be receiving a call from President Kimball, but I did not know for what purpose. But now we knew, and the dream had been fulfilled.

I set up my tepee in the BYU library. I stayed there from the time it opened in the morning until the library closed late every night. All that time I had only one thing on my mind: I had to finish the dissertation; a prophet of God had instructed me to do so. Never before had I worked as arduously on any project. I really never had a chance to be with my family, but my wife was very supportive. Without her, it could not have been done. I completed my dissertation before July 1. It was a miracle. President Kimball had made a believer out of me.

President J. Edwin Baird, my former mission president, lived in the Orem area. I visited frequently with him, learning all I could about his experiences as a mission president.

I also did a lot of reading and praying in order to prepare myself spiritually. I knew I had to be spiritual and clean in order to save souls for the Lord. My wife joined with me in this preparation.

Before I realized it, we were on our way to the mission field with our two sons, Duane and Chad, and our daughter, Tricia. The Lord had opened up many experiences for me. I was grateful for all the things the Lord had given me. My faith was stronger than it had ever been. The trial as president of the Arizona college had tempered me and helped me to learn endurance. It began to have meaning now. The Lord had fully prepared me for this calling.

On my way to the mission, I thought about a phone call I had received from Peter J. McDonald, then chairman of the Navajo Tribe. All my life I had set a desire to one day become chairman of my tribe so I could do things for them in a good way, to extend upon the good that previous chairmen had done. One of my dreams was to lead my people as chairman of the tribe.

In the call, he had informed me that he and his assistant had been surveying the Navajo population, looking for someone worthy and capable of handling such a grave responsibility. Peter McDonald was known the nation over for his able leadership ability. He had said that my name had come to the top of the list. They had wanted to groom me to be the next chairman. Of course, and not with little heartbreak, I had had to tell him the Lord had called me on another mission I could not refuse. This he had kindly accepted.

Some time later, at a BYU Indian Education Week, Peter McDonald spoke. He humorously told the audience that Jesus Christ was a better recruiter than he was, because George P. Lee was now on a mission and not training to be the next tribal chairman. Truly, it was a chance of a lifetime for me, but I have always tried to serve the Lord first.

When we arrived at our destination on July 1, 1975, the mission president had already left for the other mission that had been split off from the Arizona Holbrook Mission. The mission staff was there to greet us. We had entered the mission field in excitement and great anticipation. I could hardly wait to start teaching and to begin working with the missionaries. The idea of working with mission priesthood leaders and others was full of promise. I was in the labor of the Lord and was so thankful for it.

Of course, I had some goals. Two things I wanted to teach: Jesus Christ and the Book of Mormon. I immediately set up zone conferences with all the missionaries to have them work toward those goals. I felt that the Book of Mormon had never really been taken to the Indian people. This we needed to accomplish. All that was taught needed to be centered around Jesus Christ. This entailed changes in the lessons to center around Jesus Christ and the Book of Mormon. I was so anxious to tell my people that the Book of Mormon contained the Indian's true religion, and that Jesus Christ had in fact visited their forefathers, who had seen the nail prints in His hands and feet.

The first Sunday in the mission field, I met with President Flake of the Window Rock District. Together we traveled to the Sawmill Branch. On the way to the branch, President Flake and I spoke about the need for Lamanite leadership. La-

Mission president George P. Lee with his wife, Katherine, and missionaries at the zone Christmas conference at Flagstaff, Arizona, 1975

manites needed to be trained. We discussed ideas about seminars wherein Lamanites could be brought in and trained in leadership in the gospel. All the branches at that time were presided over by Anglos. Our goal was to change this. We discussed strengthening the Indian Placement Program. We talked of Indian parents and of summer programs to help youth coming off the placement program. We knew that the youth should be the target of our mission. Our conversation covered many things. We discussed convert baptisms and activation. I felt I had gotten off to a good start. President Flake, I found, was a dear friend to the Lamanites. I was impressed to call him as one of my counselors in the mission presidency.

As I learned my mission responsibility, I tried never to lose sight of my original goal: to teach Jesus Christ and the Book of Mormon. If success was to be had, it would be through this. I wanted to be positive in all things and to have this spread throughout the mission.

There were three mission districts, all presided over by Anglo presidents. Those districts were the Chinle District, with seven branches; the Four Corners District, with eight branches; and the Window Rock District, with six or seven branches.

At that time, mission presidents were taught to convert and baptize; they had learned that their superiors would look for only one thing—baptisms. When I arrived at Holbrook, I wanted to be obedient to this counsel, but at the same time the branches needed to be strengthened. There was a need to convert and to reactivate. I set up a rigorous program with the missionaries to make converts and to build up the districts and their branches. We wanted the new converts to attend strong branches and to be spiritually edified.

Instead of coming in and following what had been done before in the mission, I decided to come in from a different angle. Immediately I set up zone meetings and taught many things to the missionaries. I particularly taught them to think positive thoughts. I spent a lot of time trying to persuade them to rid themselves of negative attitudes and thoughts. It was my intention to help them catch the vision of the work among the Lamanites. I shared success stories to help them realize they could be the best missionaries and learn the Navajo language well. I helped them understand they could excel in obedience, goal setting, attitude, scripture study, prayer, friendliness, and happiness. I taught them that to be Christ-like, we must practice the principles of a Christ-like life now. I knew that spirituality was a key to our success. After spirituality, we concentrated on teaching principles of convert baptisms. The missionaries began to understand, and the mission rose in its successes.

I met with branch presidents and district presidents individually to give them direction and encouragement. I urged them to reduce attitudes of failure. They needed to be more positive. We spoke together of the need to disseminate strength, faith, and courage to their district and branch members. I knew that success with our priesthood leaders depended upon a simple yet strong spirit-to-spirit, one-on-one personal interview.

We set up intensive priesthood seminars to teach Lamanite leadership throughout the mission. By the end of July, I had toured the mission completely and had met with all the district and branch presidents, as well as all the missionaries. It had become evident to me that if the Indian people were to grow and progress as the Lord wanted them to, they would do it under the leadership of their own people. Accordingly, I went before the Lord with the names of three Lamanites to replace the three district presidents who were not Indians. The three presidents had done a good job, but the Lord wanted the change to take place, and so I really had no choice but to follow the counsel of the Spirit. The three Lamanite district presidents were Dan Nakai, Art Allison, and Dan Smith.

I also received special permission to call three Lamanite counselors to help me direct each of the three districts. Those men were MacArthur Norton of Blanding, Utah, to direct the Chinle District; Bahe Billy of Farmington, New Mexico, to direct the Four Corners District; and president Herbert Frazier, who was retained from the former mission presidency to direct the Window Rock District. President James Pinegar from the former mission was retained to serve as an executive secretary. The new mission clerk was David Flake, the former Window Rock District president. Both presidents Pinegar and Flake were set apart as assistants to the mission president and given administrative duties.

My Lamanite counselors and Lamanite district presidents were like the Sons of Mosiah. They had waxed strong in the knowledge of the truth, for they had a sound understanding of the gospel and had searched the scriptures diligently. They were spiritual men, dedicated to much fasting and prayer so they might be worthy of the spirit of revelation. When they taught, they taught with the power and authority of God. President Bahe Billy was one of the first Navajos to receive a doctorate degree; he was respected and loved by Navajo people. He was an outstanding father and husband, as he was a leader. Both presidents Norton and Frazier exemplified the same virtues and attributes, as did presidents Nakai, Allison, Smith, and Denetsosie.

All of the accomplishments and successes we enjoyed, I attribute to these Lamanite spiritual giants, along with our other great Anglo assistants and counselors, President Pinegar, David Flake, David Wilmore, Gary Coleman, and Nyle Randall.

Ten stakes comprised the whole of the Arizona Holbrook Mission. Each counselor in the mission presidency was assigned a number of stakes. In these stakes, they encouraged member activation and missionary work.

We also simplified the organization of Church meetings and encouraged the branches to implement this program. It consisted of holding all branch meetings within a two-and-a-half-hour block on Sunday mornings. Priesthood and Relief Society meetings were held first. Then a Sunday School class was held for about half an hour. A regular sacrament meeting followed. A great feeling of cooperation and love began to flow throughout the mission, stakes, districts, and branches.

The first Lamanite training seminar was planned for that coming October. In this seminar, selected Lamanite men would come into the mission home to be taught leadership, administration, and the gospel for two consecutive days. These seminars would be held monthly. To get these men to the

President George P. Lee teaching priesthood leaders

seminars, a member of the mission presidency would visit with each of them. These would be our future leaders. The program began to work.

Men came to the seminars who had not set foot inside a church for years and years. They were exposed to the Spirit during this seminar. Interesting and exciting things began to happen. Many whose testimonies had lain dormant, or who never had acquired a testimony, now began to move into the light of the Savior's love. Some were called into significant positions and began to operate faithfully in their calls. Some were called in spite of their struggles with alcohol and peyote. Through priesthood service, their cleansing came. They were blessed by the Lord. Lives were changed. Bad habits were broken. Homes and families were strengthened. Conversions came. A powerful, special spirit attended these monthly Lamanite training seminars. At first, only selected inactive and active Lamanite men were invited, but they became so inspired that they begged to bring their wives and children. Permission was granted to include all family members.

Distance, funds, and lack of transportation suddenly became insignificant and were no longer obstacles. Somehow the members overcame these problems and came in droves from all across the reservation to attend the seminars. They hungered for spiritual food. We started with fifty participants and ended with over seven hundred at the final seminar.

Included in the seminars were trips to Salt Lake City to attend the general conferences of the Church. At one time, the group that came to a general conference filled the whole auditorium of the Church Office Building. When President Kimball saw the group for the first time, he was overwhelmed with the Spirit, and tears filled his eyes. He was very surprised but happy. The members were rewarded spiritually as they heard President Spencer W. Kimball. For many traditional Navajos, this was their first time off the reservation and their first opportunity to witness a living prophet of God. A sweet spirit attended this historic meeting. I could not hold back my tears as I saw President Kimball kiss and hug many of them. It was a thrilling and inspiring sight. Many tender hearts were touched and strengthened by this sweet, warm, and compassionate prophet of God.

I could tell President Kimball thoroughly enjoyed himself mixing with the group who came hundreds of miles to see him and attend general conference. Some of them sold their prized turquoise jewelry just to buy gas to have the chance to see a man whom they loved, respected, and revered. It was President Kimball who had championed their cause through the years. For many years, he was the only "Indian voice" in the Church. For a long time, it seemed that Spencer W. Kimball was alone against the world regarding Indian affairs. On many occasions, he defended the Native Americans when it was not popular to do so. He was truly bold and courageous yet humble and compassionate.

It has been my privilege and honor to have known and associated with President Spencer W. Kimball. It is impossible for me to do justice through the written word to express the way I feel about him. It is difficult, at best, for me to convey the depth of his soul and the sincerity of his love for the gospel and for all people. Words cannot describe the tremendous influence he had upon the Lamanites.

He has assisted many Indians to acquire self-regard in their native culture as well as in the dominant white culture in order to transcend both. He has helped many to appreciate cultures other than their own, and in the process they have become more balanced people with positive self-esteem.

President Kimball has always impressed me as a man of great physical and moral courage. I regard him as the "man of the hour" where the Church and its needs were concerned. When he was called as president and prophet of the Church, he was the man that God needed at that particular time. The Lord had the right man at the right time as the earthly head of His church, one whom he had prepared and proved through years of experience and who came through trials and tribulations and was tested and not found wanting.

He always manifested the qualities of true leadership. I

marveled at his wisdom and at the strength of his testimony of the validity of the work entrusted to the Church of Jesus Christ. I have been awed by his great courage, his great knowledge and understanding of the scriptures, his deep spirituality, his deep compassion for all, and his thorough and complete dedication to the work of the Lord and Master.

While touring the mission, I met with an Anglo branch president who did not have Lamanite counselors. I asked him why he did not. He said there were no worthy Lamanite men in his branch who could serve. But through the leadership seminar we conducted, we found that there were many Lamanites who could serve if they were given the chance. They just had to be treated with compassion and love.

We helped the missionaries to understand that many Lamanites will respond only to the voice of the Spirit—they cannot be converted logically through the usual means of flipcharts and scriptural discussions. They move more by their feelings than by mental recognition of spiritual things.

We introduced a program called "Living with Exactness" wherein missionaries denied themselves of many worldly things, such as newspapers, movies, and radio programs. They were encouraged to write only to their parents, and not to girlfriends or boyfriends. Instead of playing football and basketball on their preparation days, they were to find other diversions that would be more uplifting to the spirit. We discouraged them from visiting members to manipulate dinners for themselves.

Soon the missionaries began coming into the mission home with stories of wonderful spiritual experiences. Many converts were coming into the Church. Also, many Lamanite members who had long been inactive began coming out to Church when they learned that one of their own, a Lamanite, was mission president.

One of the first branches I visited as mission president was the Sawmill Branch. It was slowly dying. A few weeks after our visit, I placed two missionaries there. Because the area had been very difficult for the missionaries because of the powers of darkness, the former missionaries had been taken out. There was a lot of opposition from anti-Mormons and from evil spirits.

The two new missionaries were proselyting in the area and also giving blessings to cast out the evil spirits that lurked about. Somehow, the two missionaries themselves began to be bothered by evil spirits. And it was not long until both of them were overpowered by the dark forces. Others of the area were also contaminated with the same darkness. The situation was desperate.

The Window Rock District presidency was called in to cast out the evil spirits. Along with the district presidency came some of the high council. They arrived about six in the evening and began to labor to cast the dark spirits from the afflicted individuals and the area. They worked all that evening, yet no success came. It became apparent to these good men that the Lord wanted me involved in the battle. After they had done all they could, soon they were all overcome with the maleficent spirits. Finally, the district president was able to reach a telephone and called at two in the morning, urging me to come quickly to Sawmill.

I dressed hastily and called my two assistants. After they were seated beside me, we headed to Sawmill, two-and-a-half hours away. During the drive, I instructed my two assistants about what to do to cast out evil spirits. Among other important things, I told them to think nothing but good thoughts, that we should not show signs of being afraid.

When we arrived, the two missionaries were pale, sweating, and trembling. They were the best of the missionary force, and yet they were overcome. Then I saw what they had seen: legions of spirits filled the room.

I told my assistants to stay outside, for I did not want them to see what I had seen. The missionaries were shouting, crying, and screaming. I could feel the power of the evil ones all around me in their anger, gnashing, and gnawing. But I had the confidence of the priesthood and of God with me. I thought only about good things. I gave one elder a blessing, and as soon as I had finished, all the evil spirits left him.

He was so weakened that he fell to the floor for a few minutes. When he revived, he helped me bless the other missionary, and then the others in the room, one by one. It was a most spiritual experience. I'll never forget it. Wonderful and terrible it was, all at once. So thankful were we for the power and priesthood of God. I stayed with the missionaries and the others until morning to comfort and give support.

I then went back to the mission home to plan for zone conferences that were coming up. Soon after that, while preparing to go to one of these conferences in Gallup that was only two hours away, I was impressed to stay in the mission home, even though it was time to leave. I had been reading in my office, and I was overcome by the Spirit of the Lord. A strong impression came to my mind to stay a little longer. Three times I arose to leave. But each time I felt to stay. I did not know why. Missionaries were waiting for me, and I hadn't even called them to let them know I would be late and to begin without me.

The third time I got up, I was impressed by the Spirit that I would receive an important phone call in a few minutes. In fifteen minutes, the phone rang. It was Brother Arthur Haycock, President Kimball's secretary. He told me to wait for fifteen minutes, that President Kimball would be calling back. I immediately called Gallup and told the missionaries to continue without me. In those fifteen minutes, many questions ran through my mind. What did President Kimball want with me? Had I done something wrong? What in the world could he want? Was I failing? Was he going to chastise me? My heart raced. My mind sped even faster. Soon he was on the line.

Again, as he did when he had first called me to the mission, he gave me an in-depth interview over the phone. He asked about me, my family, my wife, and the mission.

Then he said, "President Lee, the Lord has called you to become a member of the First Quorum of Seventy."

I knew there were three priesthood quorums in the Church—high priests, elders, and seventies. "What is he saying?" I thought. "Why is he calling me to be a seventy? Why is he calling me to be part of a seventies quorum in a stake, and which stake is it?"

There was total silence. He knew what I was thinking.

Then, to put it more simply, he said, "President Lee, this means the Lord has called you to be a General Authority."

As soon as he had said this, I had to repeat it twice. I blankly sat down. I could not speak. I handed the phone to Kitty. The president spoke a few minutes with her. I was overcome, overwhelmed, by the Spirit. I was crying. And when my wife handed the phone back to me, I cried the whole time I tried to speak with President Kimball. "Why me? Why me?" was going through my mind. "Why should an Indian be called to the high councils of the Church? What would the world say? What about those members of the Church who may have concerns about seeing an Indian sitting in such a high station? Would it drive some away?"

I thought, "Is the Church ready for an Indian General Authority?"

After we hung up, my wife and I embraced for a long time. Both of us wept profusely.

Questions still kept going through my mind, but I was determined to do my best for my Heavenly Father, for I knew He had extended the call. Never since the time of Samuel the Lamanite had a Lamanite sat in the high councils of the Church of Jesus Christ. Prophecy was being fulfilled. This would mean traveling the world over, working with all of Heavenly Father's children. This would mean working side by side with the Prophet of God and president of the Church as well as members of the Quorum of the Twelve Apostles.

One of my life's ambitions was to work with my fellowmen all over the world, and more particularly the Lamanites. Through my diligent prayers, the Lord saw fit that I was called into a position to do so. It has been a great blessing in my life thus far.

After this thrilling and exciting moment, I felt a need to converse with the Lord privately. The next thing I knew, I found myself on bended knees, high on a mountaintop, expressing gratitude for His blessings and humbly and sincerely appealing for His help and guidance. I did not want my prayer to be mere words, but a humble petition to our Heavenly Father.

I pleaded for His inspiration to assist me in my new calling, and I prayed for His blessings upon the Church and his children generally. I asked for forgiveness of my sins and prayed sincerely for the distressed and downhearted, particularly the Lamanites. It seemed that I prayed most of the day for my people, the Native Americans, and other Lamanites.

When I got up, I was a little weak physically, but I was greatly enlarged spiritually. With moistened eyes, I faced a most beautiful sunset, and a glorious feeling of joy overwhelmed me. I felt complete assurance that in His own due time God would fulfill all the promises He had made to His Lamanite children. I felt proud for them.

As I looked toward the setting sun, I pondered the importance of the Book of Mormon. The Church of Jesus Christ of Latter-day Saints was organized through Joseph Smith. I had absolutely no question or doubts about that. God the Father and His Son, Jesus Christ, appeared to the boy Joseph Smith to restore the truth upon the earth once again. My thoughts were on this Church as being the only church upon the face of the earth with doctrines about Indian people, about who they are, and, more especially, about the sacred role they will fill prior to the second coming of Jesus Christ.

I consider the Book of Mormon to be a sacred record of the forefathers of the Native Americans. It identifies who the true Israelites are upon this continent. It prophesies of the day when the Indian and the native Islanders will rise above poverty, illiteracy, and obscurity. It contains a most glorious message. The Book of Mormon also gives us a sterling and powerful message about why the United States of America has become the greatest nation in all the world.

These truths go along with the feelings that my father had about our people and our country. I had been called to assist in the development of the fastest-growing church in all the world. I would be associating with honorable men called to fill the office of apostle. The thought was overwhelming. I felt inadequate to the call. Upon the mountain and in solitude, I petitioned Almighty God for strength, ability, and confidence, and He answered my prayers.

I ended the beautiful day with the following thought: Only in America would something like this happen. Success, status, authority, influence, power, and prominence had come to a young Native American who had risen above poverty, illiteracy, and obscurity. I was so proud to be an Indian, and, at the same time, proud to be an American. God bless America!

Elder George P. Lee

INDEX